IMAGES
of America

NEW MEXICO IN WORLD WAR II

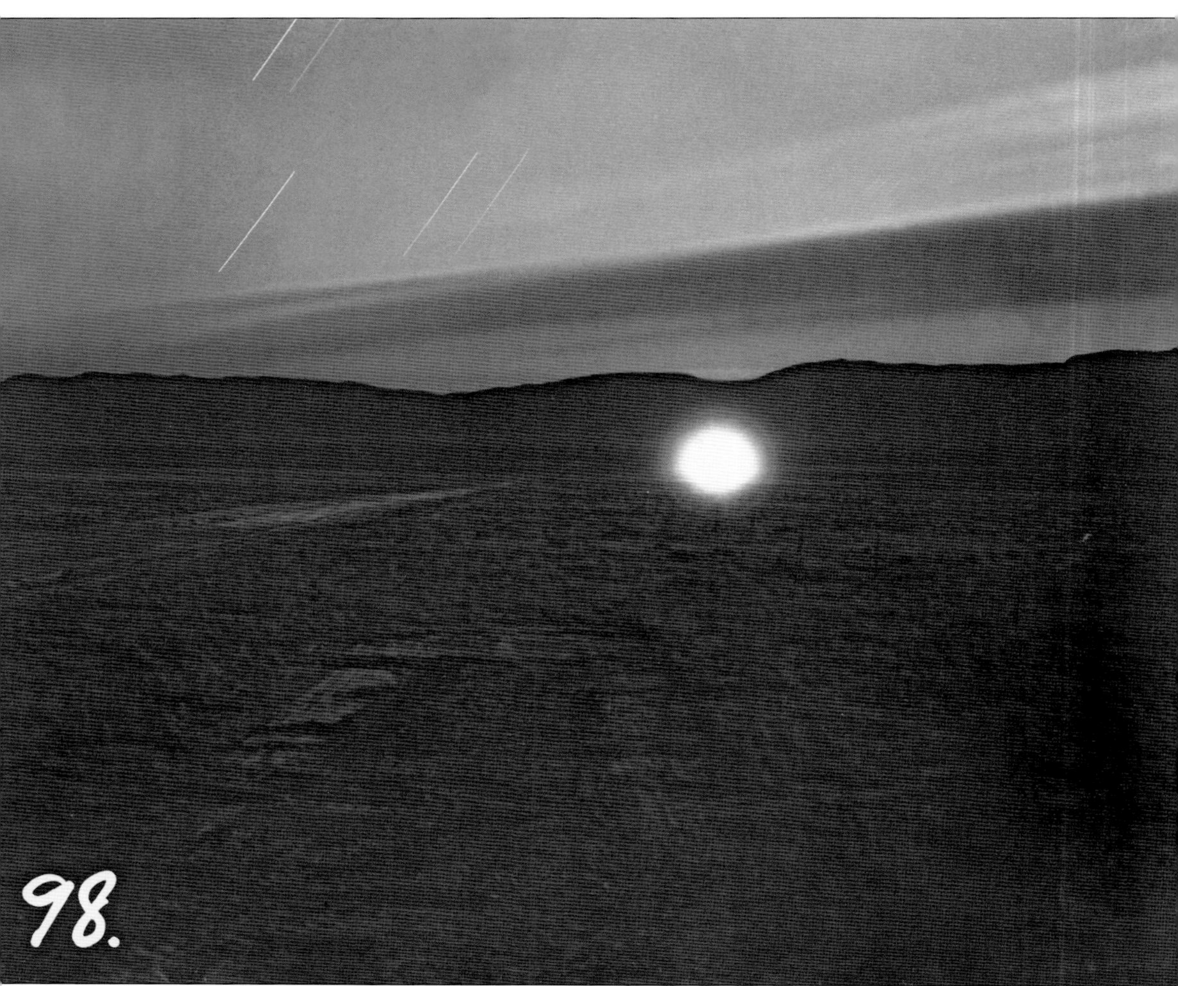

This image shows the first light from the detonation of the first nuclear weapon in the Trinity test on July 16, 1945, at the Alamogordo Bombing Range (now White Sands Missile Range) in south-central New Mexico. This could very well be described as the Dawn of the Nuclear Age. (Los Alamos National Laboratory.)

On the Cover: Units from the 200th and 515th Coast Artillery unit train in 1940 at Camp Luna in northern New Mexico prior to deployment to the Philippines. Many of these soldiers were captured by the Japanese on Bataan and subjected to the tortuous Bataan Death March. (Museum of New Mexico, JP2000.20.349.)

IMAGES
of America

NEW MEXICO IN WORLD WAR II

Richard Melzer and John Taylor

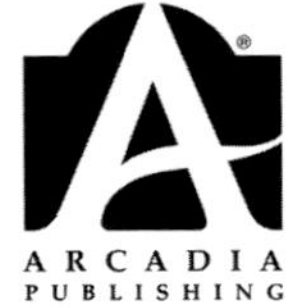

ISBN 978-1-4671-0670-2

Published by Arcadia Publishing
Charleston, South Carolina

Printed in the United States of America

Library of Congress Control Number: 2021931841

For all general information, please contact Arcadia Publishing:
Telephone 843-853-2070
Fax 843-853-0044
E-mail sales@arcadiapublishing.com
For customer service and orders:
Toll-Free 1-888-313-2665

Visit us on the Internet at www.arcadiapublishing.com

This volume is dedicated to all the men and women from New Mexico who served our country, either at home or abroad, during World War II. We especially honor those who gave their lives in the service of our country.

Contents

ACKNOWLEDGMENTS

Our special thanks go to fellow historians David Holtby, William Cass, Dennis Daily, Jon Hunner, Tomas Jaehn, Margaret Espinosa McDonald, J.P. Mendoza, Mo Palmer, Millie Pressler, Boni Seligman, and Nancy Tucker. Especially helpful photograph archivists include Hannah Abelbeck of the New Mexico History Museum, Jim Eckles, Jillian R. Hartke at the Albuquerque Museum, Robert Sherman of the Walker Aviation Museum, and Judy Basen Weinreb at Congregation Albert. Alan Carr, John Moore, and Madeline Helene Whitacre of the Los Alamos National Laboratories shared hundreds of valuable images of the Manhattan Project. Andy Hayes, Toni Hiley, and Harvey Khler helped with information about atomic spies. Rebecca Ullrich of Sandia National Laboratories lent support with proximity fuse images. Fellow Arcadia authors Donna Blake Birchell, Carolyn O'Bagy Davis, and Terrence M. Humble were generous with their images as well. Research librarians at the University of New Mexico's Valencia Campus provided inter-library access to countless hard-to-find resources; they include Kat R. Gullahorn, Cory Meyer, and Barbara Lovato.

Introduction

On December 7, 1941, a Japanese naval fleet commanded by Vice Adm. Chiuchi Nagumo and consisting of six aircraft carriers with 420 bombers and fighters, as well as battleships, cruisers, destroyers, tankers, and five midget submarines, conducted a surprise attack on the US naval base at Pearl Harbor, Hawaii. The attack, as conceived by Harvard-educated Admiral Isoroku Yamamoto, cost 2,403 American lives and destroyed or damaged 19 ships, including eight battleships. Fortunately for the American Navy, no US aircraft carriers were in port, and the fuel storage system and submarine base at Pearl Harbor were largely untouched.

In the wake of this attack, which Pres. Franklin Roosevelt called "a date which will live in infamy," the United States declared war on Japan and its Axis allies, Germany and Italy. Thousands of New Mexicans rushed to enlistment stations to sign up for military service. Volunteers were sworn in, including on the Santa Fe plaza. Others were drafted, and New Mexico earned the distinction of having the highest percentage of servicemen and servicewomen per capita of any state in the country. Volunteers and draftees represented every segment of New Mexico's population, including Hispanics, Native Americans, blacks, whites, Japanese Americans, Jews, and the descendants of recent European immigrants. New Mexicans served in every branch of the armed forces. Starting with the USS *New Mexico* (BB-40), many ships and planes were named after individuals, places, and groups in New Mexico history.

As in every previous war since New Mexico's conquest by the United States in 1846, New Mexicans were eager to prove their loyalty to America. Over 2,500 served in the Union army during the Civil War in the Southwest. About 15,000 served in World War I. Over 350 served as Rough Riders, the most famous fighting unit of the Spanish-American War. Over 1,500 served in the New Mexico National Guard in the 1920s and 1930s, preparing to help defend their nation at a moment's notice, as they were called on to do in 1941. As citizens of the second-youngest state in the country (Arizona was one month younger), New Mexicans were eager to confirm their patriotism and willingness to sacrifice for their country. With the highest casualty rate of any state in the United States, more than 2,200 New Mexicans paid the ultimate price, dying on the battlefield, at sea, in the air, in captivity, or from disease. Thousands are buried overseas or in New Mexico's national cemeteries in Santa Fe and Fort Bayard.

Every state in the United States contributed its unique assets to the American victory in World War II. The purpose of this book is to consider how New Mexico's unique assets helped the United States in ways that few could have predicted at the outset of the war in 1941. Once mobilized by state and federal authorities, these assets made New Mexico not merely one among many, but one of the few most important states that facilitated a final victory over Germany, Japan, and their allies.

The chapters of this book describe how New Mexico's diverse, talented population contributed its courage (at Bataan and with Medal of Honor recipients), its innovation (in the creation of the Navajo Code and the invention of the atomic bomb), and patriotism (in sacrificing money, time, energy, and lives). Civilians pitched in whenever possible. Women contributed by working in previously male-dominated roles, including in the military itself. Families rationed goods, wrote letters to loved ones overseas, contributed to the Red Cross, and bought war bonds. Some grew war gardens. Even children helped out, collecting scrap metal, buying war bond stamps, and attending patriotic parades and rallies.

Whole towns gladly hosted Army Air Corps bases, especially in southern New Mexico. Bases in Alamogordo, Albuquerque, Carlsbad, Clovis, Deming, Hobbs, and Roswell helped train flight crews that graduated to fight in both Europe and the South Pacific. Weapons testing took place at what is now the White Sands Missile Range. Special Army training programs were held at colleges like New Mexico A&M, now New Mexico State University.

Other chapters consider how New Mexico's natural resources, from minerals and crops to weather and terrain, allowed for everything from food and fuel to military training, atomic testing, and prisoner of war (POW) camps needed for national defense. Perhaps New Mexico's greatest contribution was the will and determination of its people to do so much with what, on the surface, looked like so little—how else could one of the poorest states in the county have contributed so much in so many ways?

New Mexicans have much to be proud of in the history of their contributions. But the events of World War II in New Mexico were marred by tragedy as well. Plane crashes and accidental bombings left many killed or wounded. Mexican laborers, recruited in a special program negotiated by the United States and Mexico, were often abused and exploited. The armed forces remained segregated. Japanese Americans were unjustly detained in internment camps in Santa Fe and Lordsburg. At least four communist spies stole top-secret information regarding the atomic bomb, leading directly to the Soviet Union's creation of its own nuclear weapons at the outset of the Cold War. And while the atomic weapons developed at Los Alamos forced the Japanese to surrender in 1945, the attacks on Hiroshima and Nagasaki came at a tremendous cost of both military and civilian lives in those cities.

Descendants of New Mexicans who lived, worked, or fought in the war might well have heard bits and pieces of the state's role in World War II in history classes, from grandparents, by visiting monuments, or by attending special events held to honor fallen heroes like the men of the Bataan Death March. But it is important for these descendants to learn the full extent of their state's sacrifices and leadership. This valuable knowledge will help make New Mexicans prouder, stronger, and more confident as they face war, disease, global warming, or whatever unexpected challenges arise in the future. We can only hope that this small volume will provide this needed knowledge in an interesting format that facilitates learning and remembrance, in good times and in bad.

One

New Mexicans in the Bataan Death March

The Japanese attack on Pearl Harbor was hardly an isolated event. It was, in fact, the first phase of a large, complex strategy meant to include the capture of key American possessions throughout the Pacific, especially Guam and the Philippines. The Japanese knew that by destroying ships, aircraft, and war matériel at Pearl Harbor, the United States would be unable to send reinforcements and supplies to defend its scattered positions. American positions would fall easily, enabling the Japanese to invade other targets, including Australia.

With this larger strategy in mind, the Japanese landed troops and attacked the Philippines within hours after the first bombs were dropped on Pearl Harbor. But the Japanese met heavy resistance in the Philippines, thanks to the determined fighting of Filipino and American forces, including 1,825 New Mexicans, former members of the state's National Guard. US forces fought as well as they could until, low on supplies and without reinforcements, they had no option but to surrender in April 1942.

The Japanese forced the defeated troops on one of the most infamous death marches in military history. Thousands died amid horrendous conditions and brutal treatment by enemy troops. Thousands more died from torture, starvation, and disease in POW camps and on "hell ships" over the next three years. With some exceptions, the Japanese largely ignored Article 27 of the Geneva Conventions of 1929, which mandated the humane treatment of all POWs.

New Mexicans helped one another at every stage of the Bataan Death March and POW confinement. Many were relatives, friends, and colleagues from their prewar lives in New Mexico's small rural villages and few urban centers.

American POWs were finally liberated with Japan's surrender in 1945. Of the 1,825 New Mexicans who had arrived in the Philippines in 1941, approximately half had perished. Survivors often suffered from physical and psychological problems for the rest of their lives.

The nightmare of the Bataan Death March is probably the most remembered event of World War II in New Mexico. It is memorialized in statues, monuments, buildings, street names, and even a marathon "reenactment" held each spring.

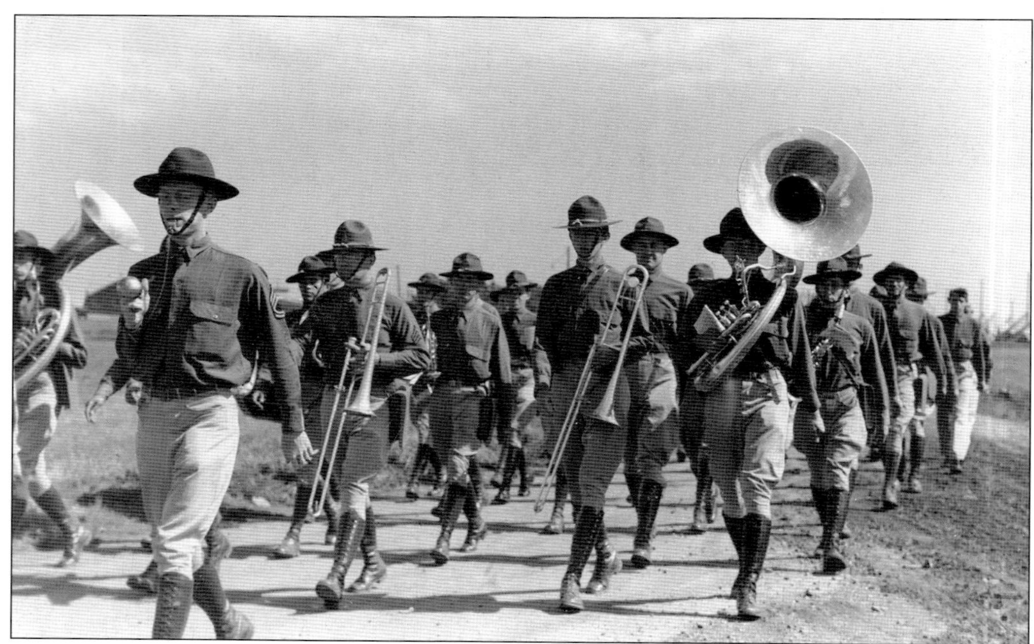

Many members of the New Mexico National Guard trained at Camp Luna, west of Las Vegas, New Mexico. The camp had been named to honor Capt. Maximiliano Luna, a Rough Rider in the Spanish-American War. In 1941, guardsmen came from large and small communities across New Mexico. The youngest, a private, was 16. The oldest, Col. Harry Peck, was 54. Most were between 23 and 27 years old. Seventy percent were Anglo, twenty-eight percent were Hispanic, and two percent were Native American. Many had relatives in the ranks, with 42 sets of brothers, many cousins, seven sets of uncles and nephews, and a father and son. They had a marching band (above) and sent postcards to their friends and relatives back home (below). (Above, Museum of New Mexico, HP2007.20,335; below, Richard Melzer.)

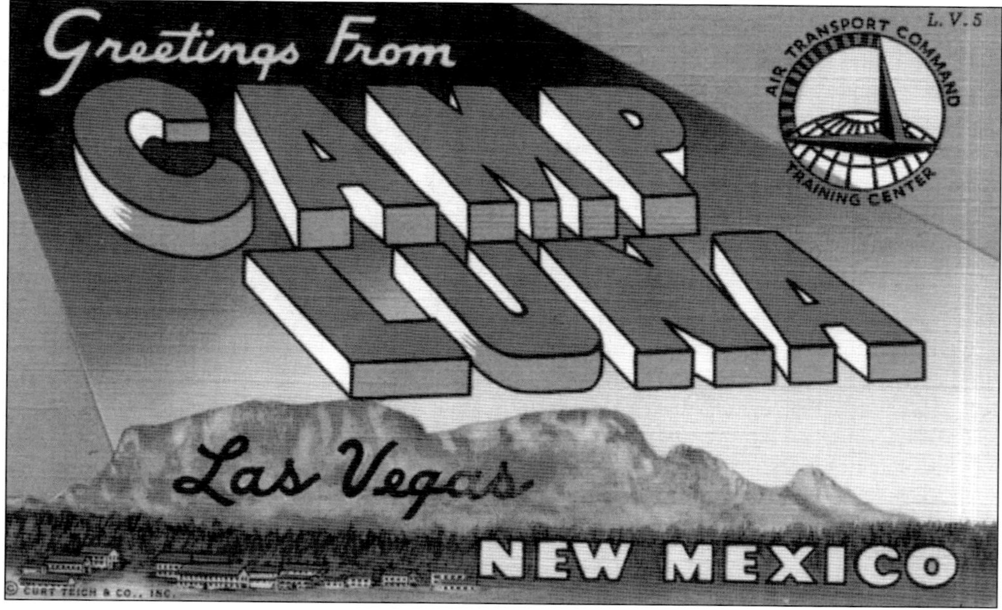

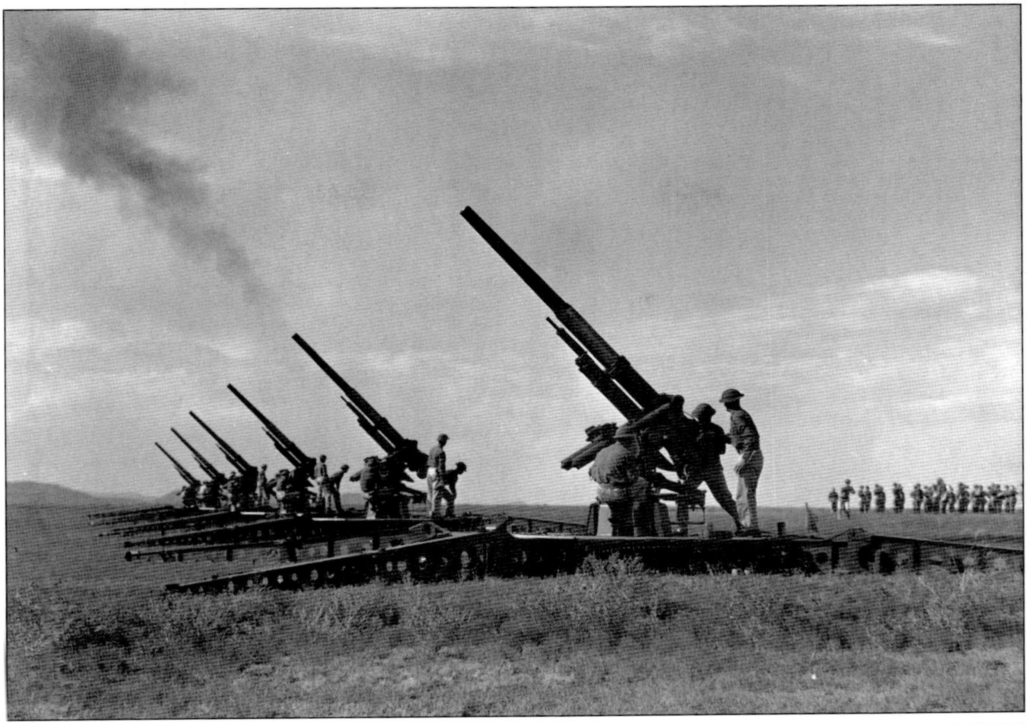

New Mexico National Guard troops knew each other not only as relatives, but also as friends who had grown up together or served together in the Civilian Conservation Corps (CCC), a New Deal program for youths during the Great Depression. After months of training, 1,825 troops from New Mexico were mobilized as the 200th Coast Artillery and the 515th Coast Artillery (above). In mid-1941, they were ordered to depart for the Philippines. Before leaving, the troops visited towns across New Mexico in a farewell tour like none other in the state's history. Large crowds, like the one shown at right, cheered the men to encourage them in their foreign deployment. Memories of this tour helped fortify the troops in the terrible days to come. (Above, Museum of New Mexico, JP2000.20.349; right, Southeastern New Mexico Historical Society.)

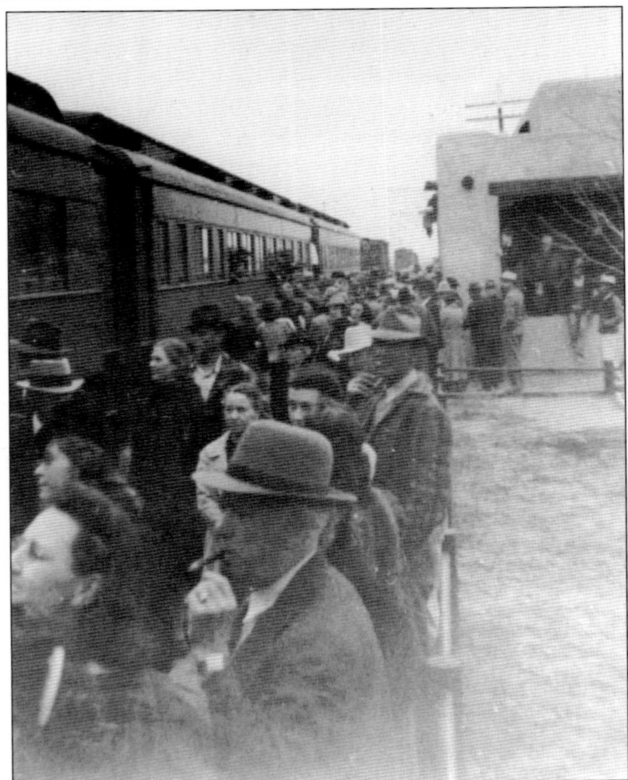

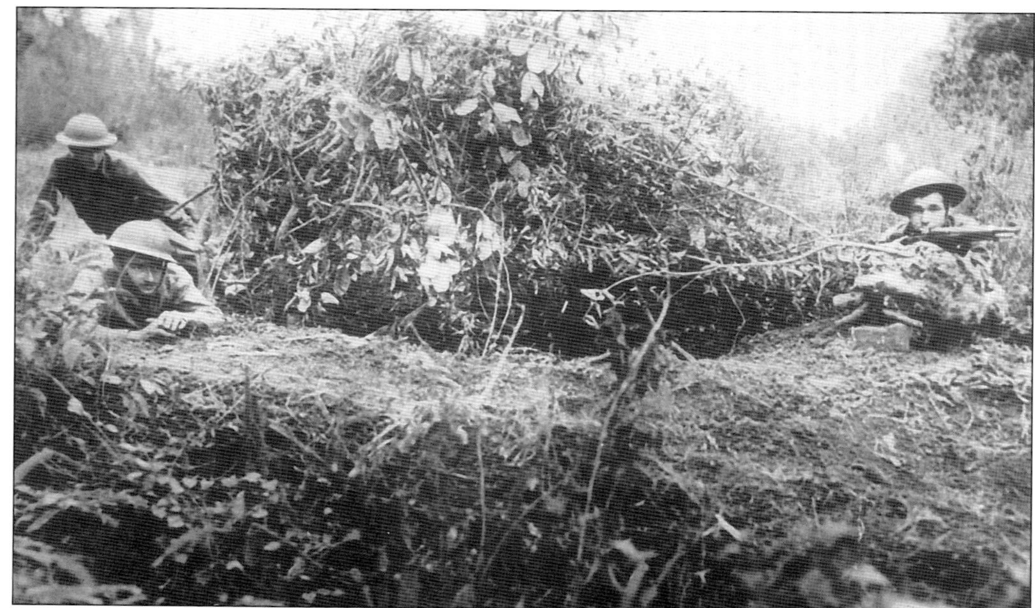

Thousands of seasoned Japanese troops stormed Luzon, the largest, northernmost island in the Philippines, on December 8, 1941. Well-supplied and prepared for a prolonged fight for the islands, the Japanese made steady progress across Luzon, ultimately driving American troops down the Bataan peninsula on the southwestern corner of the island. While more enemy troops, ships, and planes arrived daily, US forces and their Filipino allies suffered massive losses without any hope of reinforcement. The Americans soon ran out of everything, from ammunition and weapons to food and medical supplies. Medical personnel worked in makeshift outdoor hospitals, like the one shown below. Realizing their impossible position and feeling deserted, New Mexicans and other American soldiers called themselves the "Battling Bastards of Bataan." Any hope of rescue diminished by the day. (Both, Richard Melzer.)

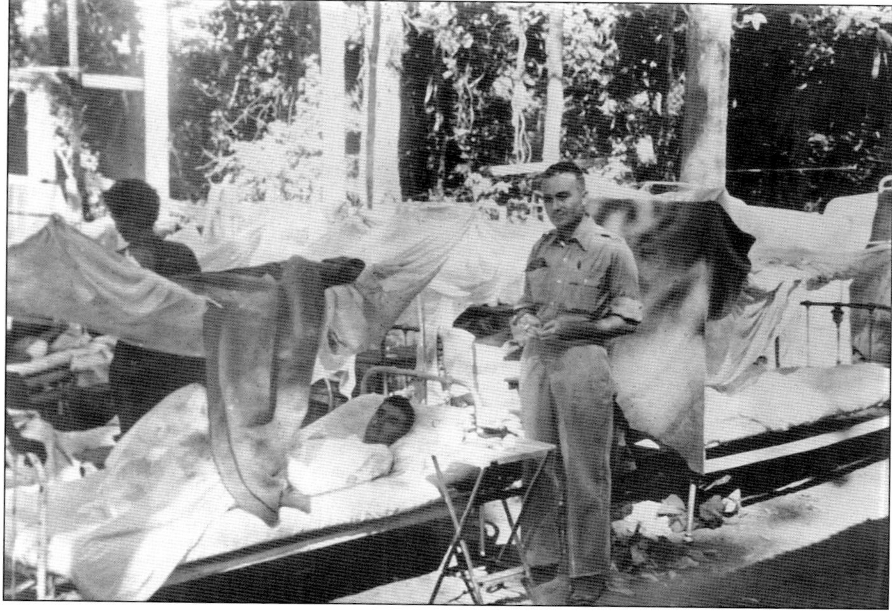

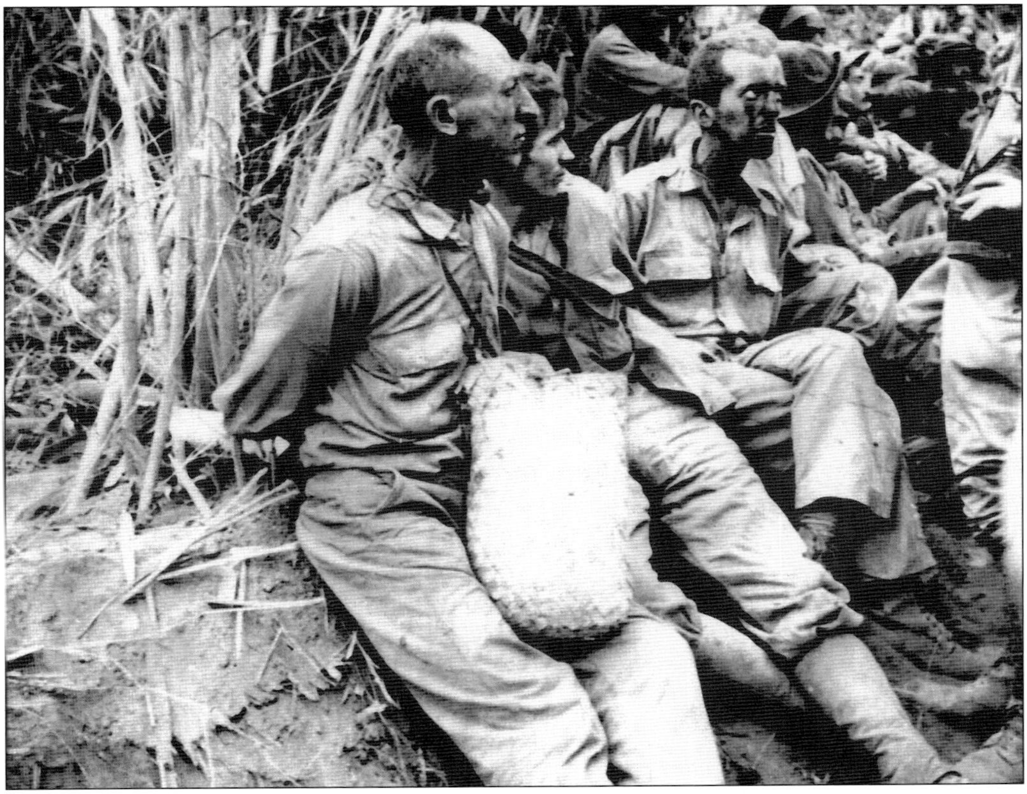

Despite the odds against them, New Mexicans in the 200th Coast Artillery and the 515th Coast Artillery were among the American and Filipino forces that fought the Japanese valiantly into early 1942. New Mexican artillery shot down 86 Japanese aircraft, including six on a single day. Knowing that they held every advantage, the Japanese were shocked that they did not defeat the Americans and capture the Philippines much sooner. But as casualties and conditions grew worse, American officers realized that they were fighting an impossible battle. Despite the opposition of almost every American soldier, Gen. Jonathan Wainwright, shown above, finally surrendered to the Japanese on April 9, 1942. New Mexicans had been among the first to fight and the last to surrender, at the cost of 19 lives. (Above, Richard Melzer; right, Dorothy Cave.)

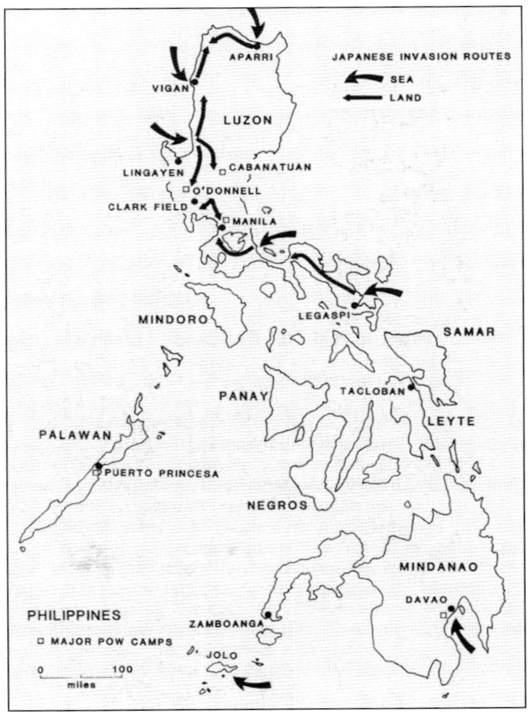

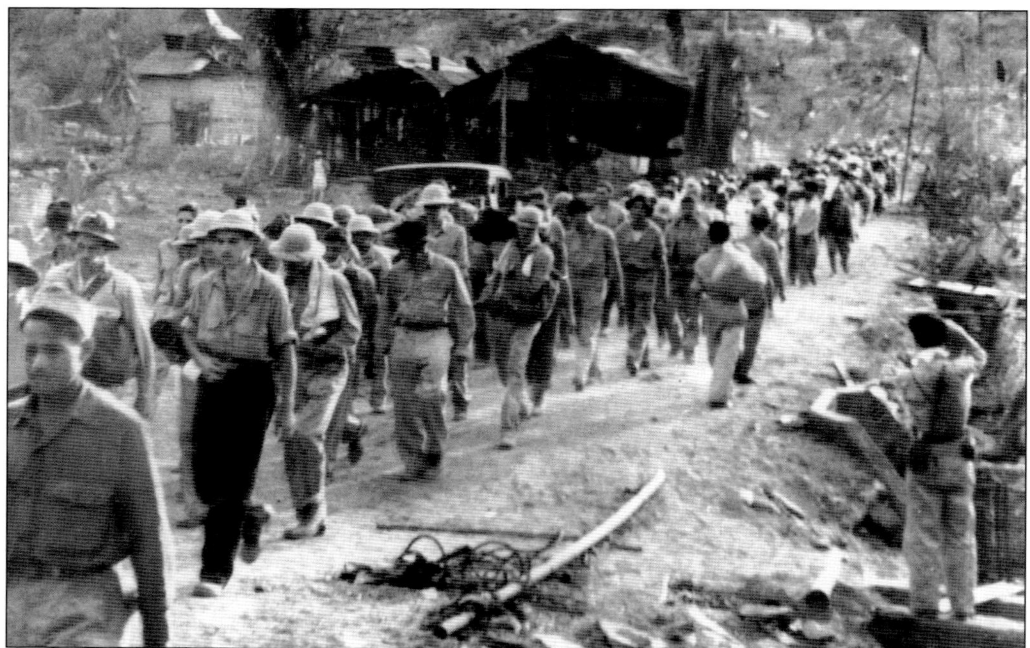

The remaining 1,806 New Mexicans joined thousands of other captured American and Filipino troops on a hellish march of 65 miles. Following a crude dirt road up the east coast of the Bataan peninsula, the prisoners suffered from thirst, hunger, filth, exhaustion, disease, and brutal treatment by the enemy. The Japanese mistreated their prisoners largely because, in Japanese culture, it was considered dishonorable for a warrior to surrender rather than fight to the death. After as many as 12 days of torturous treatment, the POWs were forced into crowded boxcars, where many more died before the trains arrived at POW camps throughout the Philippines. Conditions in the camps were no better than on the death march and trains. So many prisoners died that they had to be carried far outside each camp to be buried, as shown below. (Both, Library of Congress.)

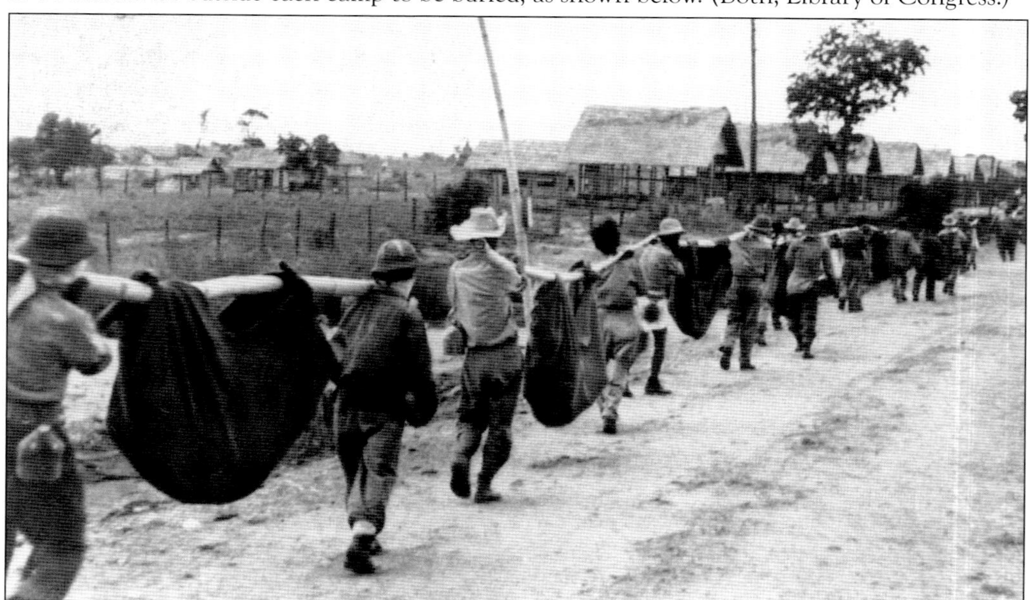

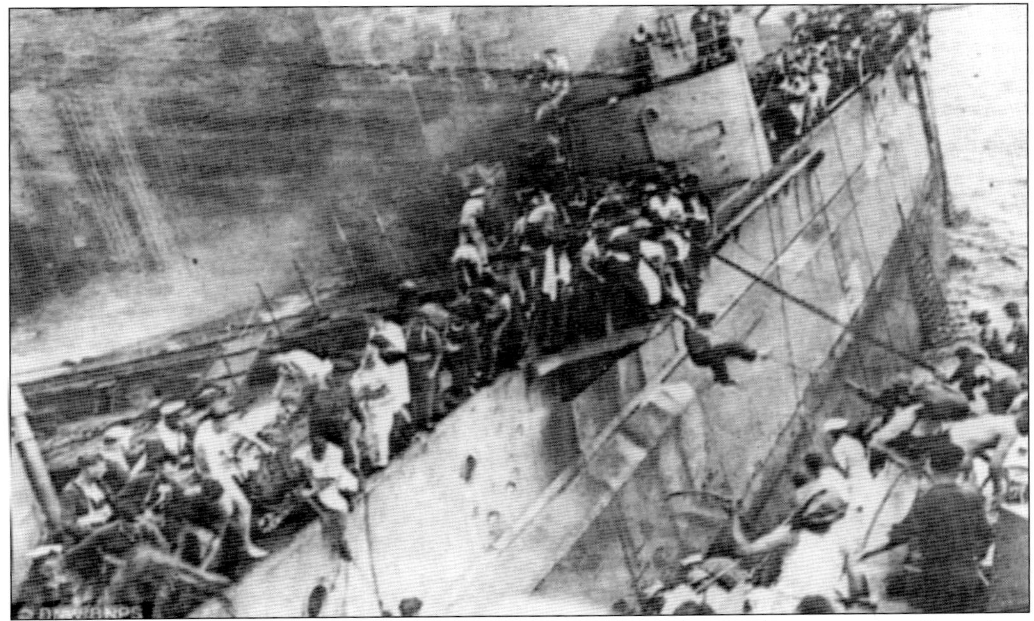

The Japanese faced a severe labor shortage. They attempted to solve this by transporting American POWs to work camps in Japan and other parts of their empire. Thousands were forced onto overcrowded Japanese ships. Many died when attacked by American fighter planes that had no idea of the human cargo held belowdecks. Suffering from starvation, thirst, disease, and attacks, more Americans died on these hell ships than in POW camps. (Dirk de Klein.)

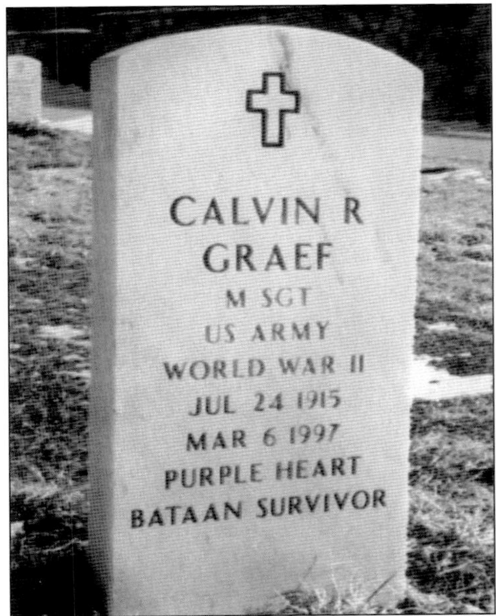

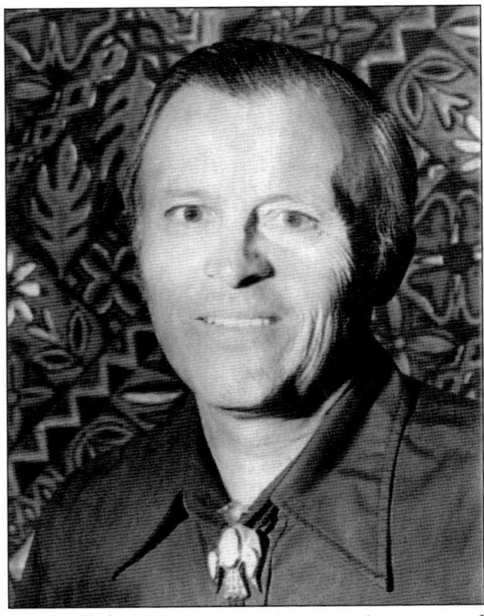

Calvin Graef of Silver City was a member of the 200th Coast Guard Artillery Regiment who survived the Bataan Death March, horrible conditions in Japanese POW camps, and a hell ship sunk in the South China Sea. The book *Ride the Waves to Freedom: Calvin Graef's Survival Story of the Bataan Death March and His Escape from a Sinking Hellship*, describes the adventures he experienced before his liberation and return to New Mexico. (Left, Richard Melzer; right, Graef family.)

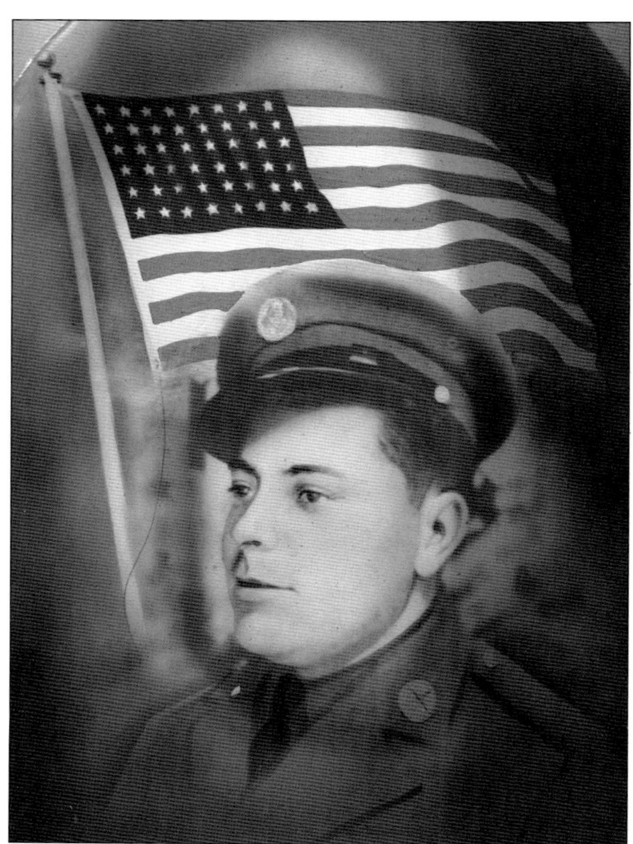

New Mexicans and thousands of their fellow POWs were liberated shortly after V-J Day when the Japanese officially surrendered to the United States and its allies on September 2, 1945. Some New Mexicans saw the nuclear explosion at Hiroshima, watching from a distance in their POW camps in Japan, but never guessing what this new weapon was or what it meant to them. Those who survived often took months to recover in Army hospitals. Many suffered physically and psychologically for the rest of their lives. Some, like Clovis G. Chavez of Peralta (left) and Vincent Ojinaga from Santa Fe (below), lived long, productive lives. Many of the same communities that had seen them off in 1941 now welcomed the former National Guardsmen with parades and festivities. (Left, Chavez family; below, Museum of New Mexico, HP.2014.14.1594.)

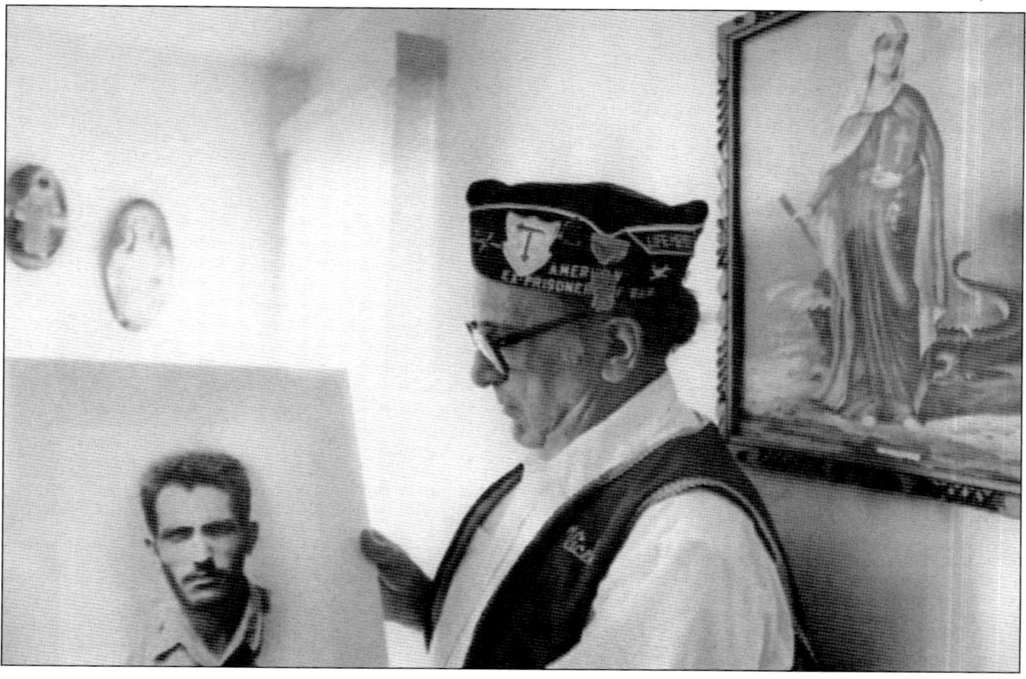

Many town parks in New Mexico include monuments or statues dedicated to the New Mexicans who suffered through the Bataan Death March. Statues of New Mexicans helping each other stand in Taos, Las Cruces (right), and Deming (below), symbolizing how New Mexicans often aided one another to survive. The largest monument is at the Bataan Memorial Park in Albuquerque. Every New Mexican who served in the Philippines is listed at the park, with the names of the 687 who died clearly identified. Some buildings, including New Mexico's former capitol building in Santa Fe and the Methodist Bataan Memorial Hospital in Albuquerque, were named to honor the New Mexicans who fought at Bataan. An Army plane and a Navy ship were also named in the soldiers' honor. (Right, Richard Melzer; below, J.P. Mendoza.)

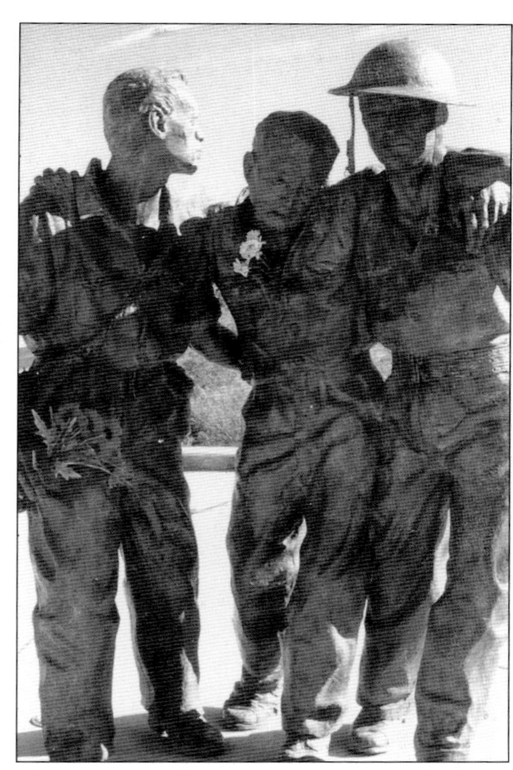

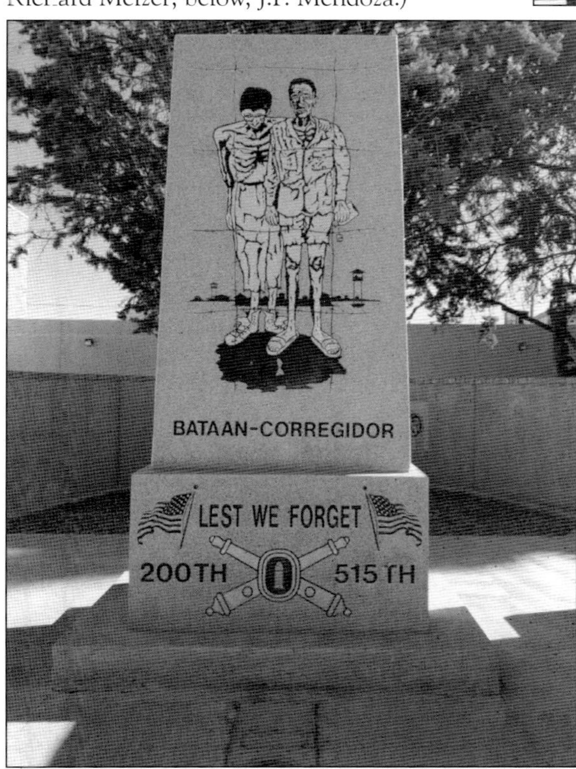

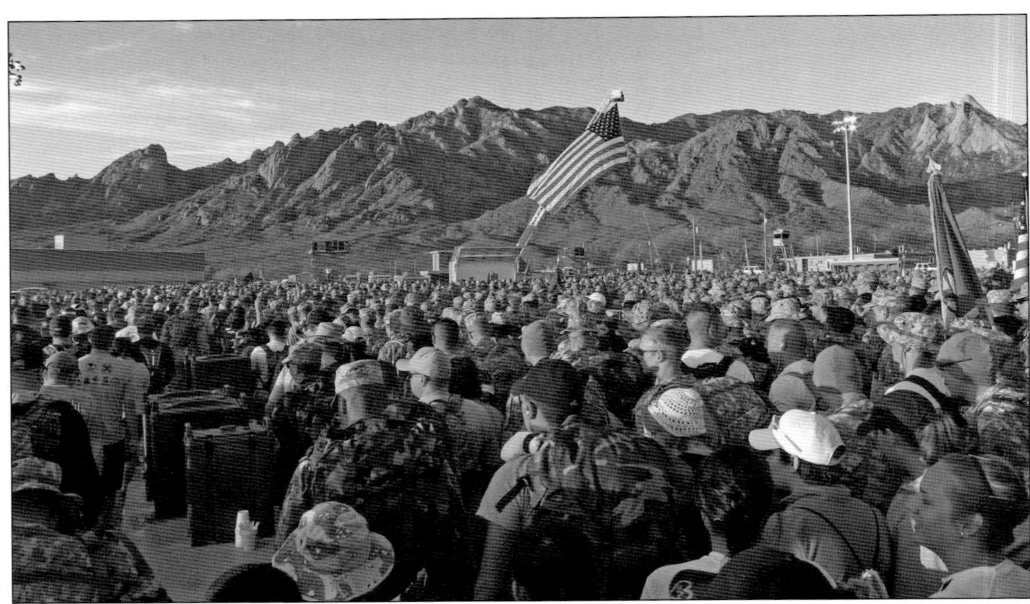

In 1989, students in the ROTC program at New Mexico State University created a unique event to honor the memory of the soldiers of the Bataan Death March. Now an annual event, as many as 8,600 participants run or walk 26.2 miles through parts of the White Sands Missile Range. Of course, participants do not attempt to recreate the horrors of the march. Most runners are physically fit, and there are 12 water stations with medical attendants available along the route. Participants come from all backgrounds, from active military personnel to descendants of the original death march soldiers. Some runners attach names and pictures of death march soldiers to their backpacks. Death march survivors are often present to cheer the runners and walkers on. (Both, Jim Eckles.)

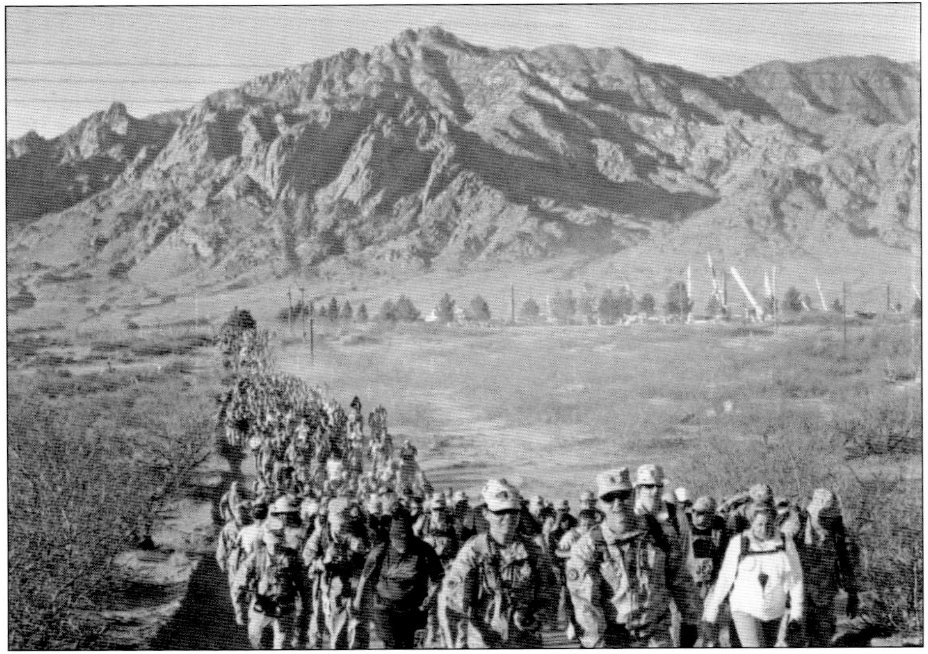

Two

Navajo Code Talkers

Good communication is essential to any military operation. Secret communication is especially essential to success in battle. But developing and keeping secret codes are among the greatest challenges in every war. The 1680 Pueblo Revolt provides the best example of a compromised code in New Mexico history. Using a well-devised code, rebel leader Popé sent runners with knotted ropes to alert the pueblos when their planned revolt would begin. Each knot in the rope represented a day until the fighting would begin. But the plan was compromised when the Spanish intercepted a runner and learned the secret of his rope and its knots.

Even the most complex, highly technical codes were eventually compromised during World War II. English codebreakers led by Alan Turing at Bletchley Park's cryptology department broke German codes used in key battlefield, naval, and diplomatic communications.

The American military searched for new answers to this age-old problem of finding a dependable code. One solution was to use a Native American language that few foreigners would know. Native American languages had been used before, as when the Army used soldiers from the Choctaw Nation during World War I. Other tribes, including Creeks and Hopis, used their native languages to send messages during operations in North Africa, Sicily, and the South Pacific in World War II.

But in each of these cases, Native Americans spoke in their own languages, meaning that the enemy could break the "code" by simply learning the language. To make matters more difficult, few of these languages had words for military items like tanks and submarines. The solution was to develop a code that related to an Indian culture and could be translated into that tribe's language. The Navajo code talkers developed such a code after joining the Marines and training for combat. Starting with just 29 members, the code talkers' code, which the Japanese never broke, was so successful that it helped lead to victory in many key battles. The Navajo code talkers have since been honored in many ways by their grateful tribe, state, and nation.

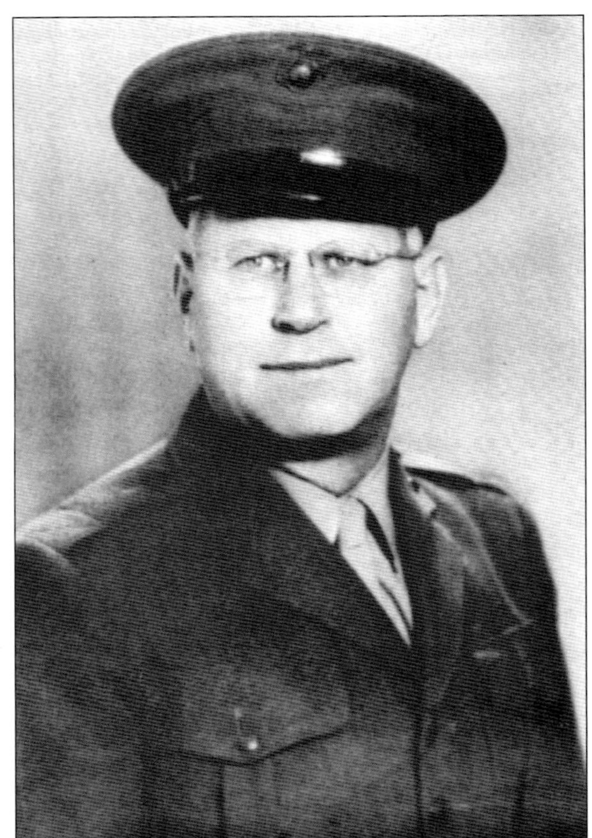

Philip Johnston is given credit for first suggesting the creation of a Navajo code. The son of a Protestant missionary, Johnston had grown up on the Navajo reservation and had learned the tribe's complex language while playing with Navajo children. In time, he served as a translator, including for Navajo leaders when they met with Pres. Theodore Roosevelt in 1901. When World War II began, Johnston contacted the Marines to suggest that a new code be created and translated into the Navajo language—a code within a code. Impressed, the Marines recruited 30 Navajos to begin a pilot program. The 29 shown here (no one knows what became of the 30th recruit) were inducted into the Marines at Ft. Defiance, Arizona, on May 4, 1942. (Left, US Marine Corps; below, Richard Melzer.)

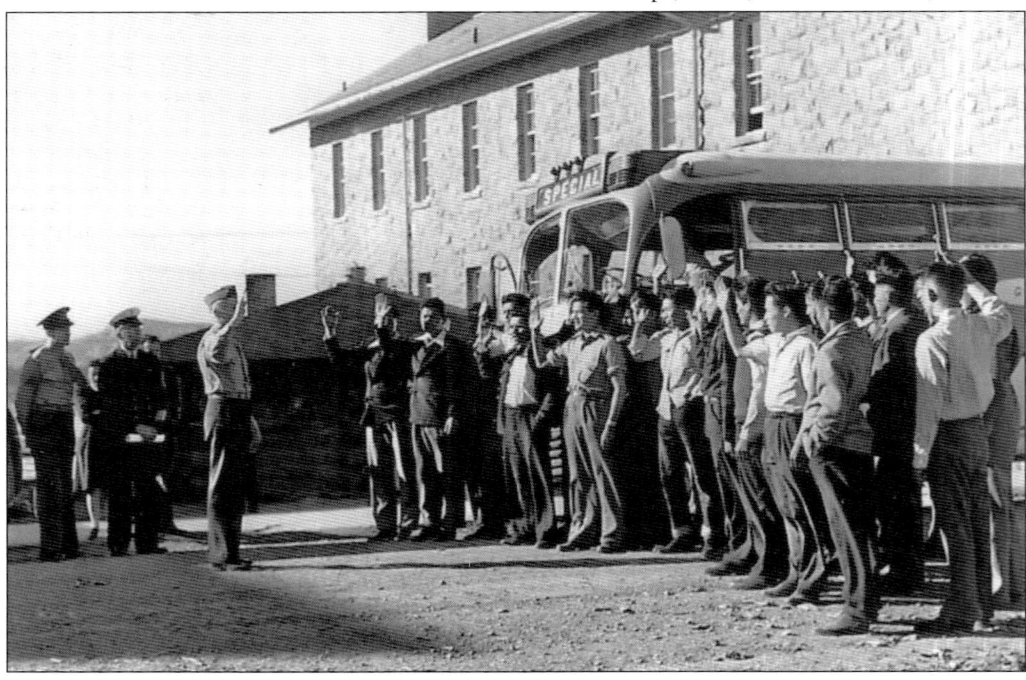

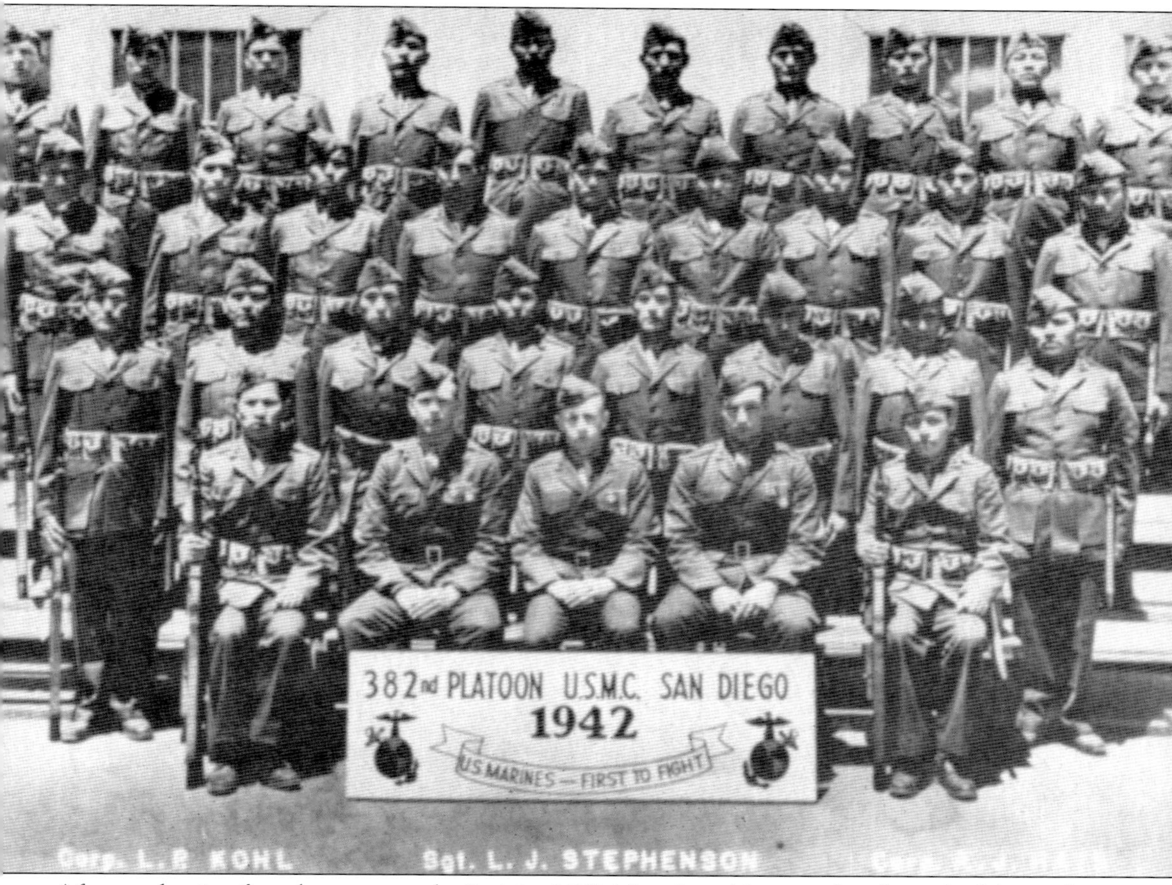

After graduating from boot camp, the "original 29" (plus three Navajos already in the Marines) undertook the creation of their unique military code. Seventy percent of the Navajos had learned to speak English at Indian boarding schools, where they had been severely punished if they spoke their native language. Now their bilingual skills became a major asset. They identified Navajo words that could be used for military terms. Words for planes related to birds: a bomber, for example, was referred to as a buzzard and a fighter plane was a hummingbird. Words for ships related to fish: a battleship was a whale, and a destroyer was a shark. These code words were then translated into Navajo. If a code word did not exist for a term, the term had to be spelled out with as many as three code words used for each letter in the alphabet. The code was never printed for fear it might fall into enemy hands. It had to be flawlessly memorized and sent at lightning speed. (Richard Melzer.)

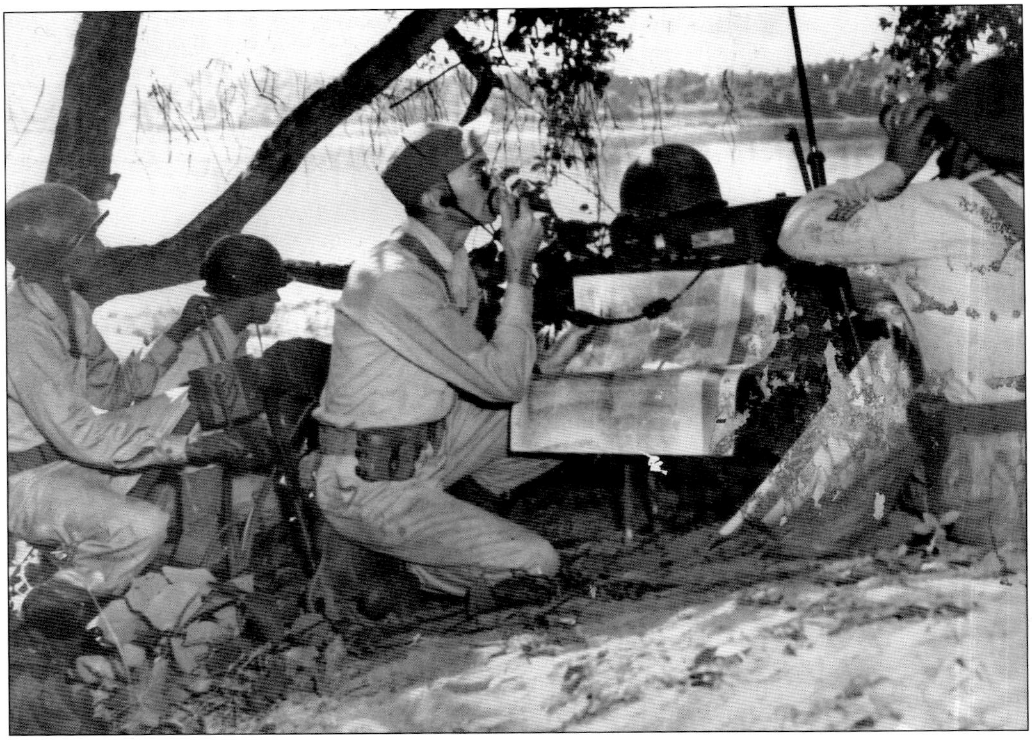

The first contingent of code talkers arrived in the South Pacific just half a year after joining the Marines. Using 28-pound radio transmitters to relay crucial messages in code, privates like Preston and Frank Toledo (below) helped turn the tide in the battles of Guadalcanal, Tarawa, Saipan, Iwo Jima, and Okinawa. At the Battle of Iwo Jima, six code talkers sent over 800 error-free messages in a 48-hour period. The Navajos fought as efficient warriors in their tribe's proud tradition. They joined other Native Americans from New Mexico and across the United States. (Both, Richard Melzer.)

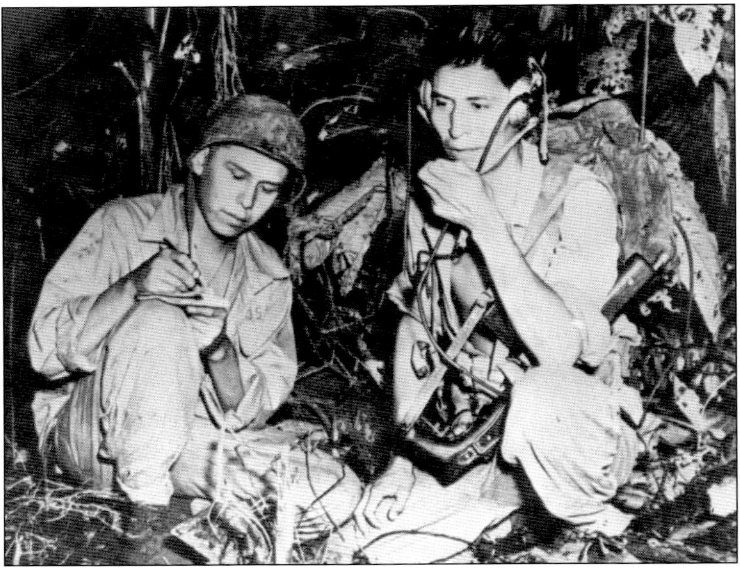

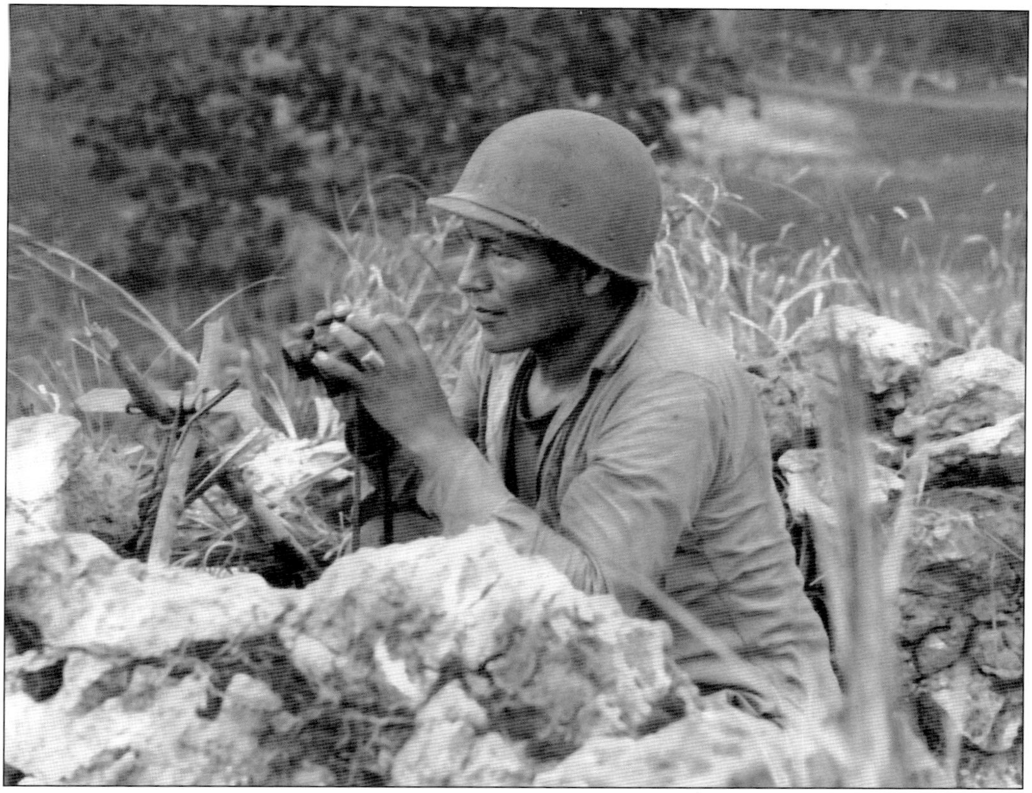

In addition to their work sending important messages in code, the Navajos fought in combat. Carl Gorman is shown here at an observation post on Saipan. An Albuquerque Indian School graduate, Gorman later became a respected artist whose son R.C. Gorman also became a famous Southwestern artist. Other former code talkers included Peter McDonald, president of the Navajo Nation, and John Pino, a respected state senator from Gallup. (Richard Melzer.)

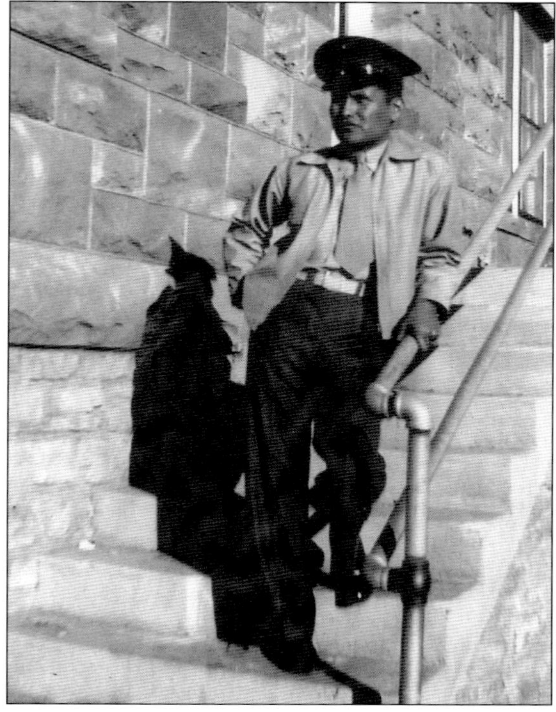

Chester Nez had attended an Indian boarding school where teachers worked to rid students of the "burden" of their language with slaps, kicks, and mouth washings. But with his new English skills, Nez was a perfect recruit for the code talkers. After serving in the war, where he always wore his Navajo medicine bag, Nez wrote *Code Talker*, the only memoir written by one of the original 29. (The Heard Museum collection.)

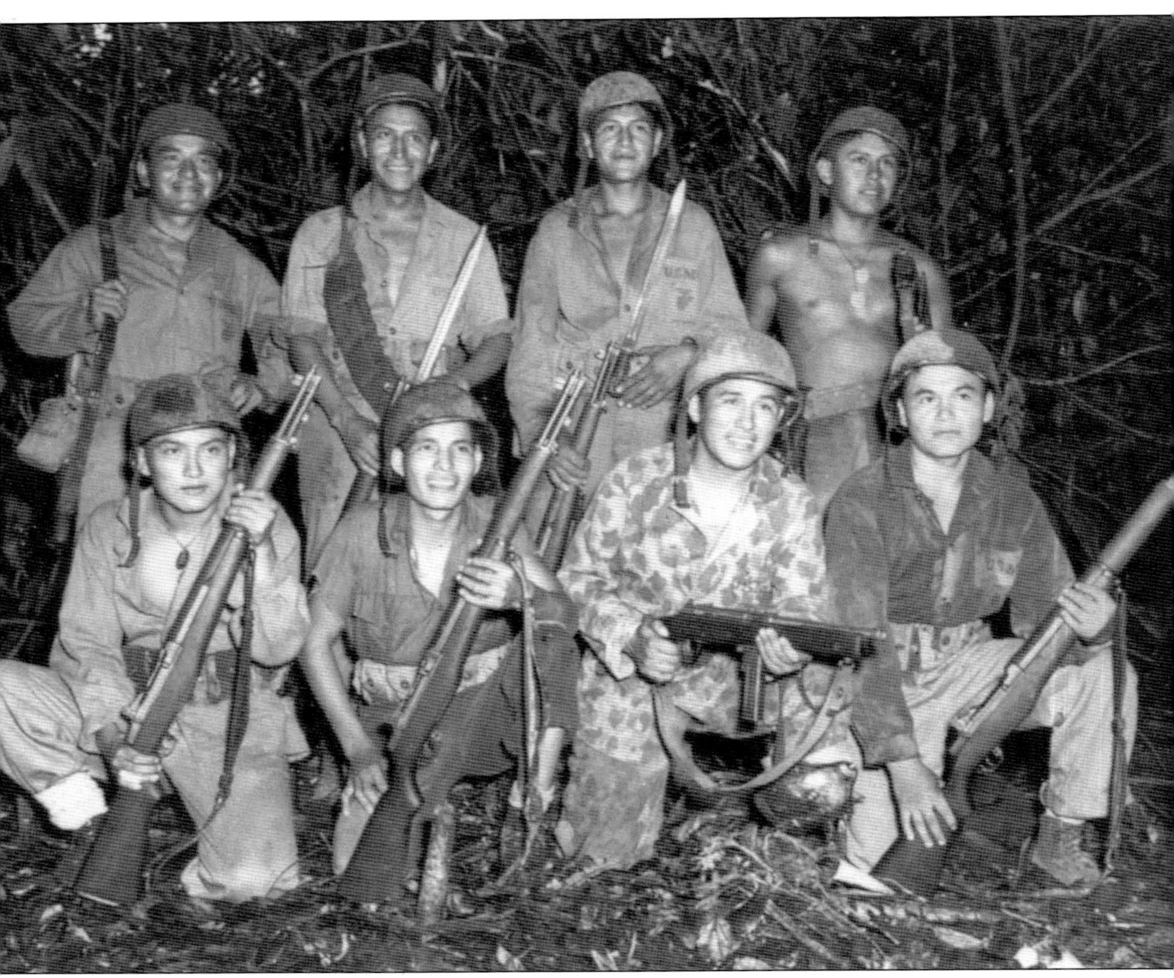

The original 29 served as Platoon 382, the first all-Navajo platoon in Marine Corps history. They were eventually joined by 352 other Navajo, recruited with the help of Philip Johnston. With time, they expanded their code to about 450 frequently used military terms. Once in the South Pacific, code talkers like those shown here on Guam faced great danger, not only as combat Marines, but especially as possessors of the code. If captured by the Japanese, they could be tortured to reveal a code the enemy coveted. The Navajos were also endangered because their fellow Americans, often unfamiliar with Native Americans, sometimes mistakenly concluded that the code talkers were Japanese soldiers disguised in US Army uniforms. As a result, white guards were assigned to protect the code talkers. None were captured, but several were wounded, and 11 were killed in action. The enemy never deciphered the code, and the code talkers never revealed it until it was officially declassified in 1968. (Richard Melzer.)

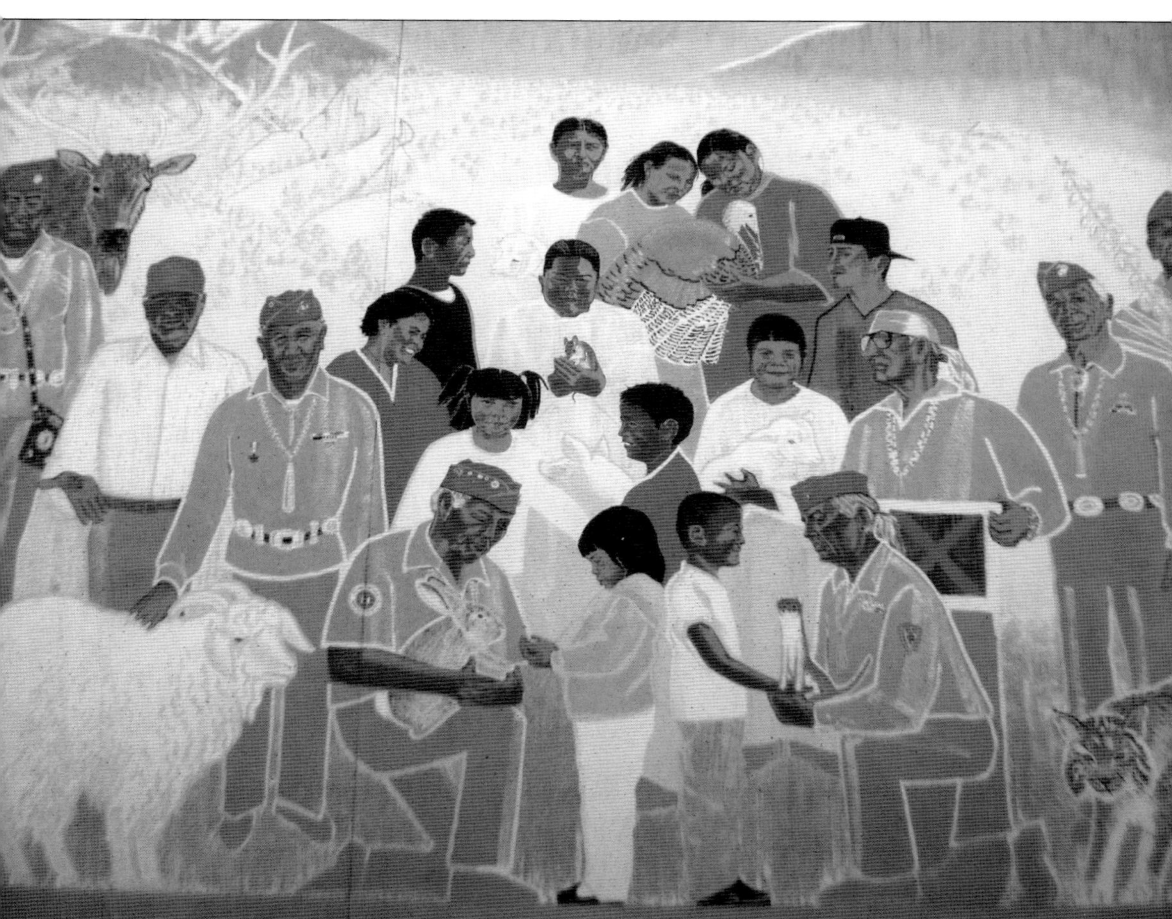

The Navajo code talkers' devotion and loyalty to the United States were remarkable, especially when the country they were fighting for had often betrayed them with broken treaties and disastrous policies meant to destroy their culture and spiritual lives. The Navajo suffered the Long Walk, followed by four years of imprisonment at Bosque Redondo in the 1860s. They were forced to send their children to Indian boarding schools where future generations were taught to reject their culture as primitive and backward. In the 1930s, the federal government destroyed as much as 80 percent of their livestock, the center of their economy and rural way of life. Despite this history, the code talkers were eager to fight for the United States because they were loyal American citizens and because they were determined to defend their families and culture. Many code talkers were purified of whatever evil they had experienced in a ceremony called the Enemy Way when they finally returned home. Their ties to traditional ways are emphasized in this mural by Be Sargent, completed in Gallup in 2001. (Richard Melzer.)

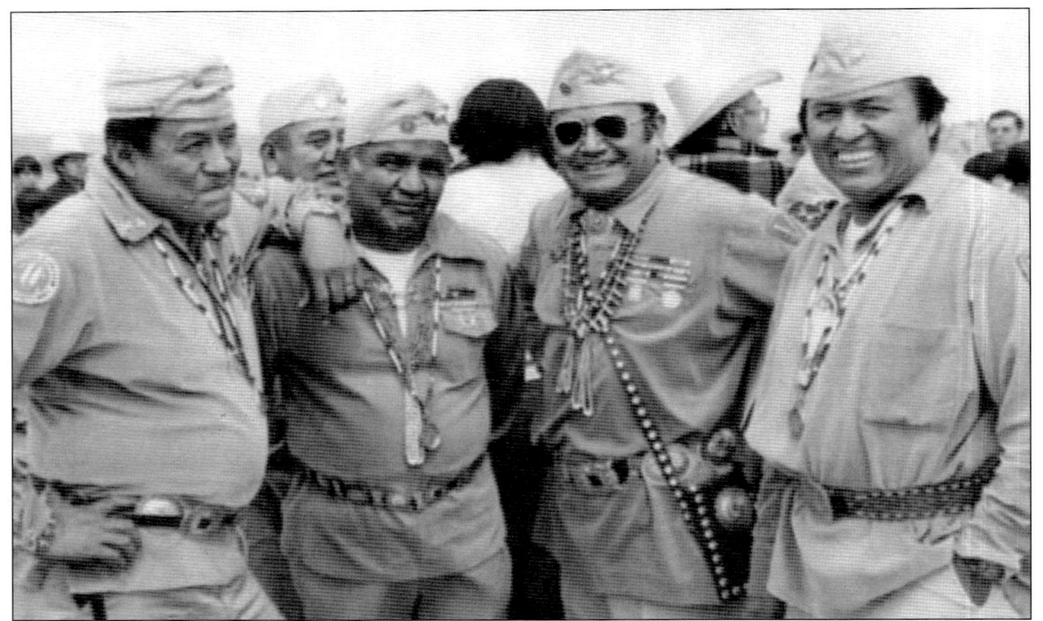

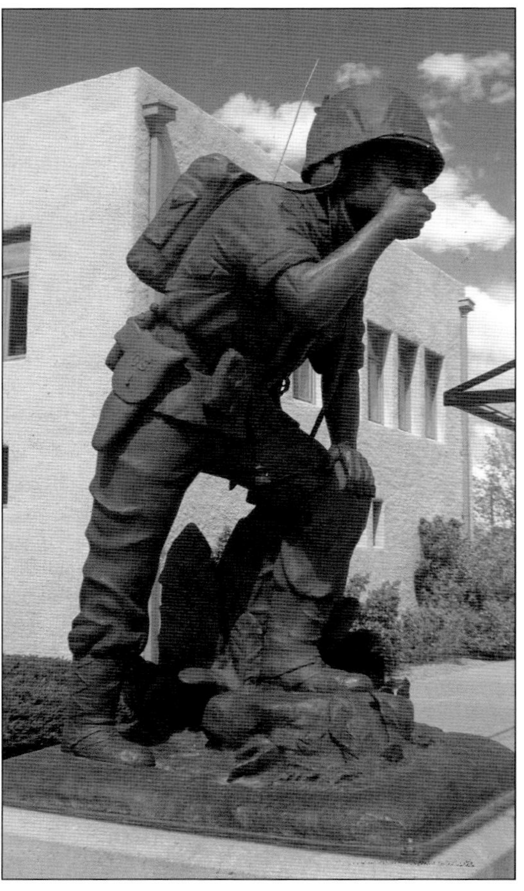

With their code declassified, the Navajo code talkers and their critical role in World War II could finally be revealed. They were publicly recognized for the first time on June 28, 1969. They have been honored ever since, including at the annual Inter-Tribal Indian Ceremonials held in Gallup. Pres. Ronald Reagan proclaimed August 14, 1982, "National Code Talkers Day." In 2000, surviving members of the original 29 received Congressional Gold Medals of Honor—the highest accommodation civilians can receive. *Windtalkers*, a movie produced with the technical assistance of several code talkers, premiered in 2002. Code talker statues by Kirtland, New Mexico, artist Oreland Joe stand outside the Gallup Cultural Center (left) and the Navajo tribal offices in Window Rock. (Above, Kenji Kawano; left, Richard Melzer.)

Three

"New Mexico's Navy" in World War II

Ninety-six ships have been named for one or another aspect of the land-locked state of New Mexico. Two ships, a submarine and a battleship, were named for the state; ten ships, mostly supply vessels, were named for counties; twenty-one ships, mostly small patrol fighting ships, were named for cities and towns; eleven ships, mostly oilers and gasoline transports, were named for rivers; twenty-three ships, mostly Liberty and Victory supply ships, were named for individuals; eight Liberty and Victory ships were named for battles and monuments; and twenty-one, mostly tugboats and supply ships, were named for Native American tribes. Of those 96 ships, 67 participated in World War II, mostly in the Pacific Theater.

The vessels ranged from the 32,000-ton battleship USS *New Mexico* (BB-40) to the 59-ton harbor tugboat USAT *Apache* (ST-724). There were submarines, troop transports, amphibious support vessels, supply ships, tugboats, oilers, and gasoline tankers. Most of the ships were directly involved in enemy action, and five were lost, costing 616 lives and thousands of injuries. Although only a few New Mexicans served aboard the ships that bore the name of their home state, 2,000 men and women from the Land of Enchantment served in the Navy, Coast Guard, and Merchant Marines during the war.

Supply ships provided the fighting forces with food, medicine, and ammunition. Amphibious support ships transported the Marines from ship to shore and provided supporting artillery cover for the troops as they landed. Tugboats pulled the landing craft off the beach, towed damaged vessels safely to repair facilities, and provided gunfire support for the troops.

The five ships that were lost included a submarine, an oiler, two supply ships, and a tugboat, all sunk by enemy action. These ships were lost to either enemy aircraft or enemy submarines. The oiler USS *Pecos* (AO-6) was sunk trying to rescue sailors from another damaged vessel, the merchant ship *Patrick Hurley* was lost trying to outrun a German U-boat, and the submarine USS *Bullhead* (SS-332) was the last US warship sunk during World War II.

This chapter examines some of these vessels and their critical contributions to the Allied victory.

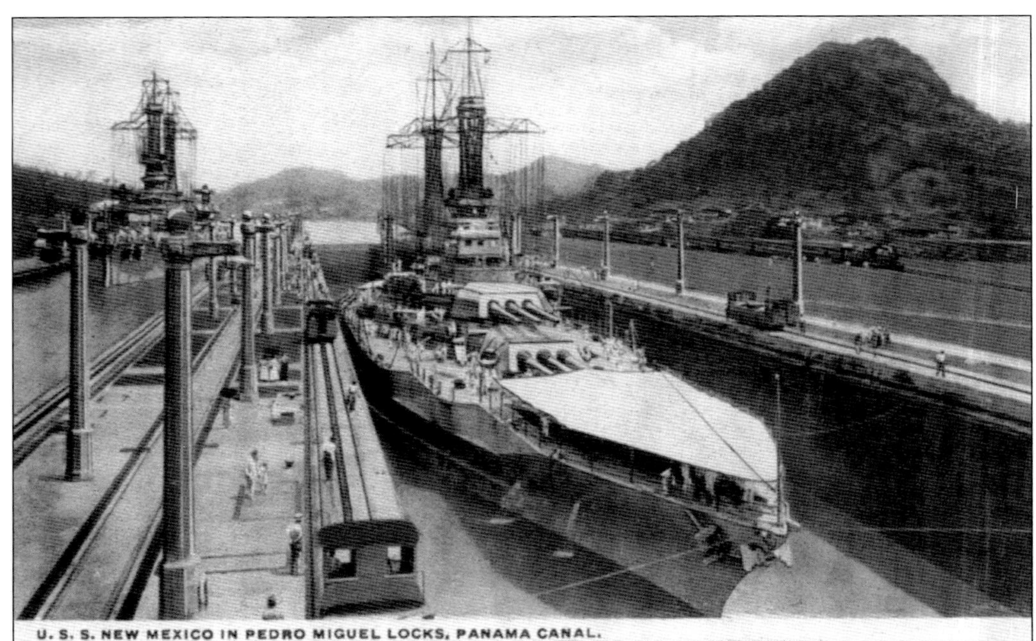

The battleship USS *New Mexico* was built at the New York Navy Yard and launched on April 23, 1917. During the ceremony, a jug containing water from both the Pecos River and the Rio Grande was broken against her hull. The postcard above shows the ship transiting the Panama Canal in the 1920s; below, the ship is pictured after its 1931 overhaul. Coming out of the overhaul with more armament and improved engines, she was assigned to the Pacific fleet for a time and was then sent to the East Coast to escort North Atlantic convoys. Following the Japanese attack on Pearl Harbor, *New Mexico* was immediately reassigned to the Pacific theater, where she spent the rest of the war years. (Both, Greg Trapp.)

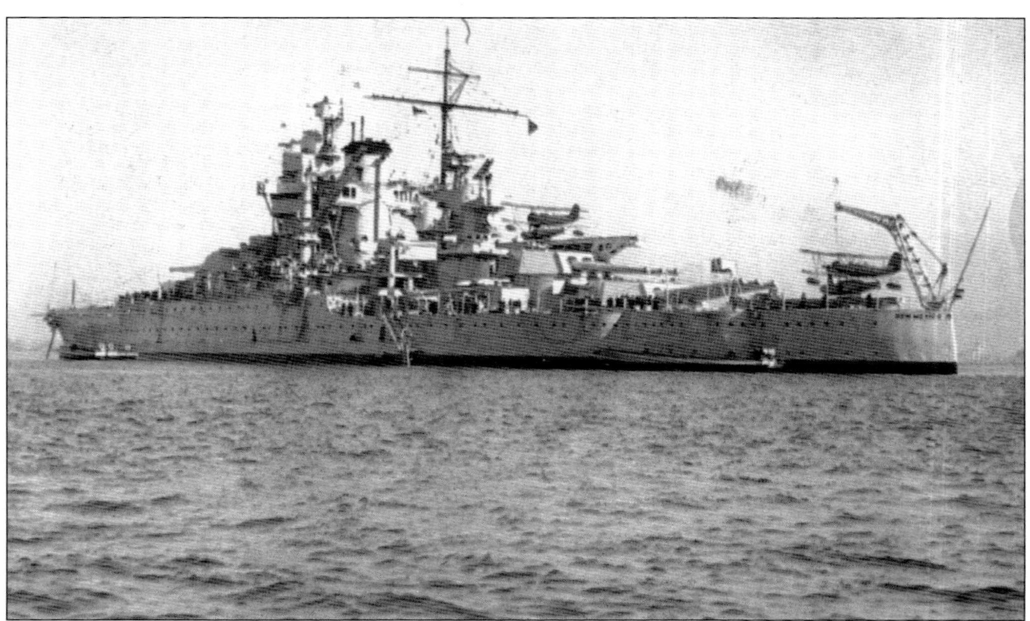

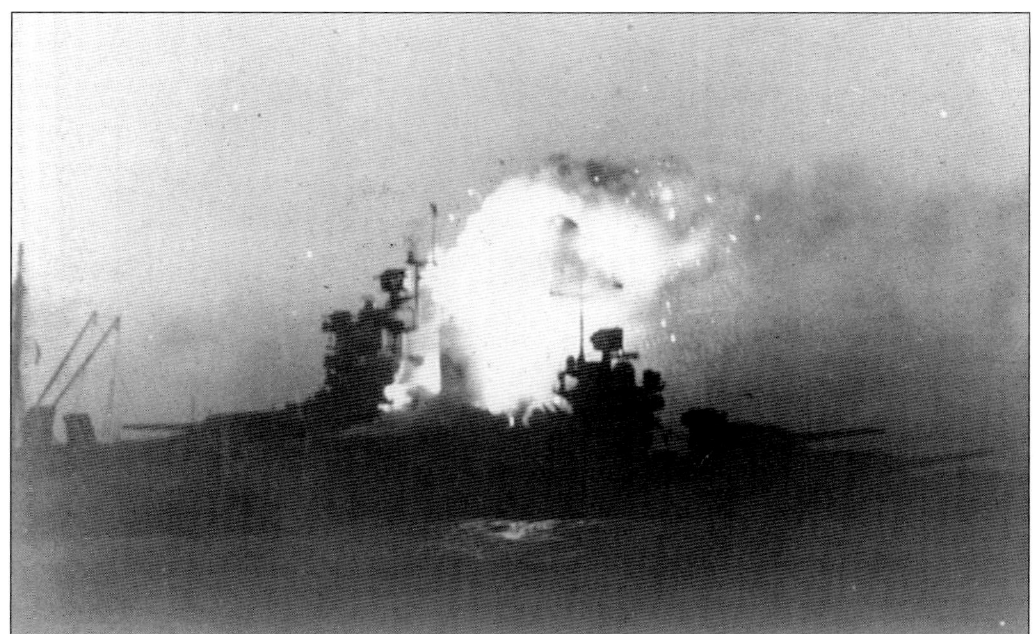

Near the end of the war, the Japanese deployed suicide planes called kamikazes (a name meaning divine wind) against American warships. During the war in the Pacific, the *New Mexico* was hit twice by these planes. During an attack on January 6, 1945 (above), in Lingayen Gulf off the island of Luzon, a kamikaze struck *New Mexico's* bridge, killing 29 men, including the commanding officer, and wounding 87. A second attack occurred on May 12, 1945 (below), while the battleship was providing gunfire support to troops assaulting the Japanese bastion on Okinawa, killing 54 men and wounding another 119. During the course of the war, she earned six battle stars. (Above, US Navy; below, Mark Stille.)

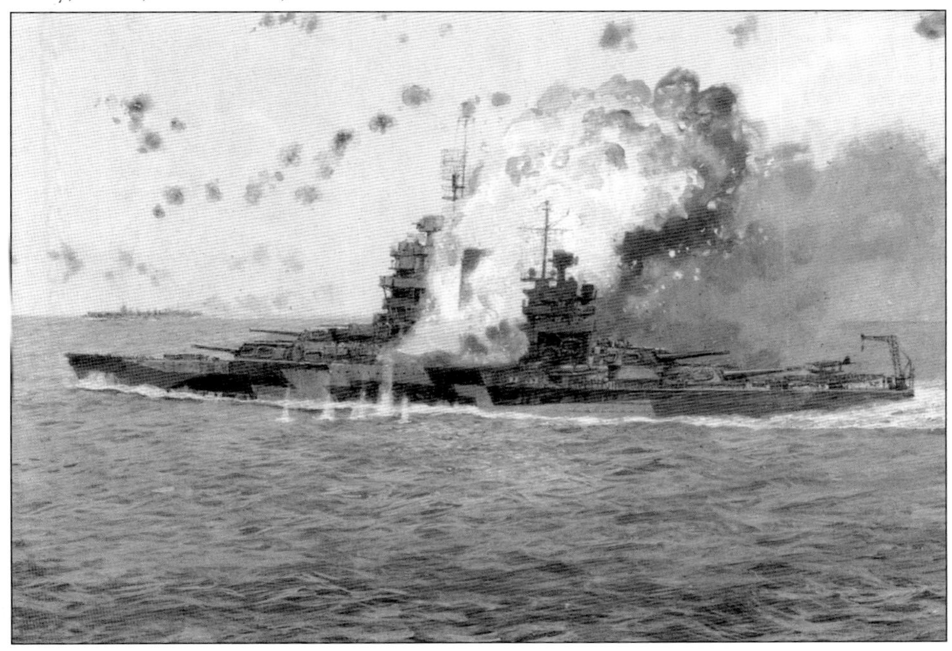

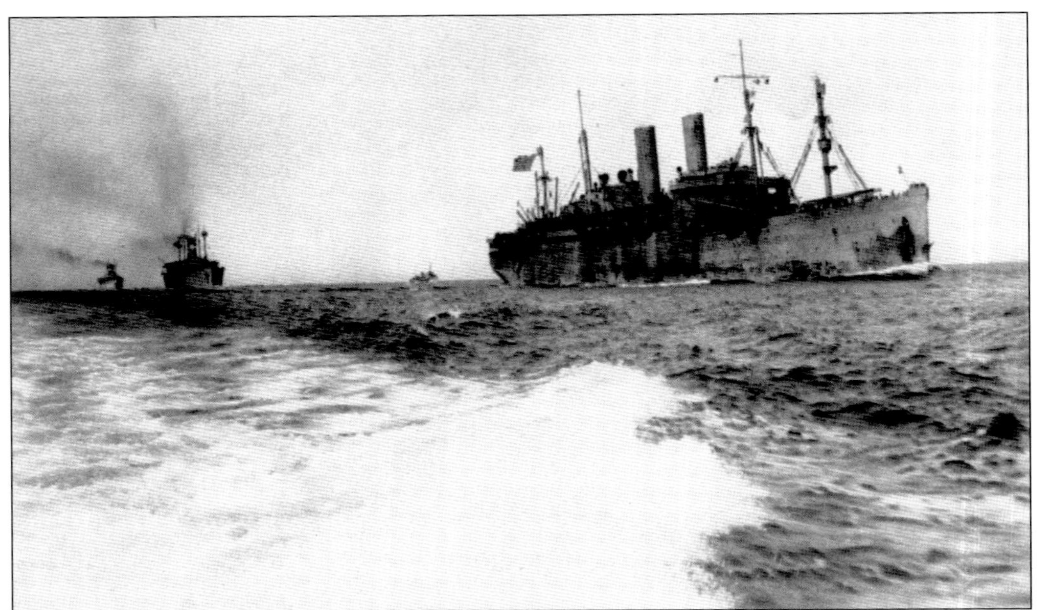

After World War I, Pres. Woodrow Wilson sailed to France aboard the SS *George Washington* (above) to negotiate a treaty between Germany and the Allied powers. The *George Washington* was escorted to France by *New Mexico*. She was also alongside the USS *Missouri* (BB-63) in Tokyo Bay when Japanese officials signed the surrender documents on September 2, 1945 (below). The presence of *New Mexico* on both occasions gave her the unique distinction of being the only naval vessel to participate in the ends of both World War I and World War II. (Above, US Navy; below, National Archives.)

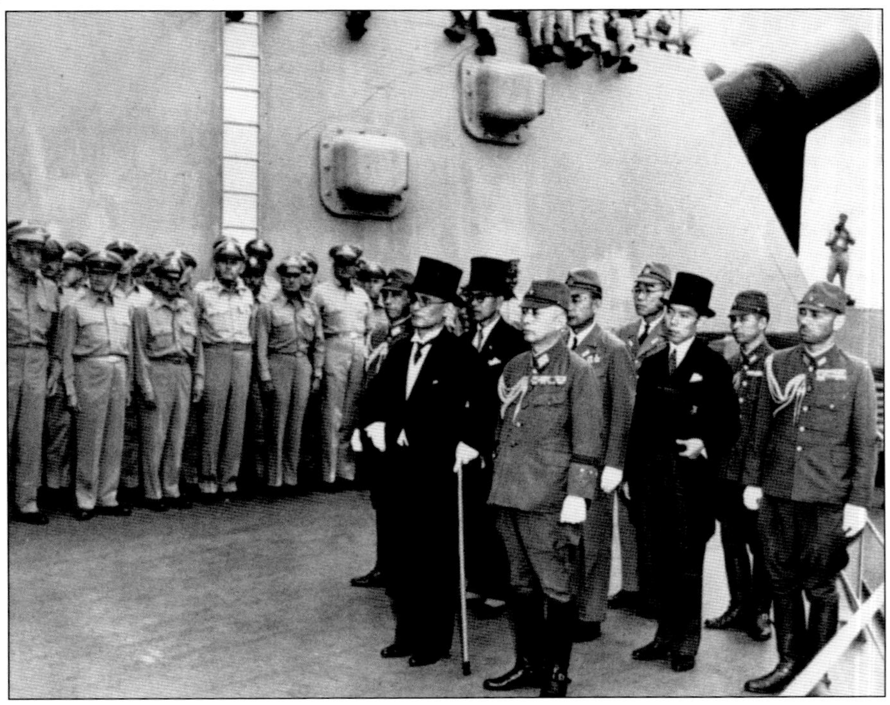

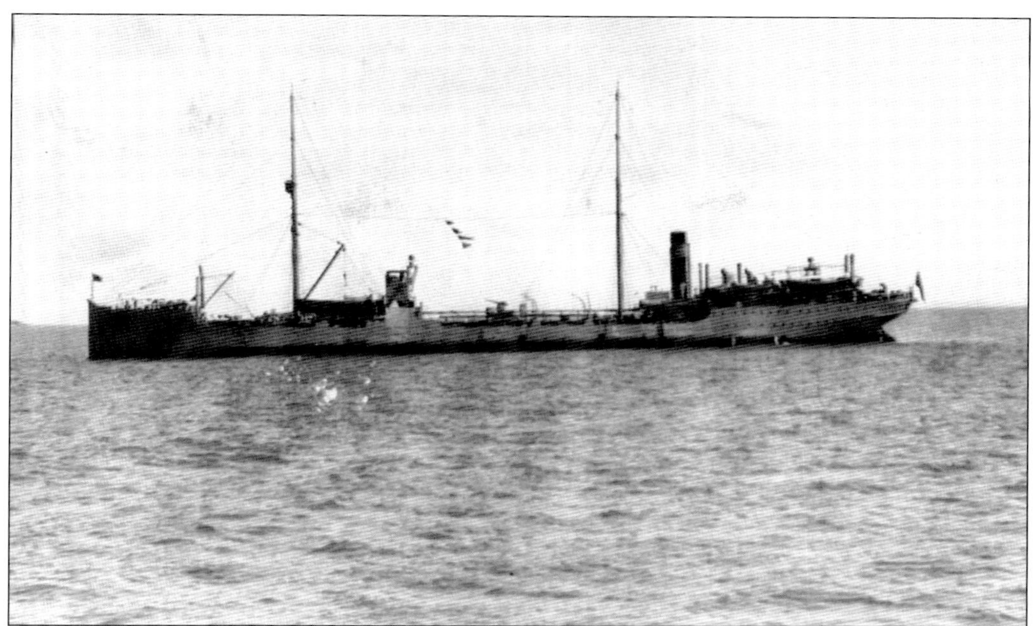

On March 1, 1942, USS *Pecos* (AO-6) was sailing in the Java Sea with two destroyers, attempting to rescue survivors from the seaplane tender USS *Langley* (AV-3). During the rescue attempt, *Pecos* was attacked and sunk by Japanese aircraft. Over 400 men aboard *Pecos*, including sailors from the *Langley*, were lost. (navsource.org.)

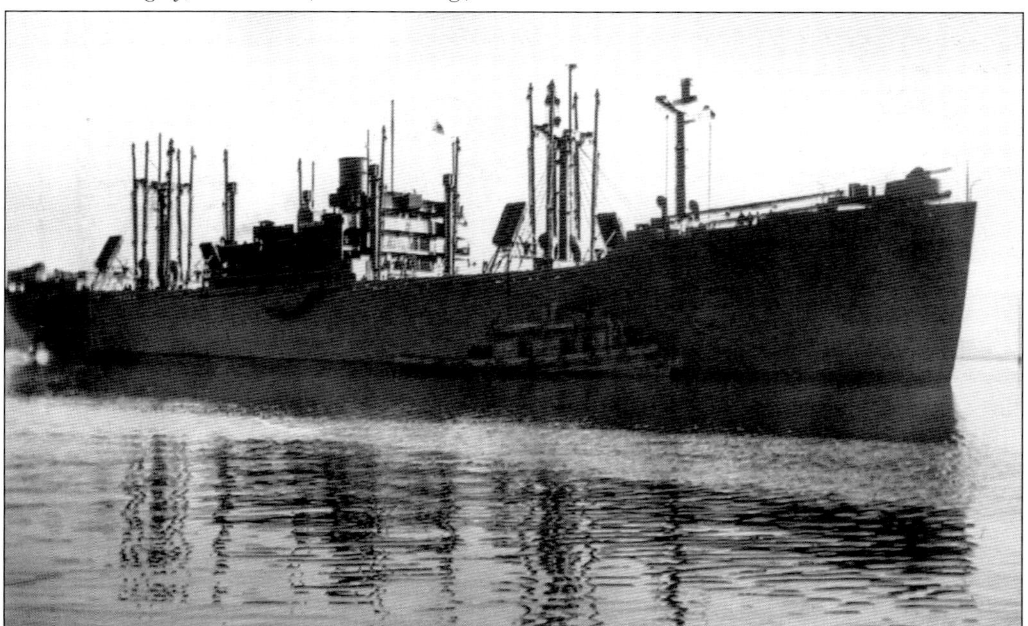

The Victory ship SS *Hobbs Victory*, named for the southeastern New Mexico town, was an ammunition carrier launched in January 1945. While supporting operations off Okinawa in April 1945, she was hit by a kamikaze. Attempts were made to control the resultant fires, but they eventually spread to the storage magazines, and part of the 6,000 tons of ammunition exploded, sinking the ship. (railsoft.com.)

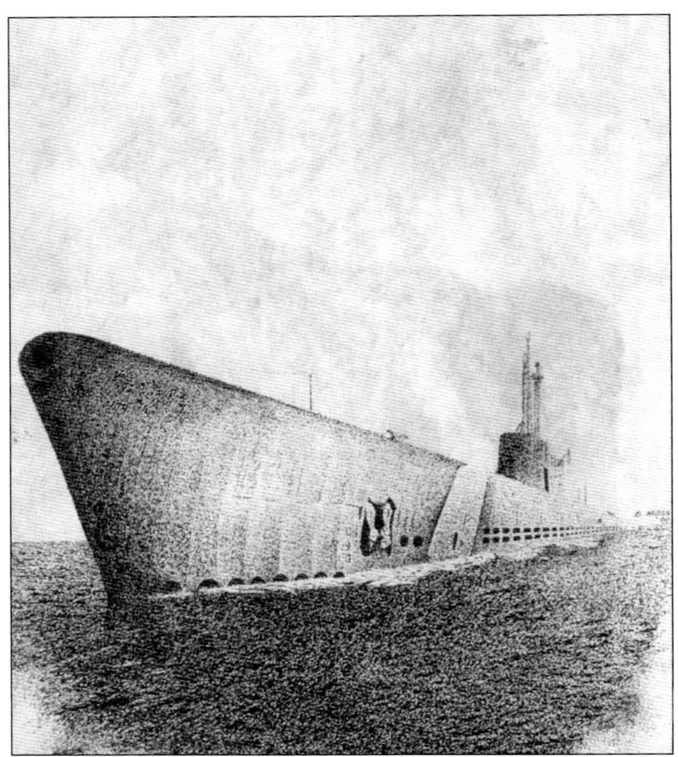

The USS *Bullhead* (SS-332) was on her third war patrol in the Java Sea off the coast of Bali when she was bombed and sunk by a Japanese Mitsubishi Ki-51 dive bomber. Her sinking occurred on August 6, 1945, the same day as the "Little Boy" nuclear weapon was dropped on Hiroshima. The *Bullhead*, shown at left in an original pencil sketch by retired Navy quartermaster Dan Moss, was the last US Navy vessel lost in World War II. In 1987, the National Submarine Veterans Association asked cities across the country to memorialize one of the 52 submarines lost during the war. Albuquerque chose the *Bullhead* and built a park dedicated to her memory (below). (Left, CQM Dan Moss, USN, Ret.; below, John Taylor.)

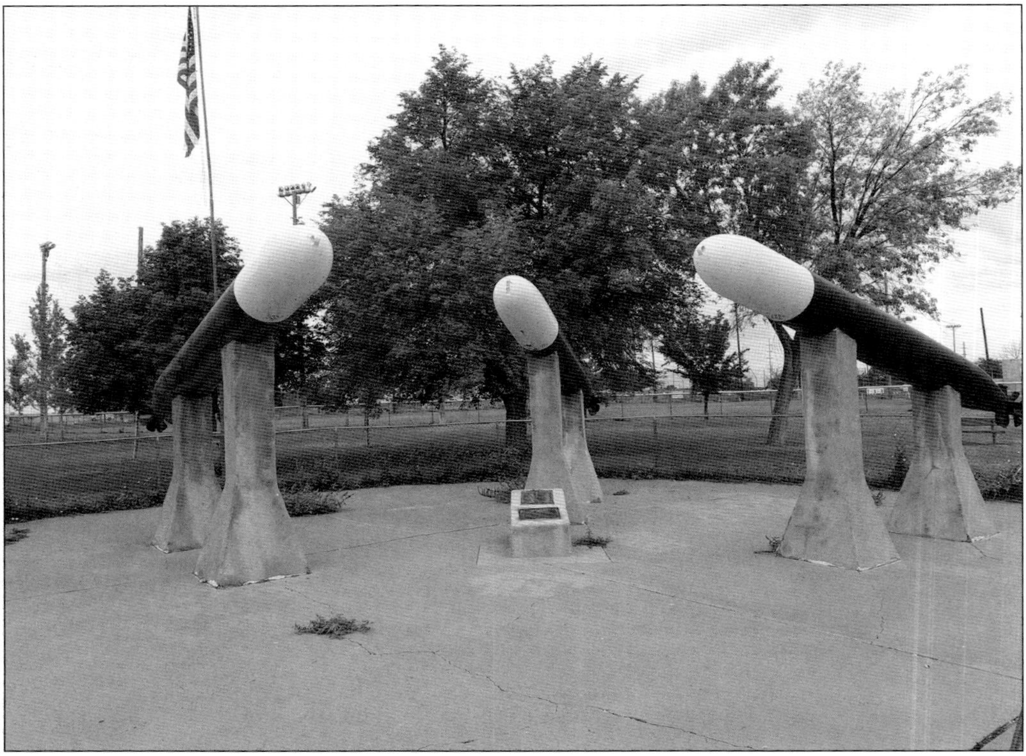

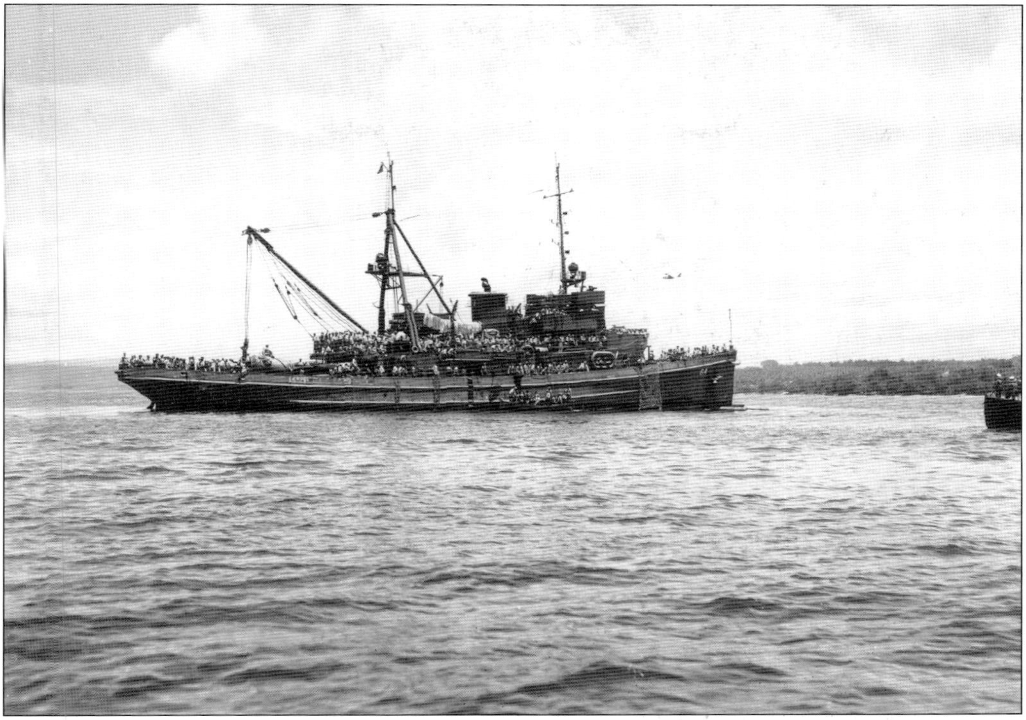

The USS *Navajo* (AT-64) was the lead ship of the Navajo class of fleet tugboats. She was launched in 1939 and was providing fleet tug services in San Diego when war was declared. From 1941 through 1943, she provided towing, repair, and salvage assistance throughout the Western Pacific. On September 12, 1943, while towing a gasoline barge from Pago Pago to Espiritu Santo, she was torpedoed and sank. Seventeen men were lost. (navsource.org)

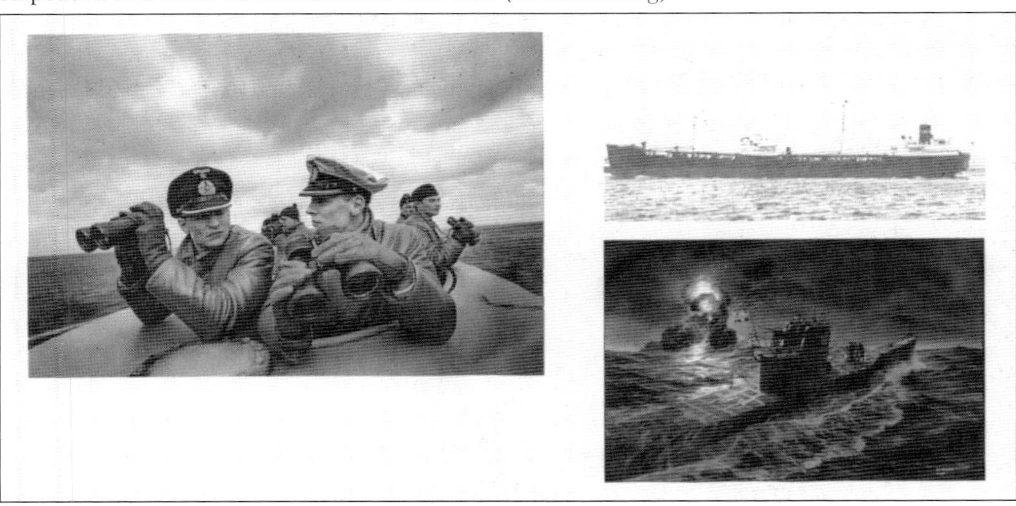

Because the steamship *Patrick Hurley* could sail at a speed of 17 knots, her crew felt that she could outrun any German U-boats operating in the Atlantic. The *Hurley* left Aruba with a load of 135,000 barrels of fuel. On September 12, 1941, the submarine *U-512* attacked the *Hurley* using her deck gun, setting the tanker ablaze. She sank with the loss of 18 sailors. (Left, New Republic; top right, nasvsource.org; bottom right, Tom Fox galleries.)

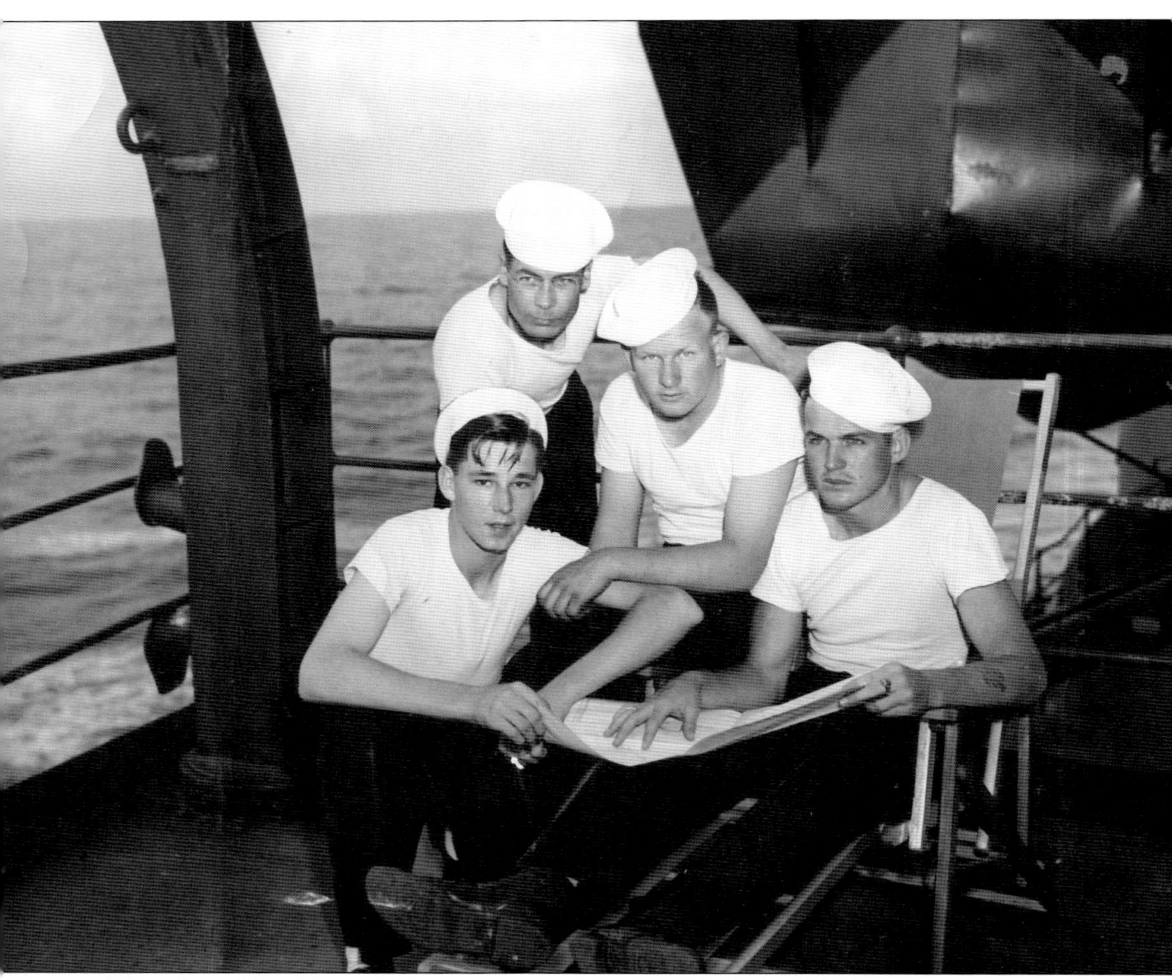

The story of New Mexico's Navy is not just about ships. It is about the sailors who served aboard them. Between 70,000 and 80,000 American sailors from the Navy, Coast Guard, and Merchant Marine gave their lives during the war, among them nearly 600 men from New Mexico. This image shows four men from New Mexico who found themselves serving together aboard USS *Appalachian* (AGC-1), an amphibious support ship that won four battle stars during World War II. From left to right are Clifford Hopkins (Albuquerque), Lynn Brown (Roswell), Richard Smith (Las Cruces), and Hershal Rutledge (Grants). Brought together aboard the *Appalachian* far from home, they represent all of the men and women of New Mexico who served in and supported the war effort. (Gregg Trapp.)

Four

THUNDER (AND BATS) FROM THE SKIES

New Mexico had a confluence of characteristics that brought the US Army Air Corps (the US Air Force after 1947) to the state. New Mexico was centrally located and far from coastlines, making it a secure location for military operations; the state was relatively unpopulated (only 530,000 people, most of whom were located in Albuquerque, Santa Fe, and Las Cruces); it had millions of acres of empty, government-owned land; the state offered a wide variety of terrain; and the weather was uniformly excellent all year long. As a result of these factors, the Army established eight bases, five dispersal sites, and thirteen bombing and gunnery ranges across the state. Thousands of men passed through these training facilities on their way to both the European and Pacific Theaters.

During the war, the Army Air Corps used New Mexico facilities to train new pilots and bombardiers, which was especially necessary given the Corps' tremendous attrition during the war. From December 1941 to August 1945, the Army Air Corps had 53,173 battle casualty deaths. In addition, it lost 65,164 aircraft—43,581 overseas and 21,583 in training or transport flights in the United States. This put tremendous pressure on the training activities in New Mexico and elsewhere to keep the bombers and fighters flying.

In addition, New Mexico scientists at the various Army Air Corps facilities developed important new technology such as the proximity fuse and the short-lived "bat bomb." They also used facilities in the state to develop the first nuclear weapon, tested at the Alamogordo Bombing and Gunnery Range, an Army Air Corps facility. The story of the atomic bomb is of sufficient significance that it is treated separately in chapter five.

Many of these locations, such as the Belen Bombing Range and the Los Lunas Bombing Range, have faded from memory. Some of the sites, such as Roswell Army Air Field and Deming Army Air Field, have become local municipal airports. Four of the locations—Kirtland Air Force Base in Albuquerque, Holloman Air Force Base near Alamogordo, Cannon Air Force Base near Clovis, and the White Sands Missile Range—remain critical elements of US national security.

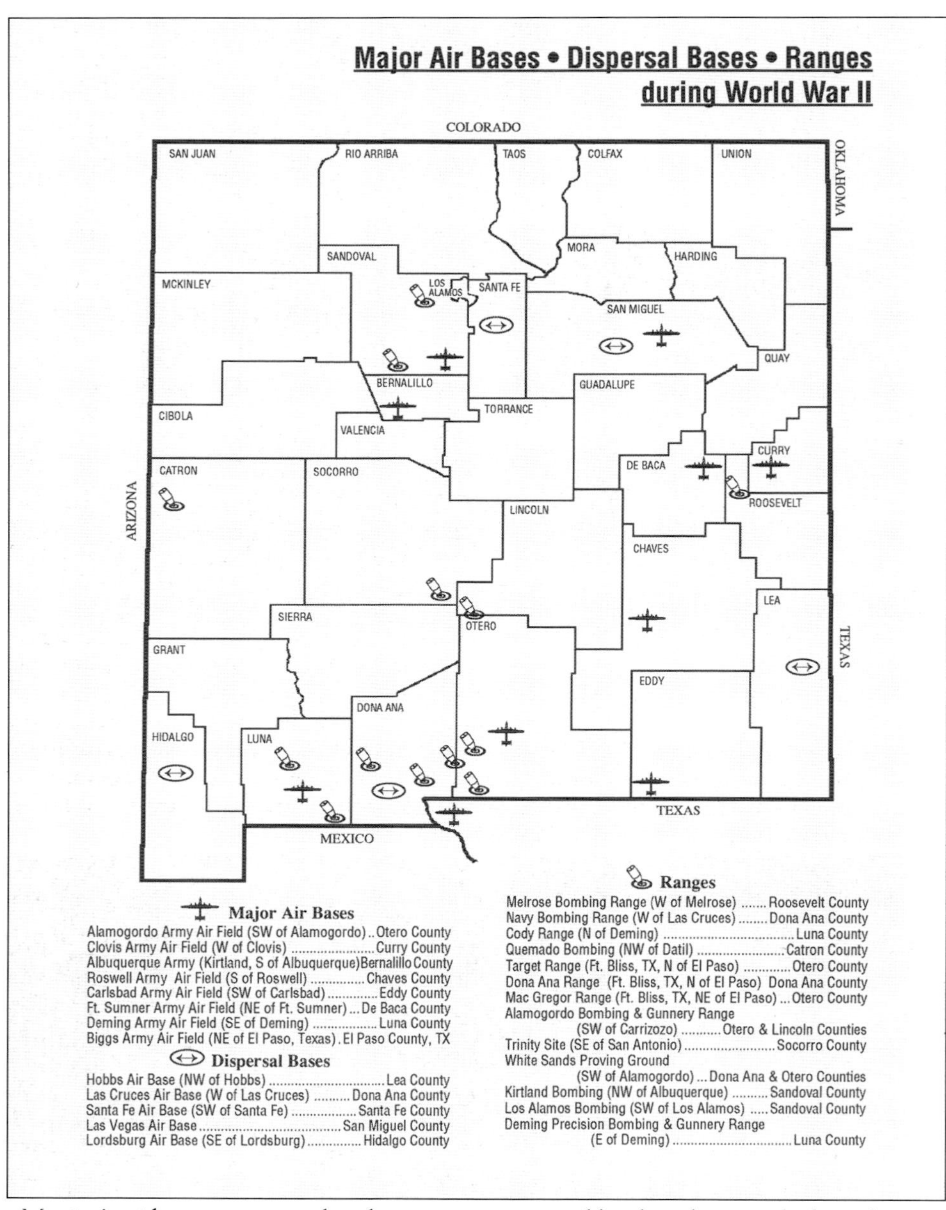

New Mexico's wide open, unpopulated, government-owned land made it an ideal site for training bomber crews in navigation, bombing, and day/night flying. The state's distance from more vulnerable coastlines also contributed to its desirability for hosting sensitive military installations. Sites ranged from airfields, where pilots and bombardiers had both classroom and flying experience, to bombing and gunnery ranges, where crews could prove their expertise. Sites such as Kirtland Air Force Base, Holloman Air Force Base, and Cannon Air Force Base that served the country so well during the war remain critical facilities. Sites such as the Carlsbad Army Airfield and the Hobbs facility have been incorporated into local commercial or municipal airfields, while many have been memorialized with monuments to recognize the brave men and women who served and died during training missions, while others, such as the Los Lunas and Belen bombing ranges, are no more than faded memories. (New Mexico State University.)

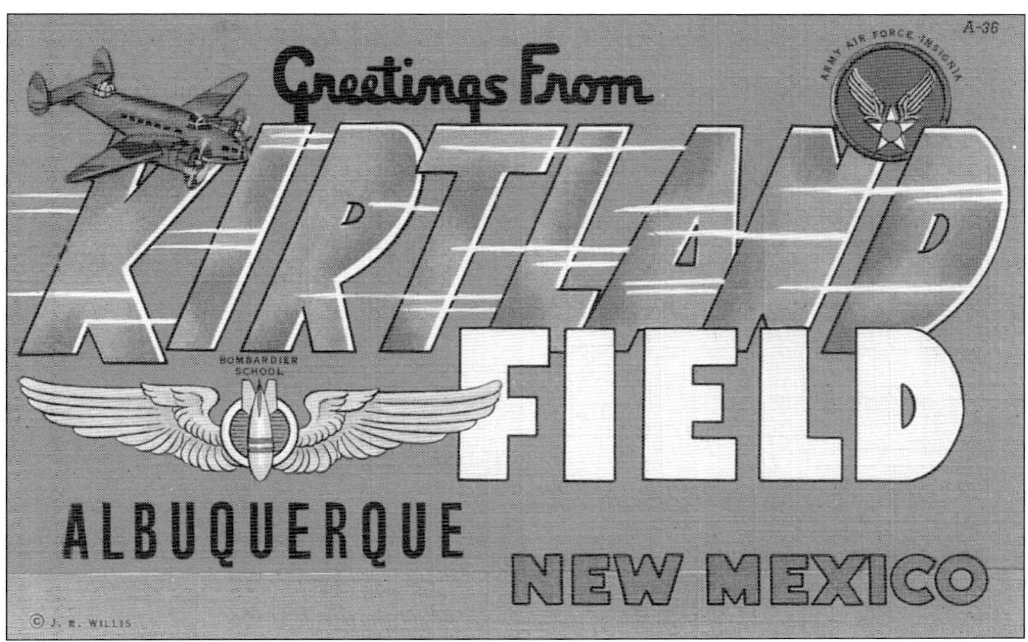

In February 1942, Albuquerque Army Air Base was renamed Kirtland Army Air Field in honor of one of America's aviation pioneers, Col. Roy C. Kirtland. During World War II, Kirtland Army Air Field was used to train pilots, navigators, and bombardiers. Actor Jimmy Stewart and the future president of the Republic of China, Chang Kai-Shek, both trained at this facility. The facility was also used as the air hub for Manhattan Project operations. The photograph below shows a student and instructor after an instrument training flight in an AT-6 trainer at Kirtland. (Above, Richard Melzer; below, Harold F. Blackburn.)

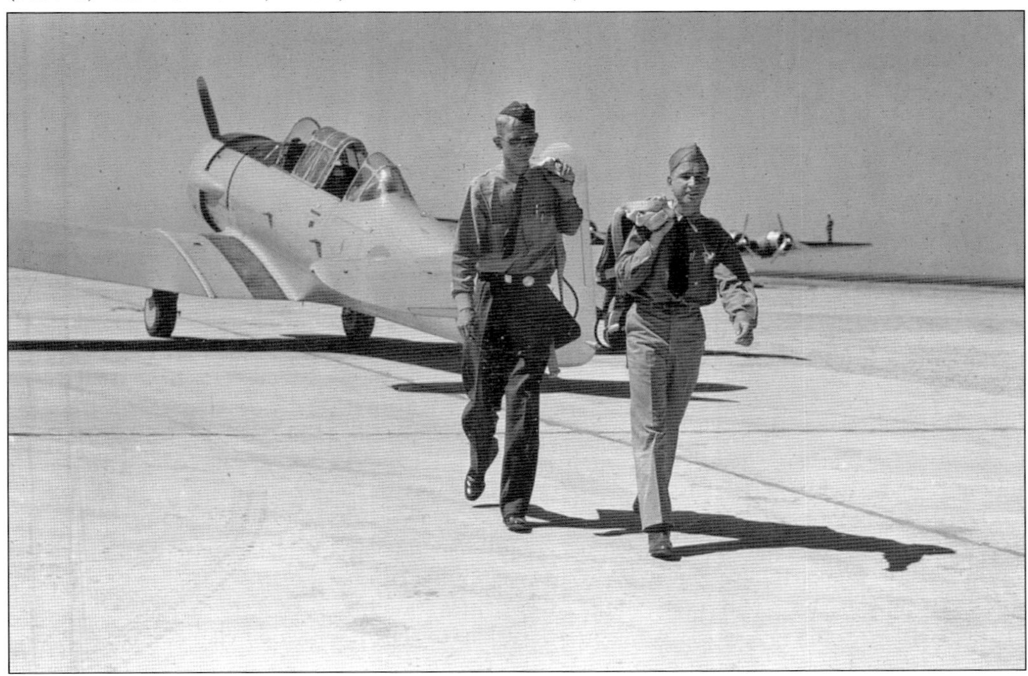

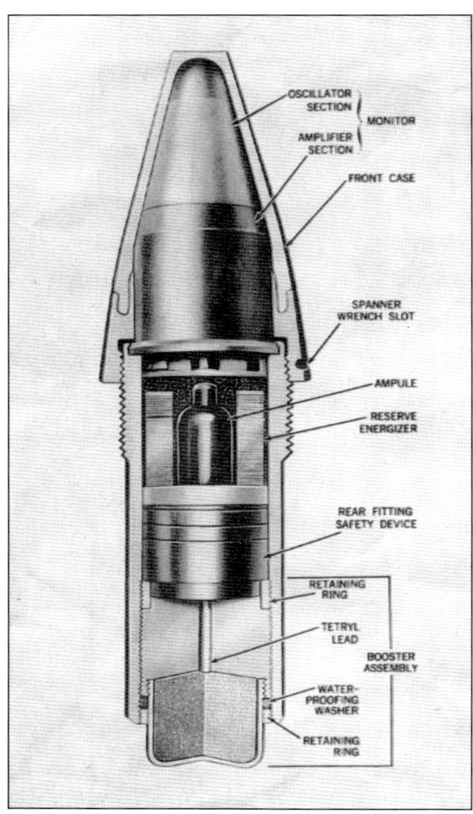

The concept of an artillery fuse that would explode near a target was first conceived in 1925, but the level of technology was not yet up to the task. During World War II, the National Defense Research Committee restarted the effort. Fuses using various technologies were designed at Johns Hopkins University in Baltimore, and designs that appeared favorable were shipped to Kirtland Army Airfield, where Dr. Everly John "EJ" Workman (below), a professor of physics at the University of New Mexico (UNM) and future president of the New Mexico Institute of Mining and Technology (now New Mexico Institute of Technology) field-tested the valuable units. (Left, historynet.com; below, UNM Center for Southwest Research, UNMA 175, Box 1, folder 7.)

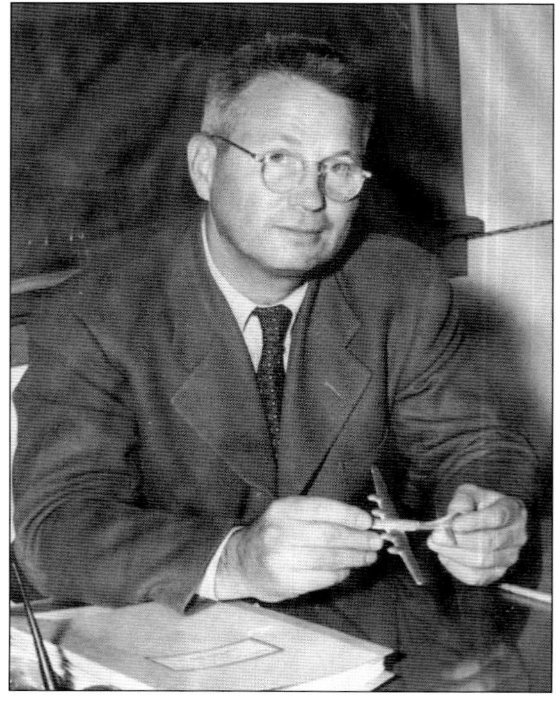

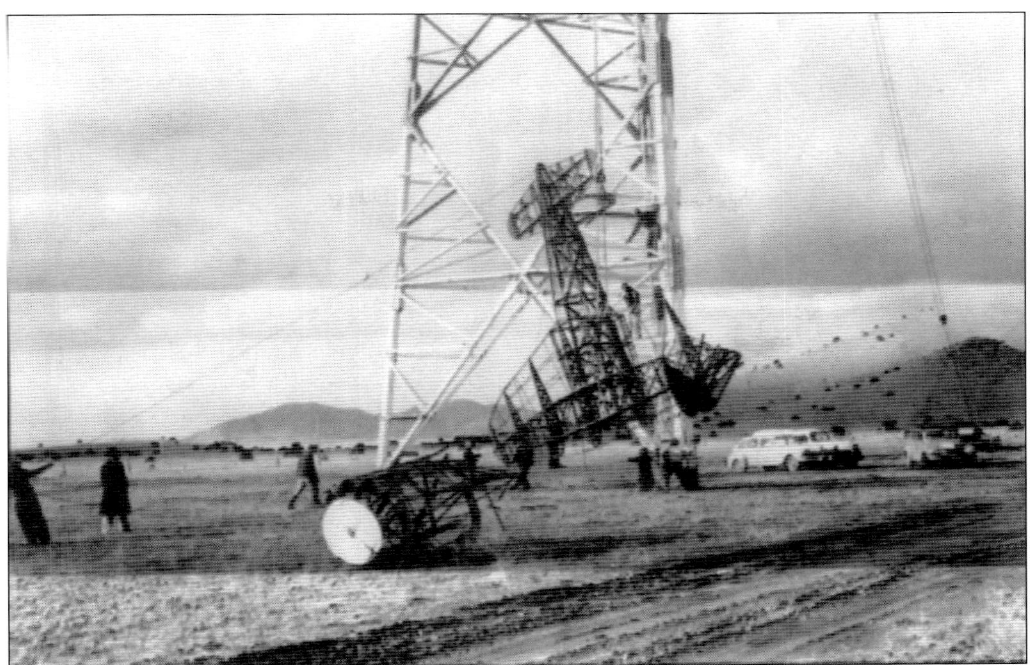

During the war, the highly classified development of the proximity fuse was considered by many to be more important than the development of the nuclear weapon because such a fuse would have an immediate impact on the warfighters' capabilities. Workman and his crew hung simulated Japanese aircraft constructed from wood between downrange towers on the south end of Kirtland Army Air Field, and shells with the experimental fuse designs were fired from nearby artillery pieces. The proximity-fused shells were eventually used by both the Navy and the Army in combat in Europe and the Pacific. (Both, Sandia National Laboratories.)

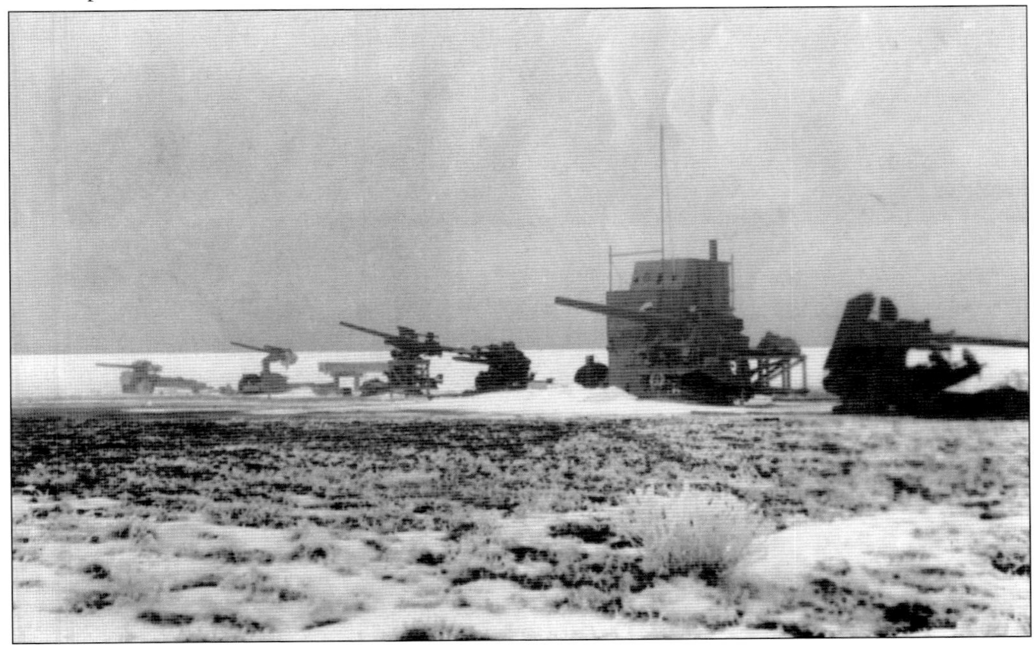

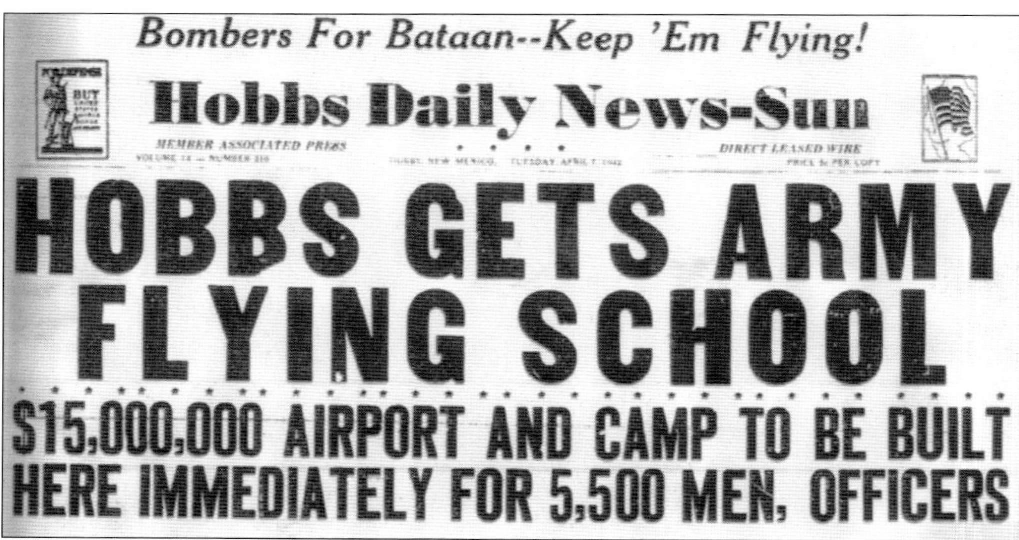

Bombers For Bataan--Keep 'Em Flying!

Hobbs Daily News-Sun

MEMBER ASSOCIATED PRESS

DIRECT LEASED WIRE

HOBBS GETS ARMY FLYING SCHOOL

$15,000,000 AIRPORT AND CAMP TO BE BUILT HERE IMMEDIATELY FOR 5,500 MEN, OFFICERS

The four-engine B-17 Flying Fortress was a mainstay of the Army Air Corps during World War II. In 1942, the Air Corps established a new training facility north of the oil-patch town of Hobbs in southeastern New Mexico. At its peak, the air base had a population of nearly 5,500 men and women, increasing the population of Hobbs by almost 50 percent. Today, the former air base is home to the Hobbs Industrial Air Park and serves as the town's municipal airport. The training base is memorialized by a sculpture of a B-17 with its crew beneath the wing (below). (Both, Richard Melzer.)

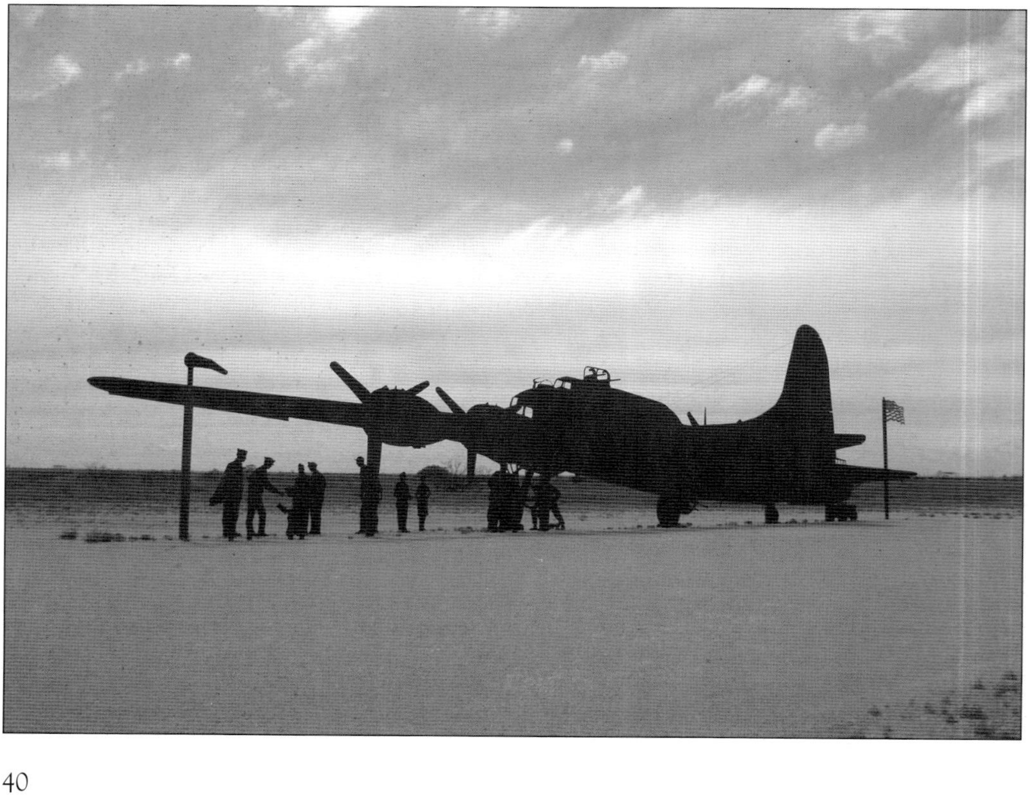

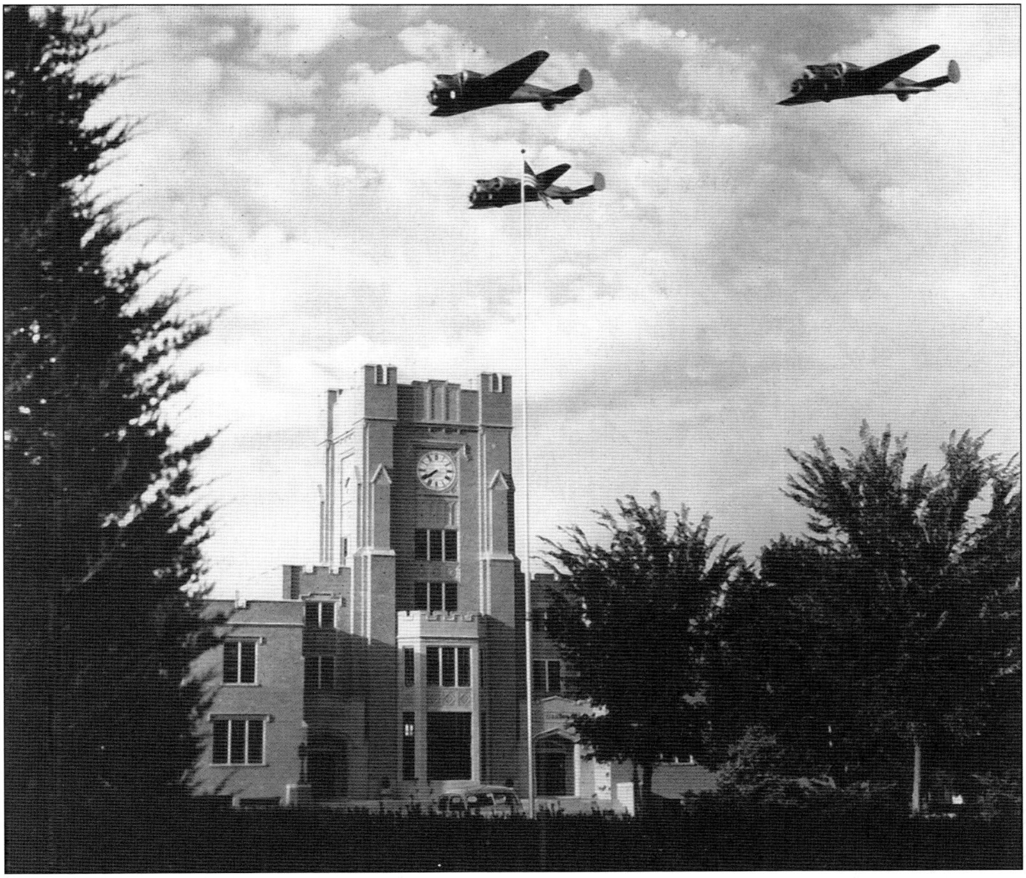

The Roswell Army Flying School (matchbook cover pictured below) was established in 1941 to train pilots, co-pilots, and bombardiers. It initially used Beechcraft AT-11, Cessna AT-17, Vultee BT-13, and Vultee BT-15 trainers. From 1944 until the end of the war, training for B-29 Superfortress pilots, co-pilots, and flight engineers was conducted at Roswell. Planes from the Roswell training facility are shown flying over the New Mexico Military Institute in Roswell above. From 1948 until 1967, the facility was named Walker Air Force Base in honor of New Mexico's posthumous Medal of Honor winner Gen. Kenneth Newton Walker. In the aftermath of the war, Walker was the headquarters of the 509th Composite Group under Col. Paul Tibbets, the pilot who had dropped the first atomic bomb on Hiroshima. (Above, Southeastern New Mexico Historical Society; below, Richard Melzer.)

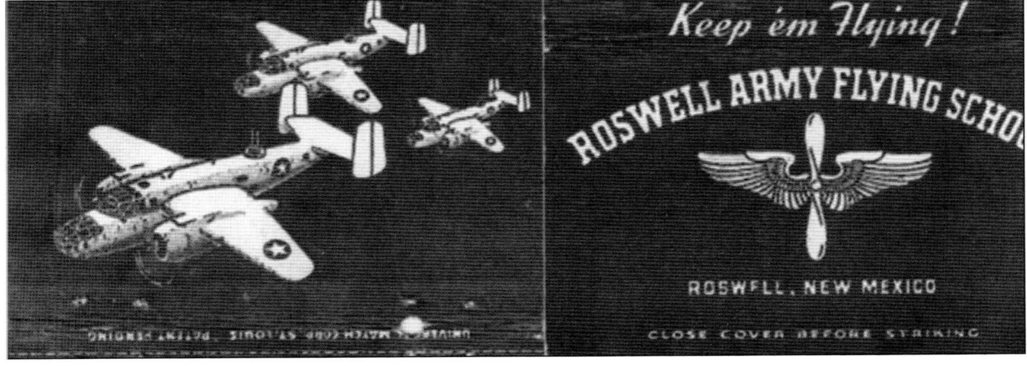

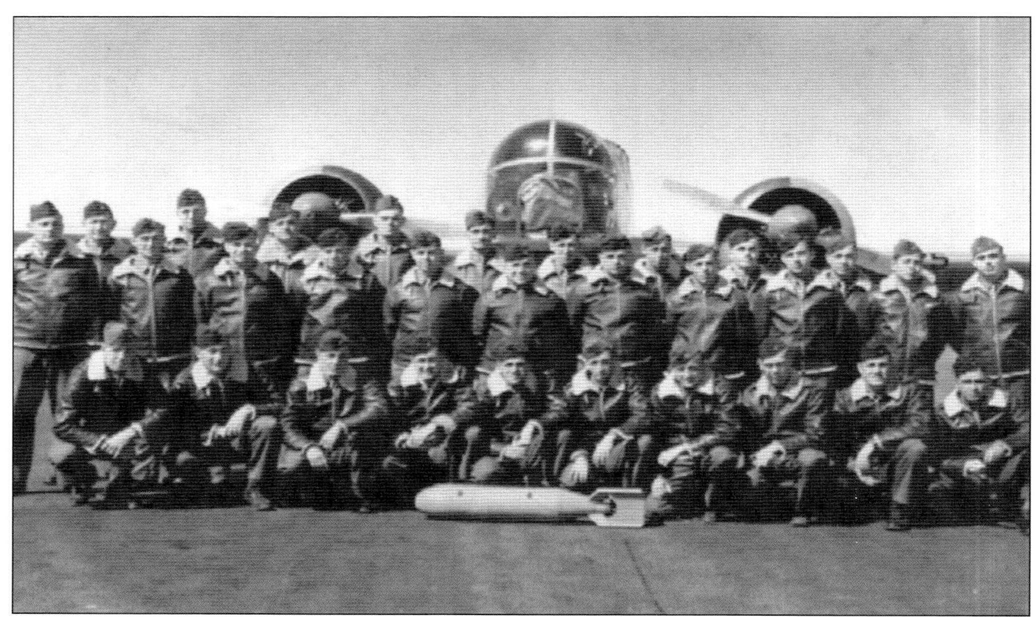

The Carlsbad Army Airfield was established five miles south of the town of Carlsbad in the summer of 1942 to train bombardiers. It principally used the Beechcraft AT-11 Kansan bombing trainer and students trained on the highly classified Norden bombsight. Once students graduated, such as the class shown above with an M38A2 practice bomb in front of an AT-11, they went on to Kirtland, Alamogordo, or other facilities for advanced training on specific aircraft such as the B-17 Flying Fortress and the B-24 Liberator. The image below shows a crew being briefed for a nighttime practice mission. (Both, Southeastern New Mexico Historical Society.)

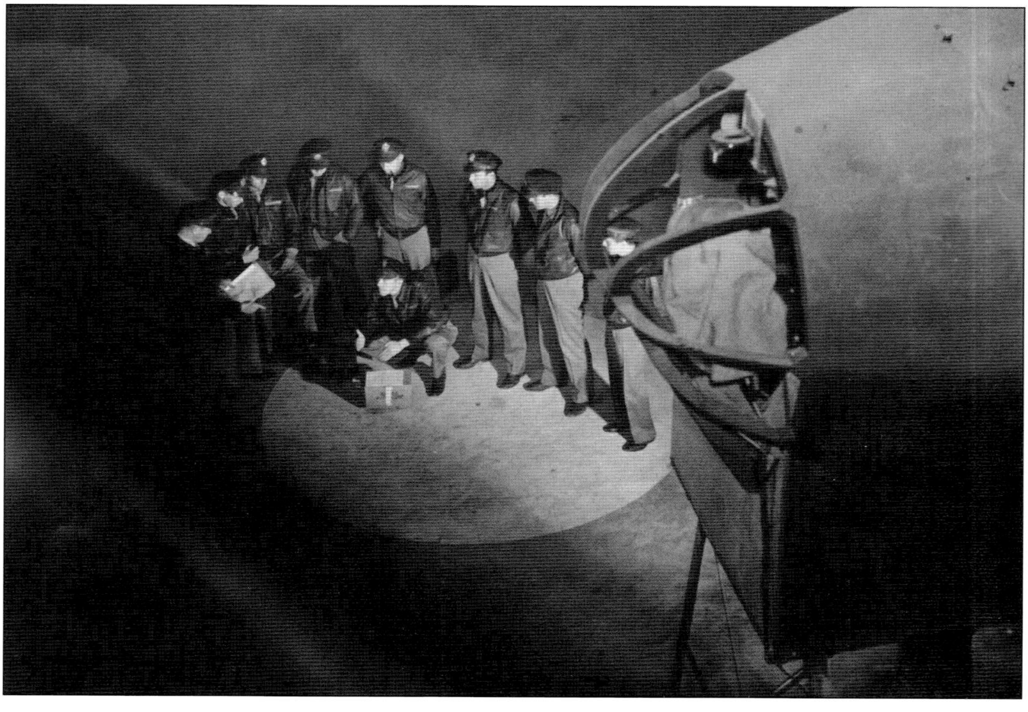

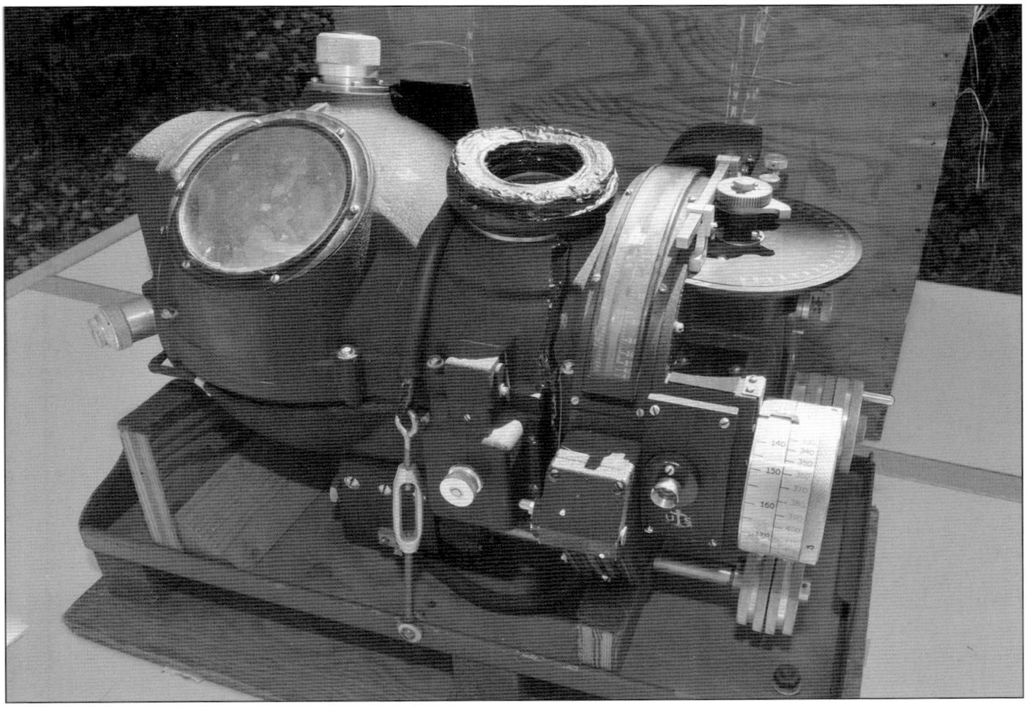

One of the most highly guarded secrets of the Army Air Corps was the Norden bombsight. Developed by a Swiss engineer in the 1930s, it was used by both Army and Navy aircraft during the war. Although more accurate than other bombsights, it failed to live up to its reputation of being able to drop a bomb into a pickle barrel from 30,000 feet. In addition, although a carefully guarded secret, it turned out that one of the Norden corporation's engineers had given a complete set of plans to the Nazis in 1938. While at Carlsbad, the valuable Nordens were stored in the building shown below, now in Veteran's Park in Carlsbad. (Above, US Air Force; below, Donna Blake Birchell.)

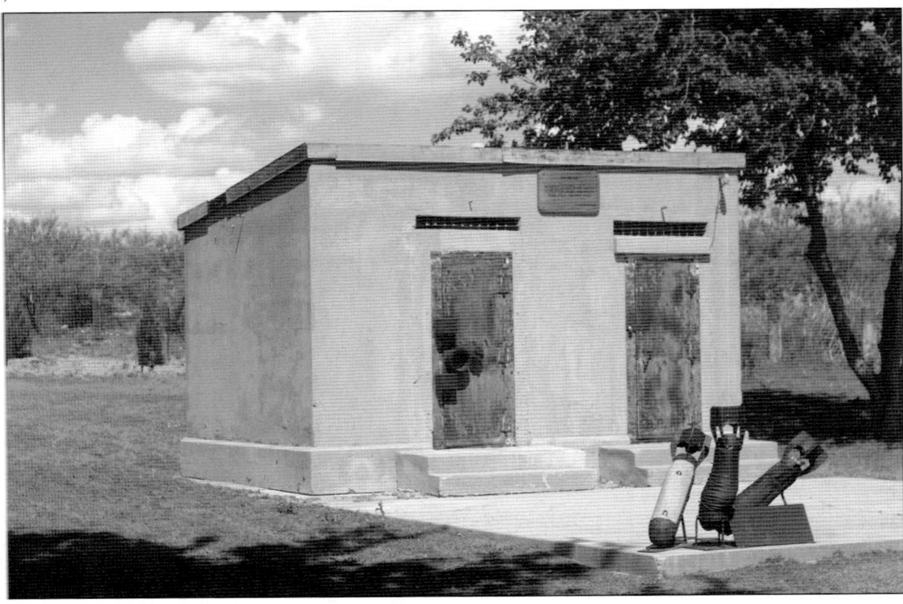

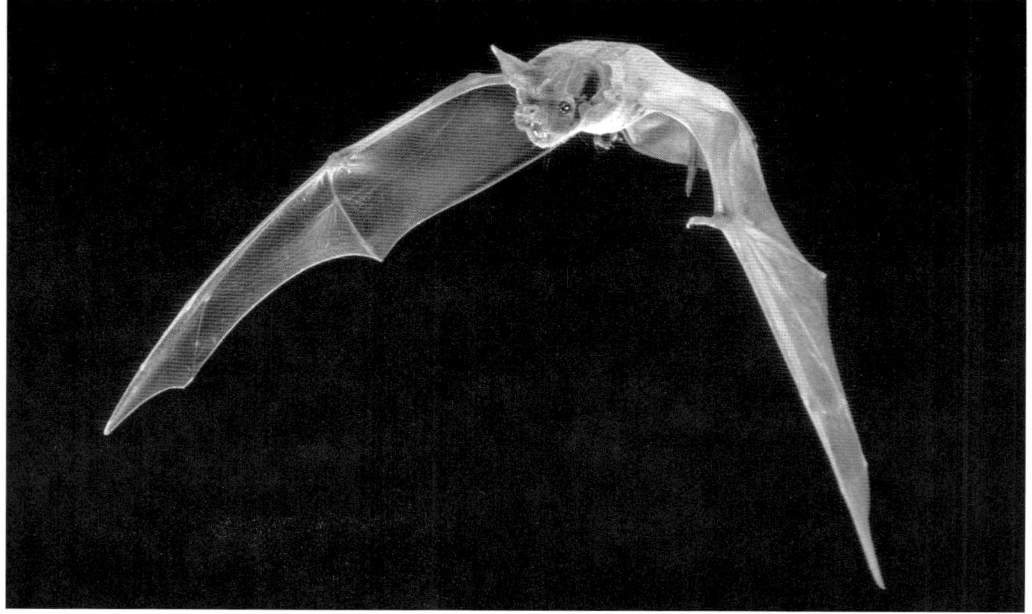

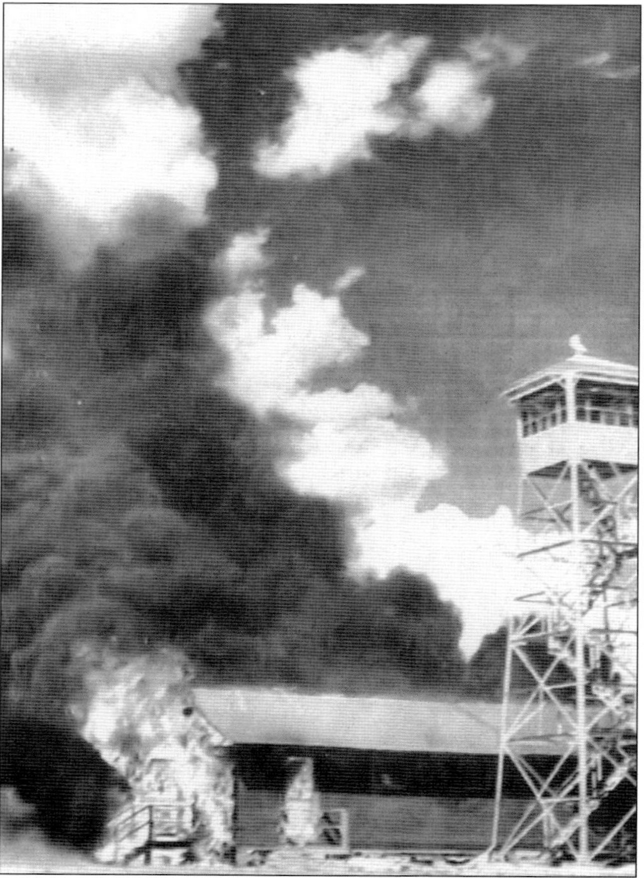

The vulnerability of Japanese cities to fire was well known, so a scheme to deliver incendiary ordnance using bats was developed (and eventually abandoned) at the Carlsbad training facility, well known for its proximity to the large bat population in Carlsbad Caverns. The bats would be rigged with an incendiary device and then inserted into a canister, which would be dropped from aircraft. Before hitting the ground, the canister would open, releasing the bats, which would fly to nearby buildings where the incendiary device would detonate. Unfortunately, during testing, bats flew into a nearby Carlsbad Air Base building and started a large fire (left). Shortly thereafter, the project was terminated. (Above, Scott Altenbach; left, Washington State University.)

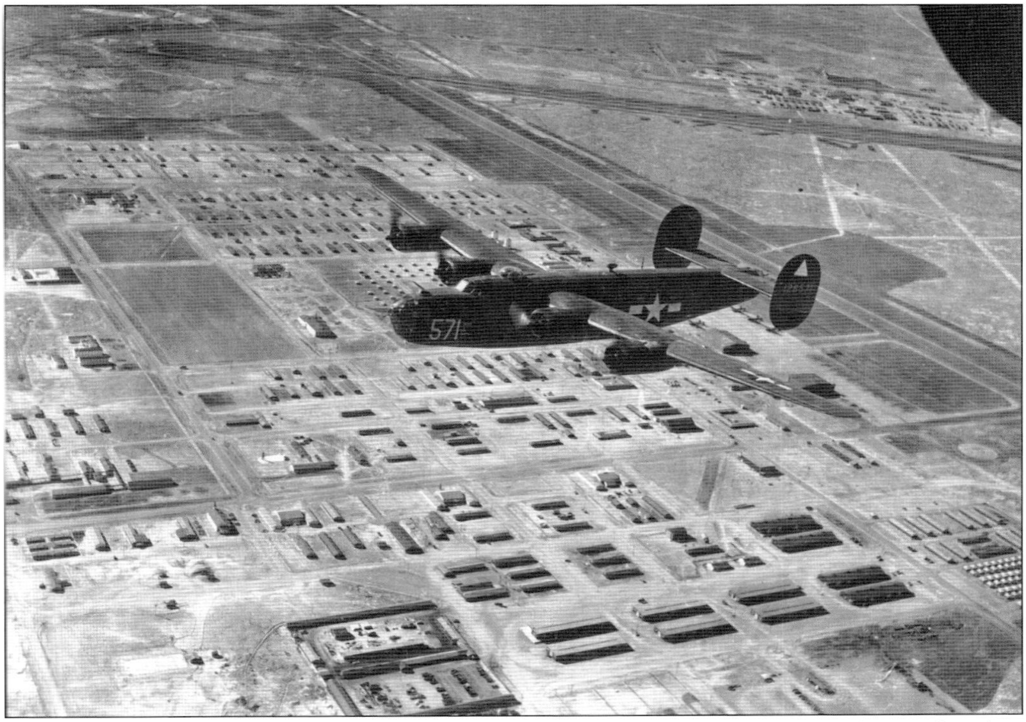

Both the Alamogordo Army Airfield, shown above being overflown by a B-24 Liberator bomber, and the Alamogordo Bombing and Gunnery Range (now White Sands Missile Range) were established in 1942. The airfield was home to the training squadrons, and the nearby bombing and gunnery range was used to sharpen the trainees' skills before sending them overseas. The facilities provided both classroom and operational training for over 20 different groups, principally bombardiers, using B-17 Flying Fortresses and B-24 Liberators. In 1948, the facility was renamed Holloman Air Force Base in honor of missile pioneer Col. George P. Holloman. (Above, Holloman Air Force Base; below, Richard Melzer.)

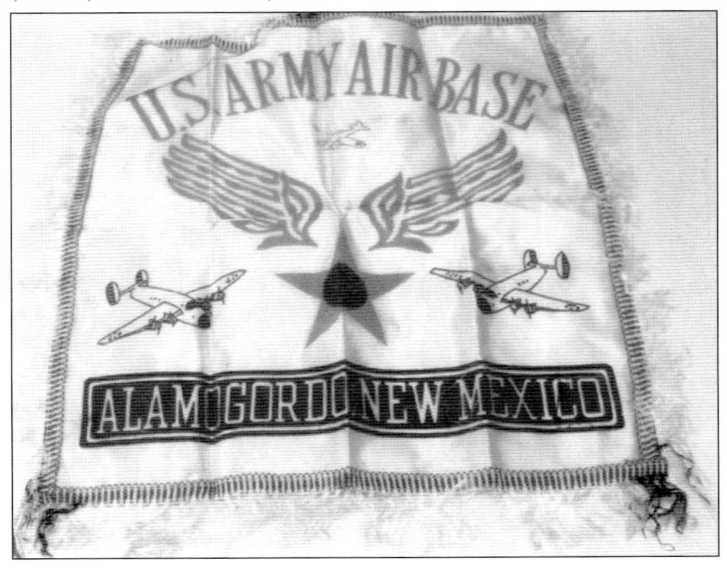

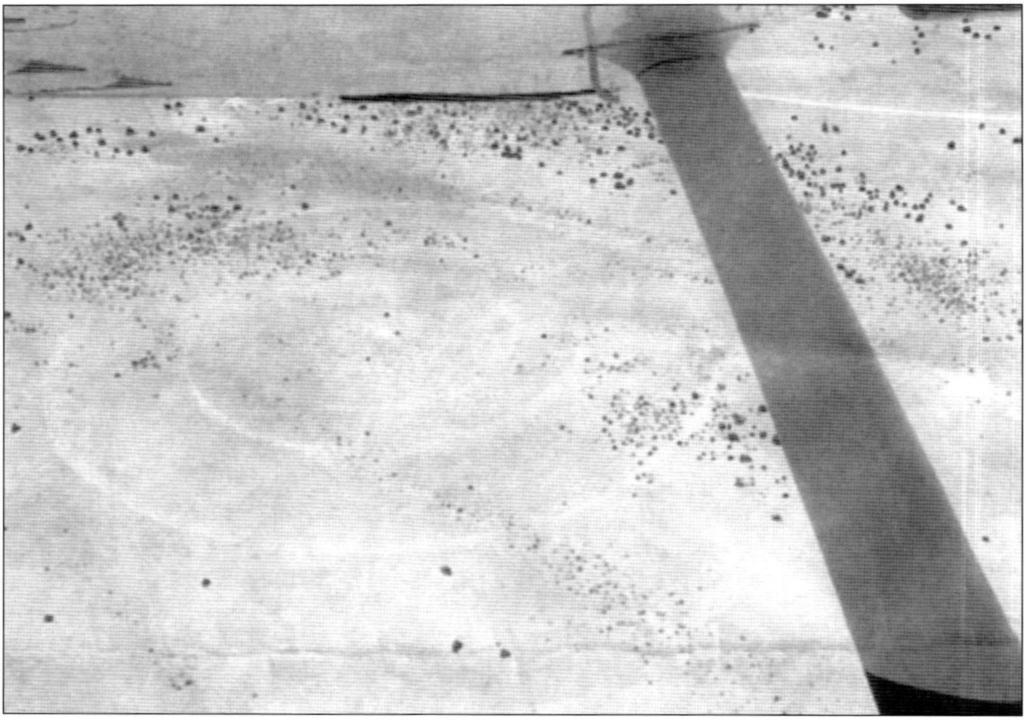

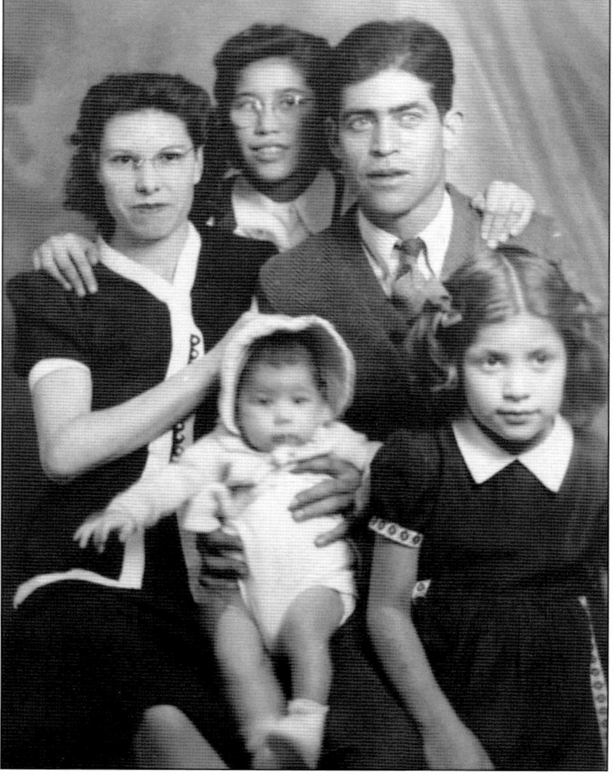

Although training crews used practice bombs filled with either sand or concrete, the bombs had small spotting charges consisting of a few pounds of black powder activated by shotgun shells. When the spotting charge hit the ground and detonated, the bombardier and pilot would know how accurately they had delivered the bomb. One day in August 1945, two children from the Montoya family (left) were horseback riding on the edge of the Belen Bombing Range (above). One of them spotted the tail of a bright blue practice bomb. They could not dislodge the bomb but were able to remove the spotting charge and bring it back to the family ranch. (Above, Helen Kirchner; left, Montoya family.)

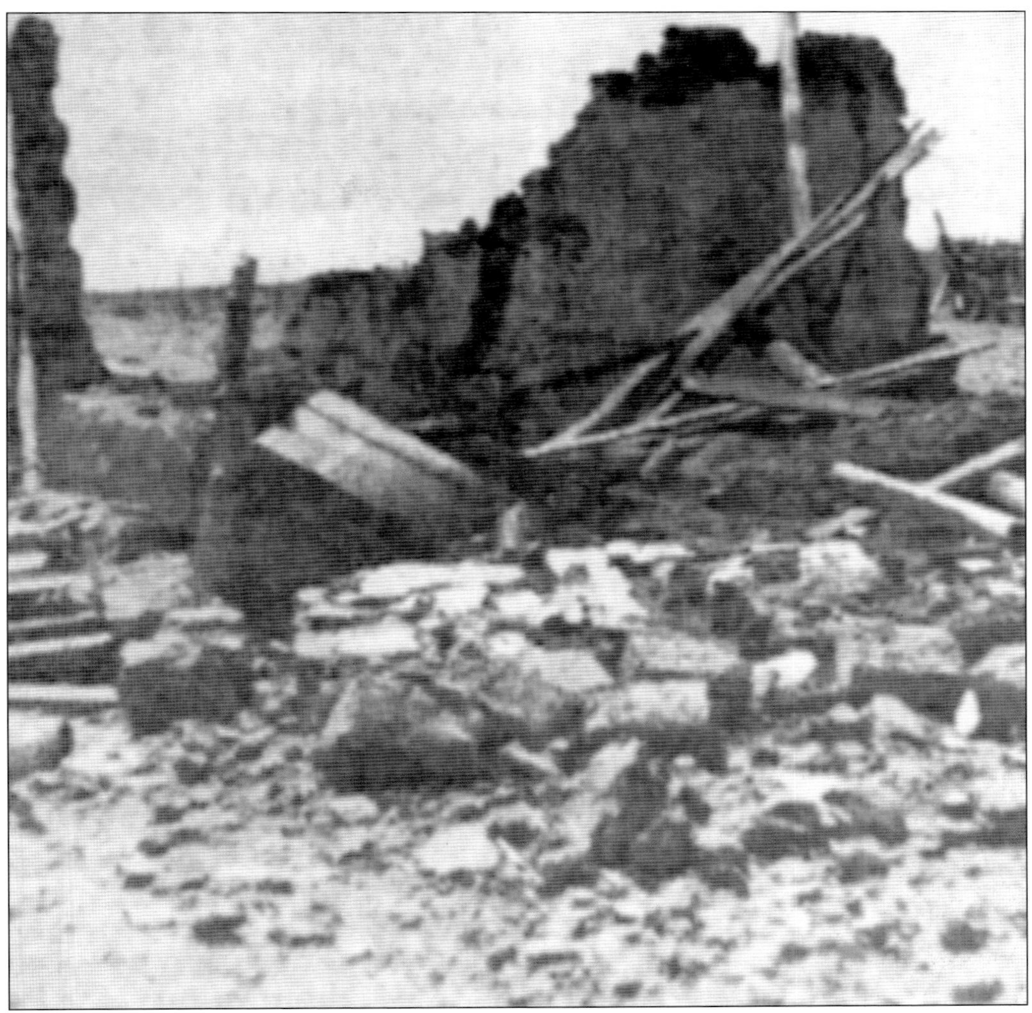

While most of the family was preparing for a meal, one of the children started fiddling with the spotting charge. Suddenly, there was a huge flash and a deafening boom, and the room was filled with black smoke. As the smoke cleared, the carnage from the explosion was revealed. A child's left foot had been blown off, and her left leg was mangled below the knee. Another girl had bruises and burns on her face and hands. Two of the men had burns and cuts and were in shock. One of the women was found in what was left of the kitchen where a viga had fallen, breaking her back. Although everyone survived, the hazards of unexploded ordnance would last well into the 21st century. (*Albuquerque Journal.*)

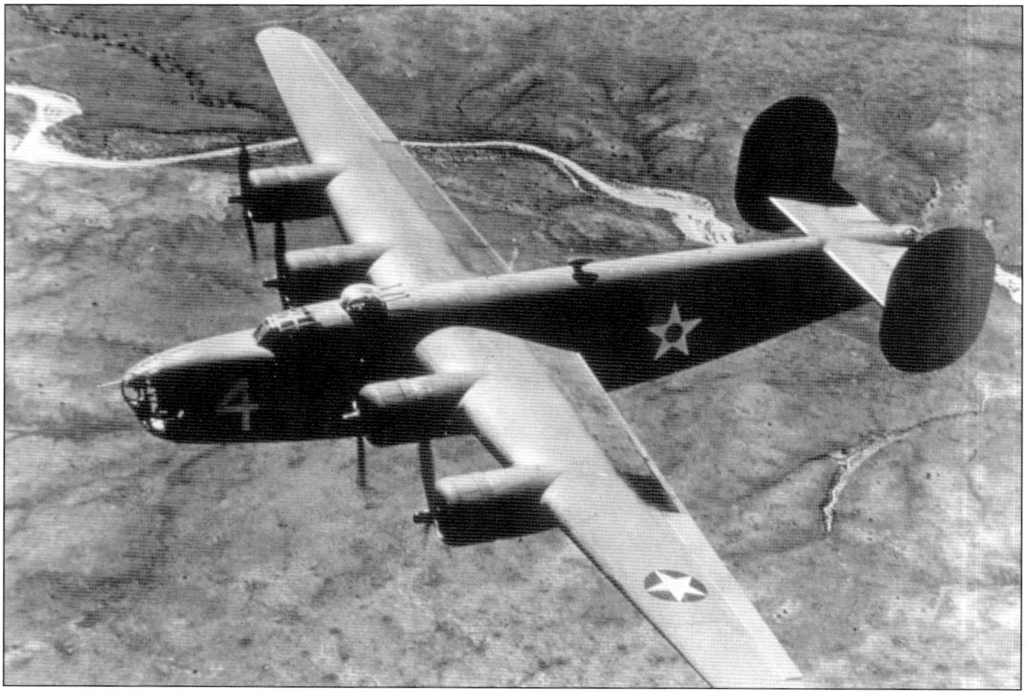

Unexploded ordnance was not the only training hazard. On April 22, 1942, B-24D bomber 41-1133, similar to the B-24D pictured over the Rio Grande above, left Kirtland for a round-trip navigational training mission to Kansas City. The crew headed back to Albuquerque at about 5:00 p.m. Coming into New Mexico from the northeast, they lost an engine and encountered a violent thunderstorm. At about 8:29 p.m., the bomber, flying straight and level at about 200 mph, crashed into Trail Peak on the Philmont Scout Ranch. Experts believe that the plane encountered a microburst causing it to drop about 4,000 feet. The crash site (seen below in 1948) is considered the most-visited crash site in New Mexico. This was only one of over 100 fatal aircraft crashes in the Southwest during World War II, claiming more than 1,400 lives. (Above, National Archives; below, Harry F. Blackburn.)

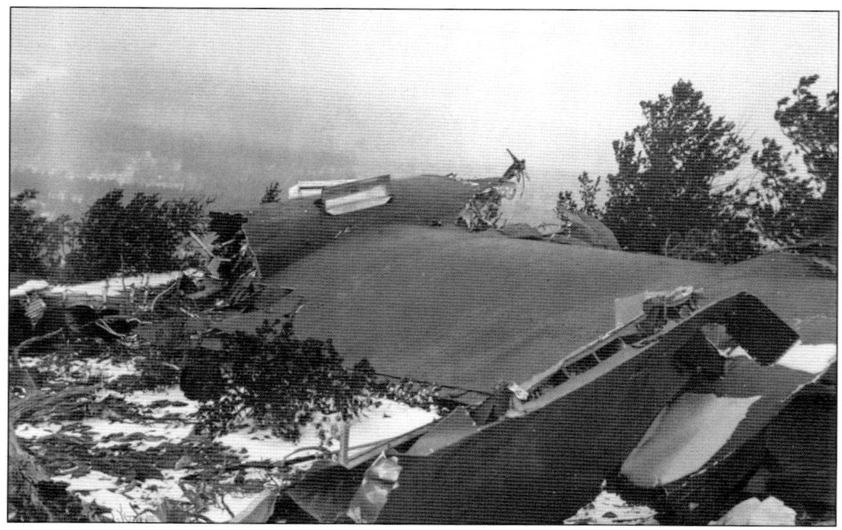

Five

The Manhattan Project

In 1938 and early 1939, German physicists Otto Hahn, Fritz Strassman, Lise Meitner, and Otto Frisch discovered that striking the nucleus of a uranium atom with a neutron resulted in the splitting, or fissioning, of the nucleus, releasing a tremendous amount of energy and additional neutrons that could fission more uranium nuclei in a chain reaction. Almost immediately, physicists around the world recognized the implications of this phenomenon for military explosives—if enough fissionable material could be compacted sufficiently, the chain reaction would expand exponentially in an extremely short period of time.

Both Albert Einstein and Leo Szilard, an expatriate Hungarian physicist, were very familiar with the German physicists and their capabilities. In particular, Werner Heisenberg, perhaps the leading German physicist at the time, was a known supporter of the Nazi regime. Einstein and Szilard were concerned that the Nazis would acquire this capability and use it in their quest for European, or even world, domination. The stakes could not have been higher.

On August 2, 1939, Einstein wrote a letter to Pres. Franklin Roosevelt expressing his and Szilard's concerns. This letter eventually led Roosevelt to establish the Manhattan Engineering District, now popularly known as the Manhattan Project, a $2 billion program to develop an American nuclear weapon before the Germans could finish theirs. The war in Europe ended before the bomb had been completed, so the direction of the project turned to using this new weapon against Japan.

The Manhattan Project eventually had more than 100 sites across the country, with some devoted to mining and milling uranium ore, some devoted to refining and enriching the uranium, some devoted to using the uranium to make a new element (plutonium), and one focused on bomb design. The center of operations was the top-secret Los Alamos Laboratory, hidden in the Jemez Mountains north of Santa Fe. Initially known only as Project Y, Los Alamos would play a critical role in ending World War II and in the nuclear age to come.

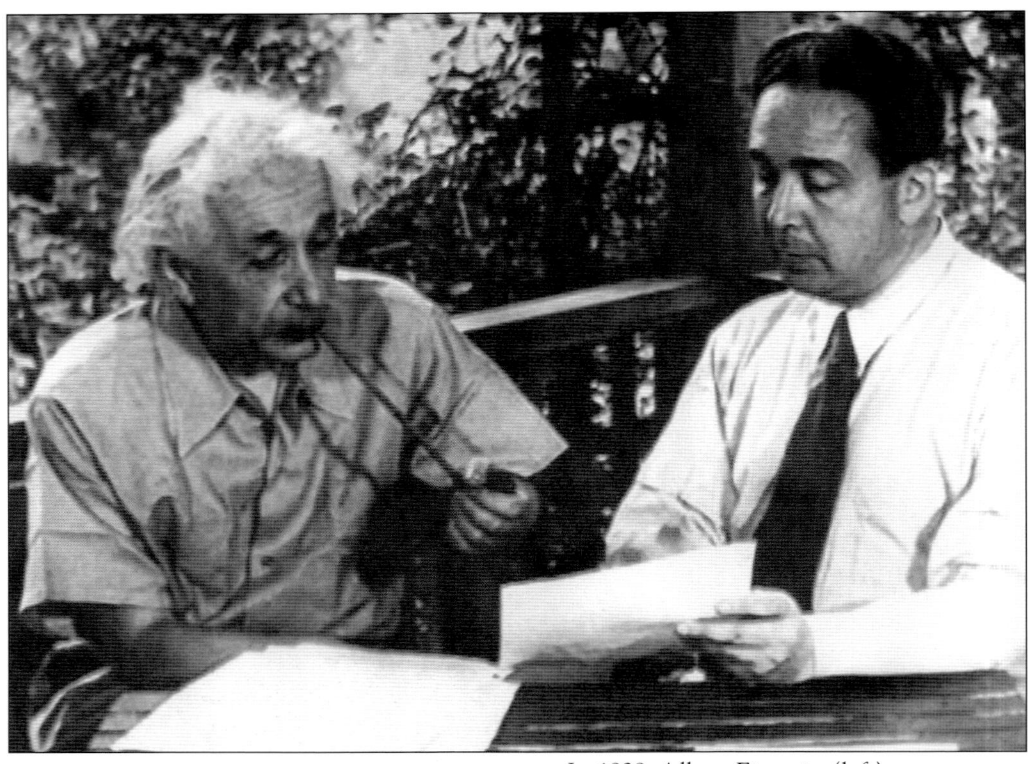

THE WHITE HOUSE
WASHINGTON

October 19, 1939

My dear Professor:

I want to thank you for your recent letter and the most interesting and important enclosure.

I found this data of such import that I have convened a Board consisting of the head of the Bureau of Standards and a chosen representative of the Army and Navy to thoroughly investigate the possibilities of your suggestion regarding the element of uranium.

I am glad to say that Dr. Sachs will cooperate and work with this Committee and I feel this is the most practical and effective method of dealing with the subject.

Please accept my sincere thanks.

Very sincerely yours,

Franklin D Roosevelt

Dr. Albert Einstein,
Old Grove Road,
Nassau Point,
Peconic, Long Island,
New York.

In 1939, Albert Einstein (left) wrote a letter to Pres. Franklin Roosevelt on behalf of himself and Leo Szilard (right) expressing the concern of the physics community that Germany would develop a superweapon using the newly discovered phenomenon of nuclear fission. The letter noted, "This phenomenon would also lead to the construction of bombs, and it is conceivable—though much less certain—that extremely powerful bombs of a new type may thus be constructed. A single bomb of this type, carried by boat and exploded in a port, might very well destroy the whole port together with some of the surrounding territory. However, such bombs might very well prove to be too heavy for transportation by air." Roosevelt's response is shown at left. (Above, National Archives; left, Los Alamos National Laboratory.)

President Roosevelt and his advisors took the Einstein recommendation to heart and established the Manhattan Engineering District (so named because its headquarters were in New York City) to develop an American bomb. They appointed Col. James C. Marshall as head of the new top-secret program. Army Chief of Staff Gen. George Marshall and Roosevelt's science advisor, Vannevar Bush, soon became dissatisfied with Colonel Marshall, who, although a competent engineer, had not moved fast enough on the urgent new program to satisfy Roosevelt. They then appointed Leslie Groves (right), another colonel in the Army Corps of Engineers, to relieve Marshall. Groves's previous assignment had been oversight of the construction of the Pentagon (below). Having completed this massive undertaking both ahead of time and under budget, Groves was an obvious choice to head the critical new program. (Right, Atomic Heritage Foundation; below, Richard Melzer.)

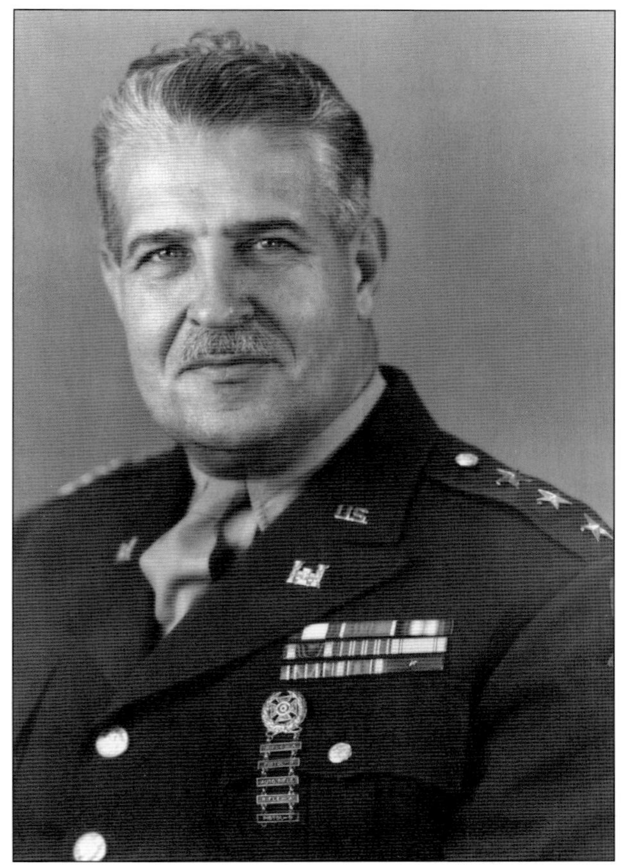

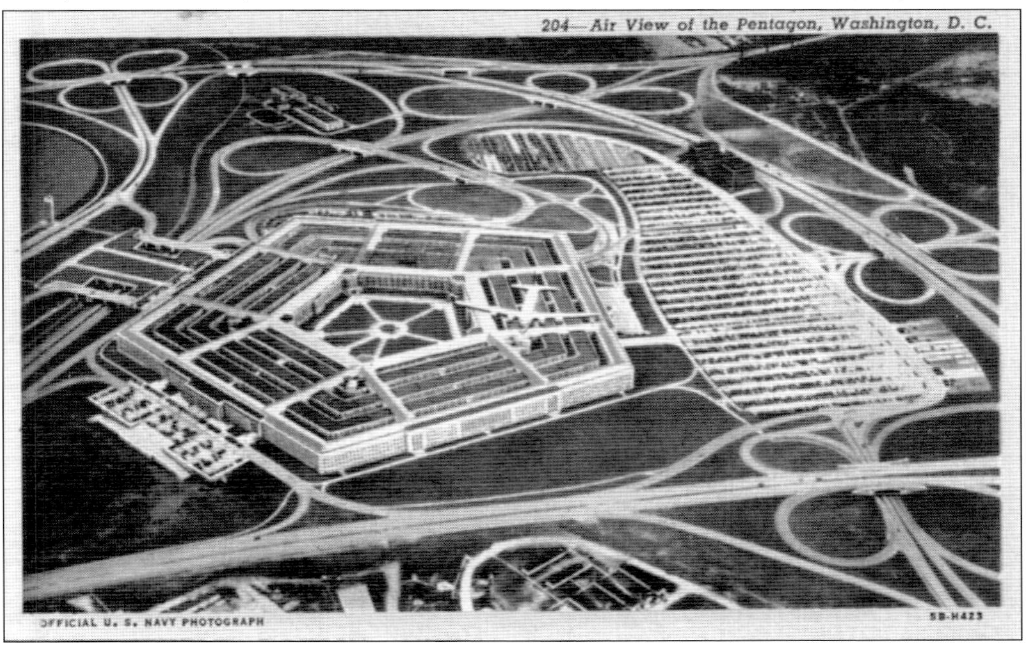

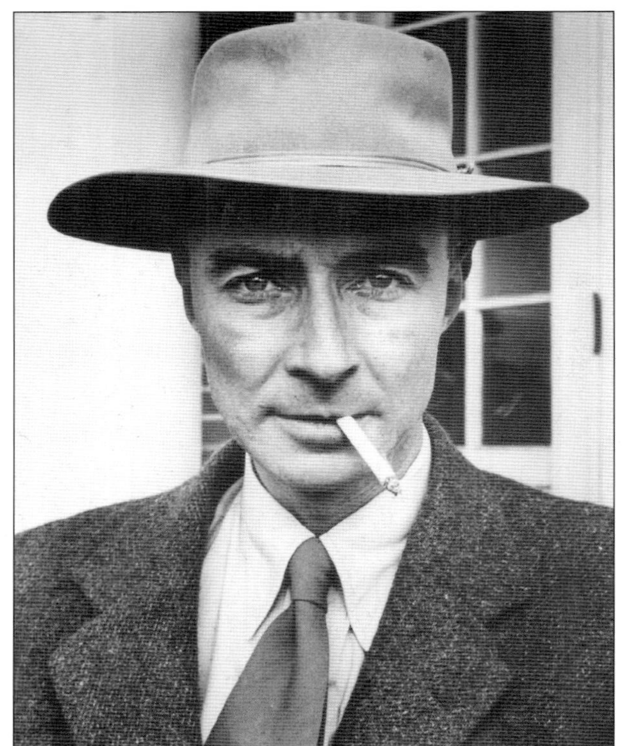

Colonel Groves chose J. Robert Oppenheimer, a physics professor at the University of California at Berkeley, to lead the nuclear weapon design effort. Oppenheimer gathered a cadre of the most prominent physicists and engineers in the country and persuaded them to come to "the end of the world" to work on a project that he could not tell them about until they were at the site. Oppenheimer and some of the more prominent of the distinguished cadre of scientists eventually lived in housing referred to as "Bathtub Row" because their houses were the only ones on the secret site with bathtubs. Oppenheimer's house is shown below. (Left, Los Alamos National Laboratory; below, Richard Melzer.)

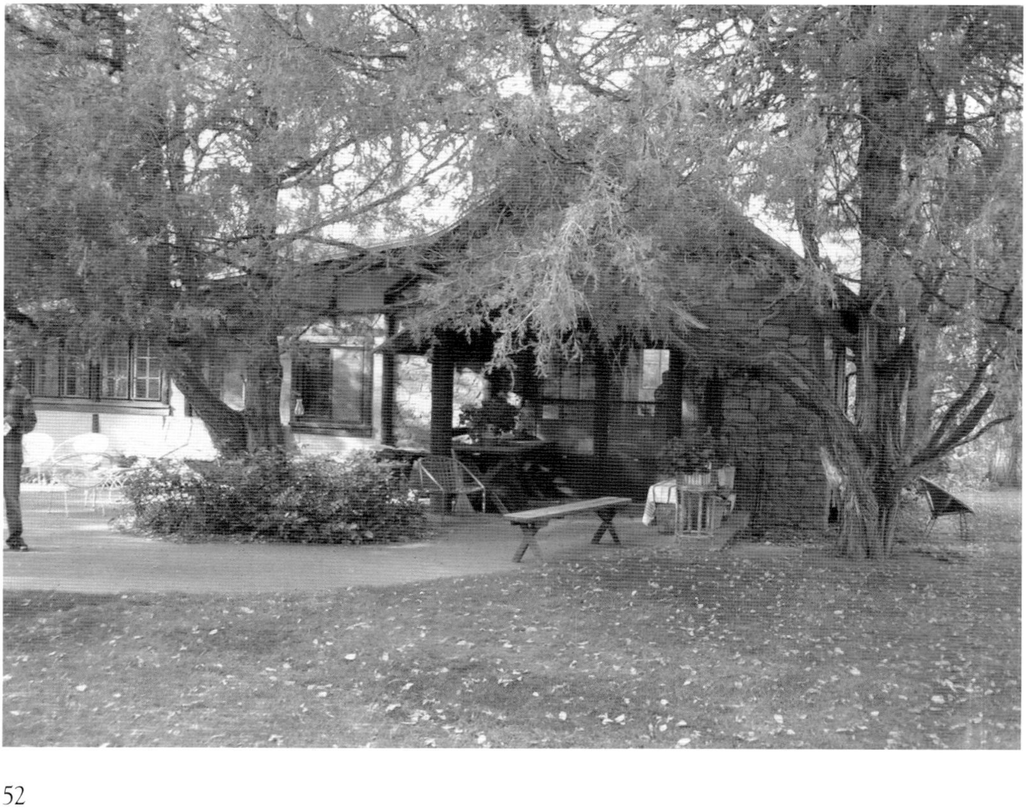

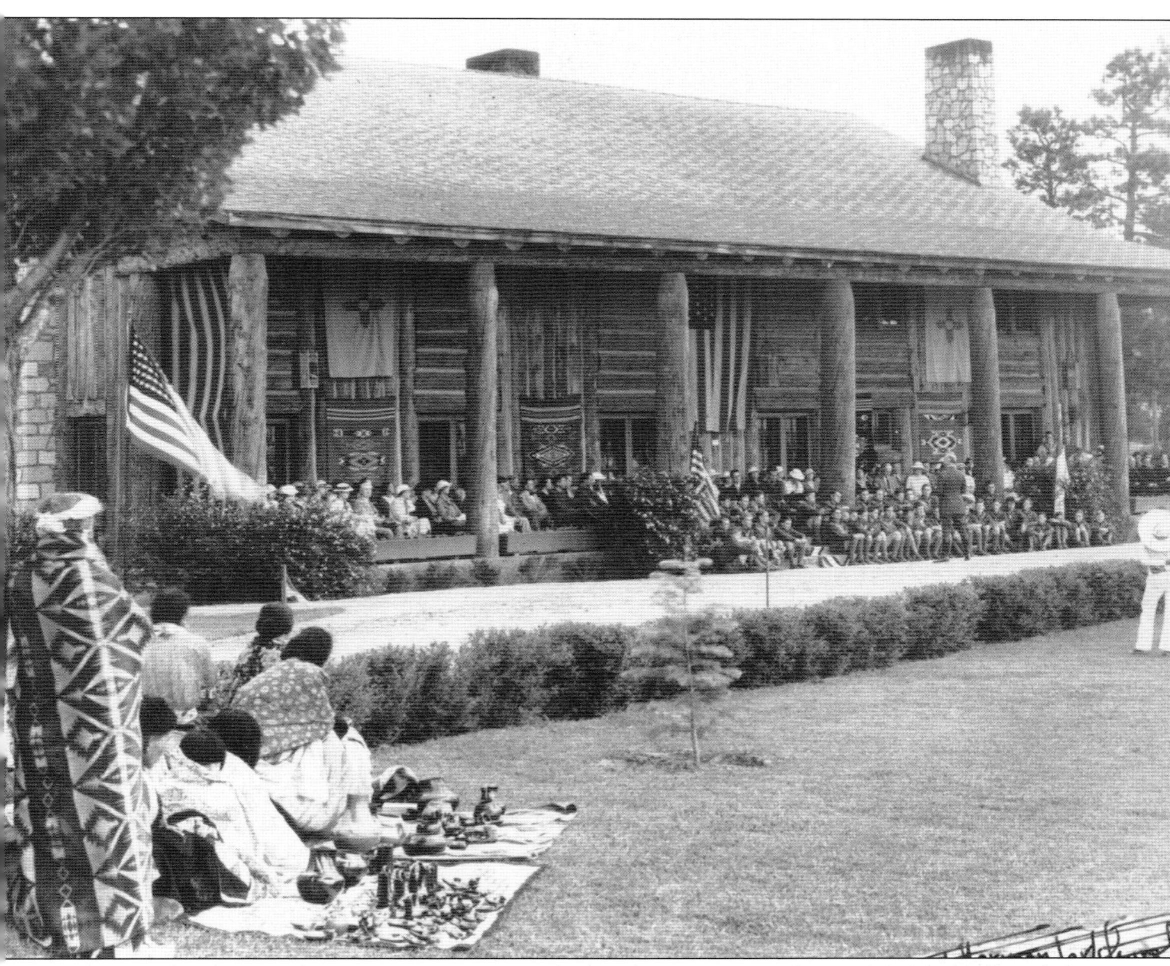

The site for the Manhattan Project's scientific headquarters was chosen by Groves based on recommendations by Oppenheimer and others. Oppenheimer had spent vacations in northern New Mexico and knew that this site met the requirements for a top-secret facility. It was isolated with limited access roads and had sufficient water, and much of the surrounding land was already owned by the federal government. The site, known as Los Alamos (the cottonwoods), had been occupied by the Los Alamos Ranch School (seen here) for 25 years. Secretary of War Henry Stimson wrote a letter to the school's director, A.J. Connell, saying that the property was needed "in the interests of the United States in the prosecution of the war." The government bought the school for $350,000, and the 40-some boys currently enrolled rushed to complete their studies before the Manhattan Project took ownership of the property in February 1943. In addition, about 25 homesteads and another ranch property were purchased, providing a 50,000-acre site for the nuclear endeavor, originally designated Project (or Site) Y. (Los Alamos National Laboratory.)

109 EAST PALACE
1943 SANTA FE OFFICE 1963
LOS ALAMOS SCIENTIFIC LABORATORY
UNIVERSITY OF CALIFORNIA
All the men and women who made the first atomic bomb passed through this portal to their secret mission at Los Alamos. Their creation in 27 months of the weapons that ended World War II was one of the greatest scientific achievements of all time.

Secrecy demanded that individuals assigned to work at the site were not given a name or address to which to report. Instead, they were sent to a nondescript office at 109 East Palace Avenue in Santa Fe. There they were met by Dorothy McKibbin, later known as the "Gatekeeper to Los Alamos." McKibbin would arrange to have the people transported 35 miles north to the site's main gate (below), where they were met by military police. The original location of 109 East Palace Avenue is now commemorated by a simple plaque in the back corner of a small shop (above). The existence and location of Los Alamos were so restricted that birth certificates for children born at the site showed an address of P.O. Box 1663, Santa Fe, New Mexico. (Above, John Taylor; below, Los Alamos National Laboratory.)

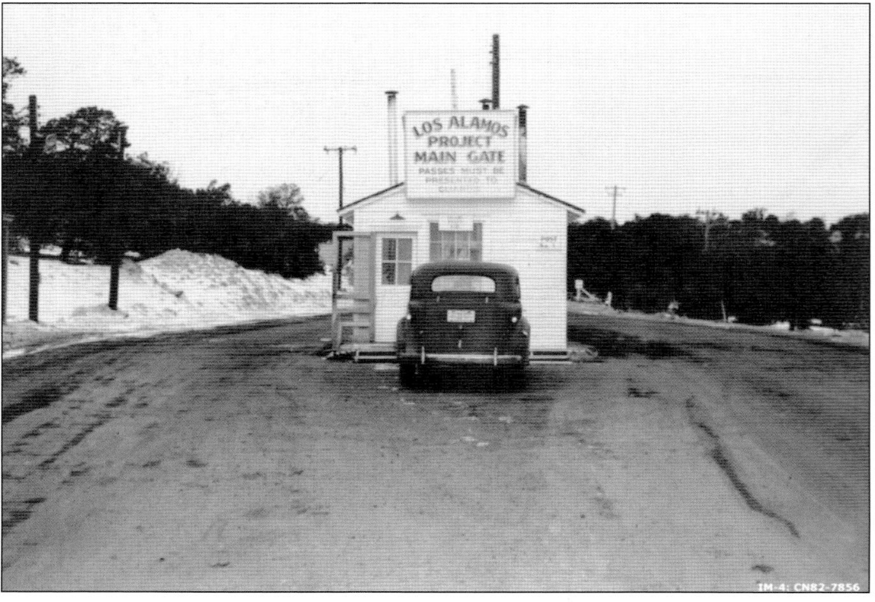

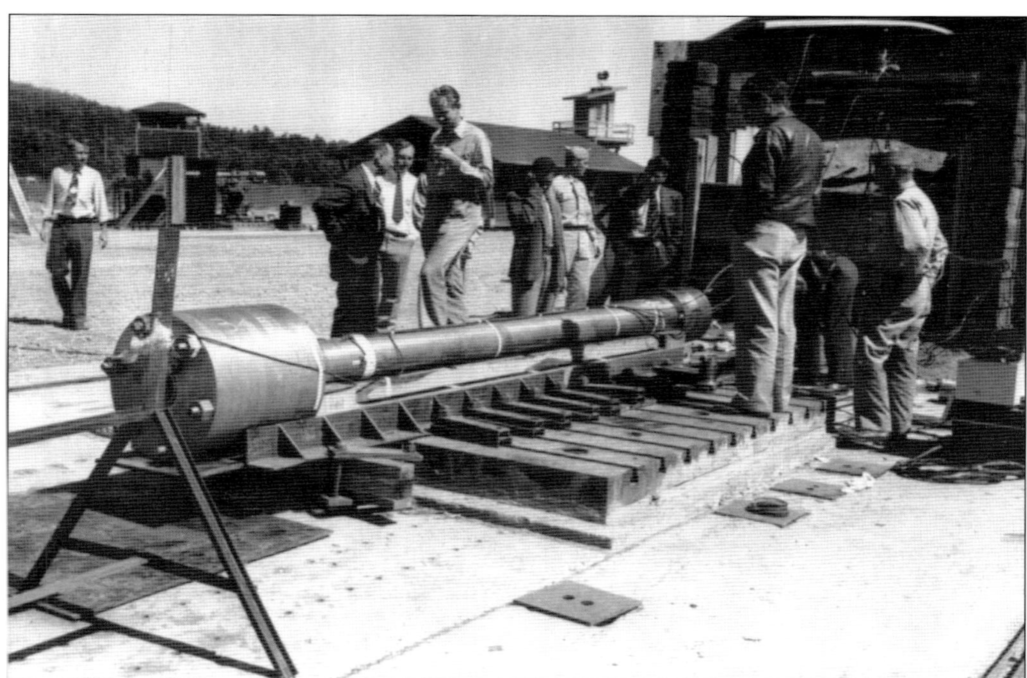

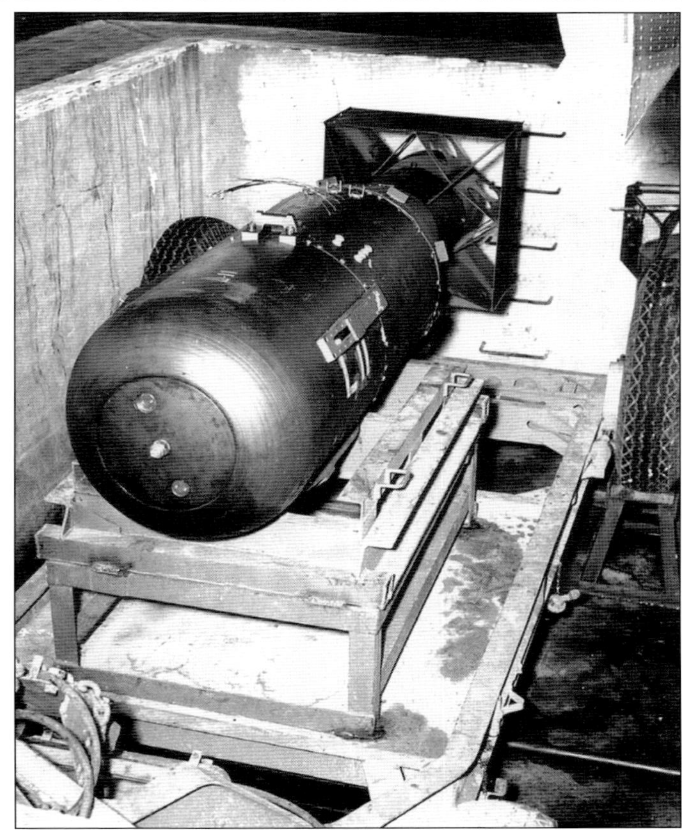

The weaponeers at Los Alamos initially focused on a design in which one small, subcritical mass of material was fired down a gun barrel at another small, subcritical mass. Together, the two masses were sufficient to cause a nuclear explosion. Two approaches were worked in parallel, with one using uranium and one using the newly-discovered element plutonium. For physics reasons, the plutonium design, called the "Thin Man" (above), was rejected, and the uranium version, eventually made into a bomb called "Little Boy" (right), was developed. Designers were so confident that the Little Boy design would work that they decided a full-scale test was not required. (Both, US Department of Energy.)

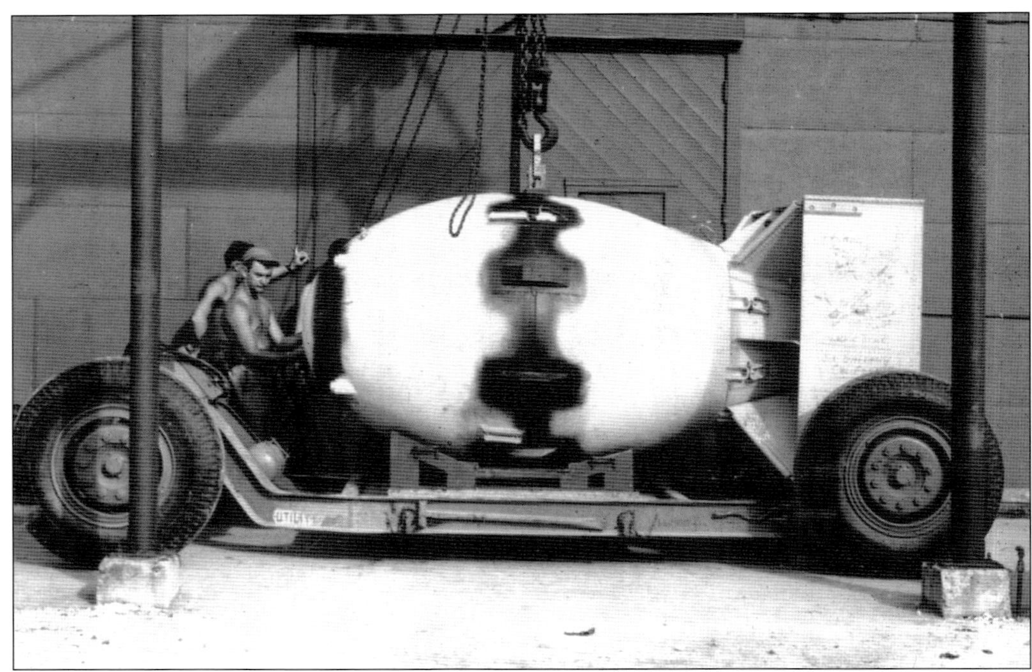

Although the physics of the Thin Man design did not prove feasible, Oppenheimer and the other engineers and physicists at Los Alamos believed that the potential of plutonium as a bomb material was too great to ignore. In addition, the particular isotope of uranium required for the Little Boy design was much scarcer. Therefore, they decided to try a completely novel approach called implosion, in which a central core of subcritical material is uniformly compressed until it becomes critical. The resulting device was developed into a bomb called "Fat Man" (above). Because the concept of implosion was unprecedented, it was felt that it needed to be fully tested before it was deployed. This incredible advance in physics was accomplished by scientists who lived and worked in the ramshackle village of Quonset huts and hastily thrown-together buildings at Site Y (below). (Both, Los Alamos National Laboratory.)

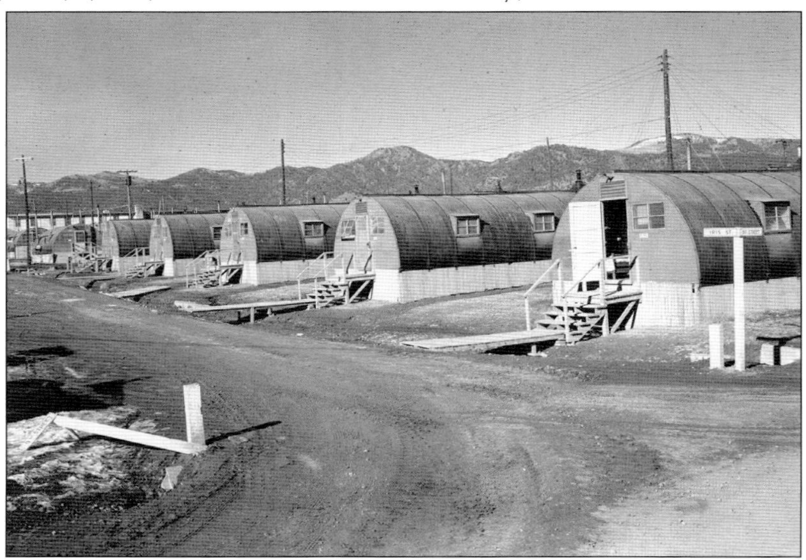

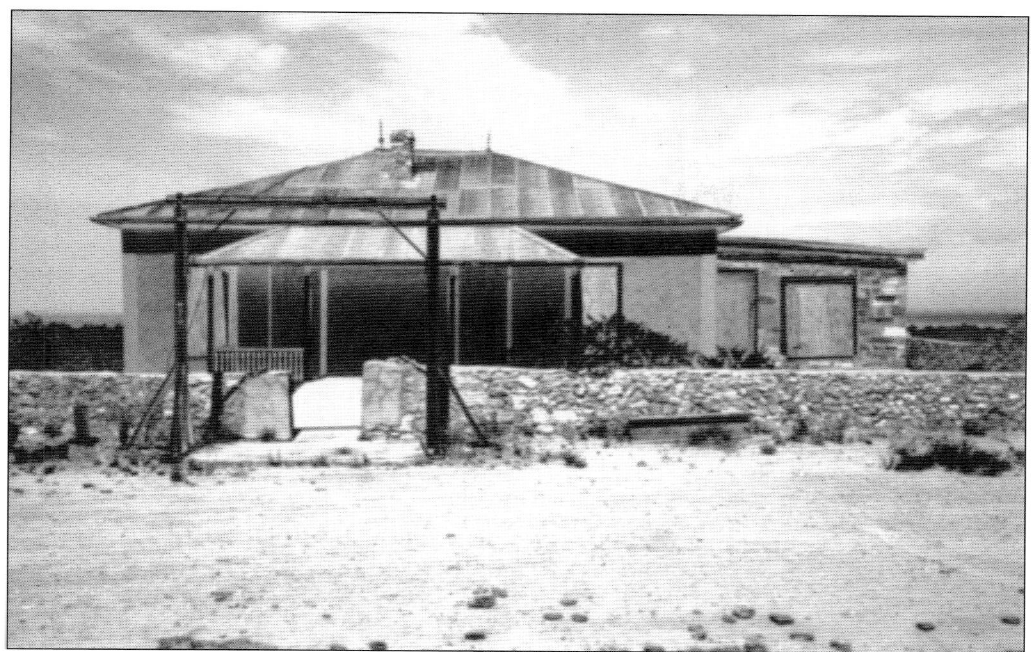

A site on the Alamogordo Bombing and Gunnery Range (now part of White Sands Missile Range) in south-central New Mexico was chosen for the test because of its isolation, flat terrain, and low wind conditions. The George McDonald family, ranchers on the range, had been forced to vacate their land under protest in 1942 when the bombing range was established. Although they never reoccupied their ranch (shown above and now listed in the National Register of Historic Places), they were eventually awarded $60,000 from the government. The test device was assembled in the ranch house. A small town (below) was established at the site, code-named Trinity, to house the men and equipment needed for the test. The name of the site was chosen from a John Donne poem, a favorite of Oppenheimer's. (Both, Los Alamos National Laboratory.)

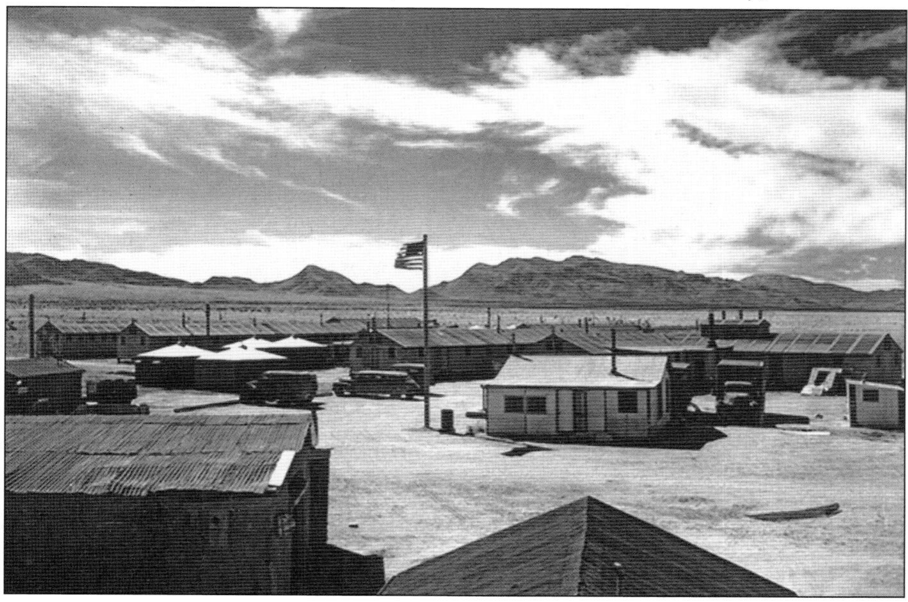

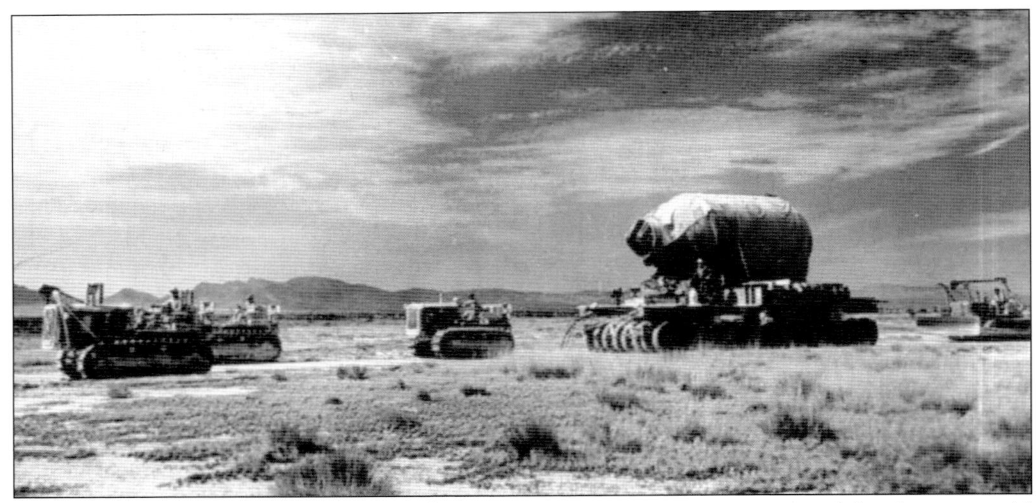

Due to the radical nature of the new design, some scientists were not sure if the device would even detonate. In fact, there was a betting pool among the scientists on what the eventual yield, if any, of the device, called the "Gadget," might be. Groves was sufficiently concerned that he had a 214-ton steel container, code-named Jumbo (above), constructed to house the explosion and salvage the extraordinarily valuable plutonium if the device failed. In the end, Jumbo was not used. However, because of the large amount of high explosives in the device, stories were contrived to explain to the public the large explosion that was anticipated. One was that a large ammunition facility on the Alamogordo range had exploded. (Above, Los Alamos National Laboratory; below, *El Defensor Chieftain*.)

SOCORRO LIGHTED AND SHAKEN WHEN ALAMOGORDO MAGAZINE EXPLODES — NO ONE INJURED

An explosives magazine at the Alamogordo air base blew up Monday morning, and the flash, sound and and shock were seen, heard and felt in Socorro, more than 100 miles away, as well as in Magdalena, Datil and Reserve.

The Associated Press said the explosion rattled windows in Gallup, 235 miles away.

The time was 5:35 a. m., according to Mrs. Leona Cope, who looked at a clock when she saw the flash. The sound did not reach here until several minutes had passed.

The flash was intensely white and seemed to fill the entire world. It was followed by a large crimson glow. The flash lasted only a second or so. It was so bright that Miss Georgia Green of Socorro, blind student at the University of New Mexico, being driven to Albuquerque by her brother-in-law, Lieutenant Joe Willis, asked, "What's that?"

No one was injured by the explosion, it is stated. Cause of the explosion is not indicated.

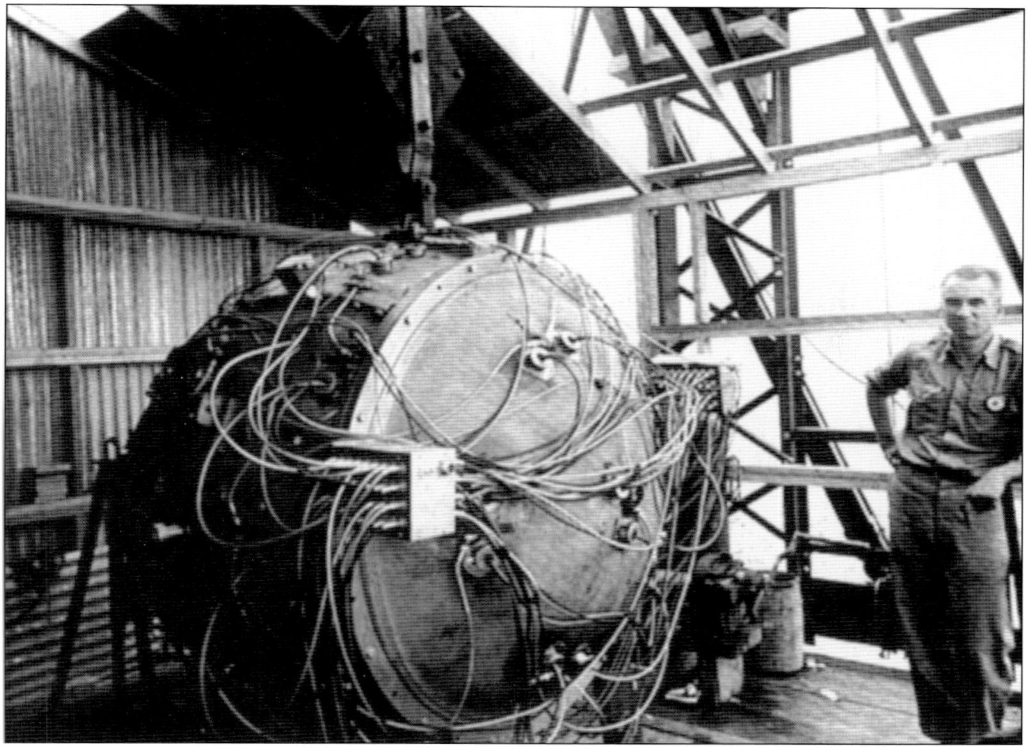

On the morning of July 16, 1945, after a series of worrisome thunderstorms had delayed the countdown, the skies in central New Mexico cleared, and the countdown resumed. At 5:29:45 a.m., the sky lit up with the light of day for a few seconds. From Clovis to Socorro, windows cracked, and items fell off shelves. People said that this was "the day that the sun rose twice." The Gadget exploded with a yield of between 15 and 20 kilotons. Oppenheimer, viewing the successful completion of his colleagues' work, is said to have remarked, "I am become death, destroyer of worlds," a quote from the Hindu Bhagavad Gita. (Both, Los Alamos National Laboratory.)

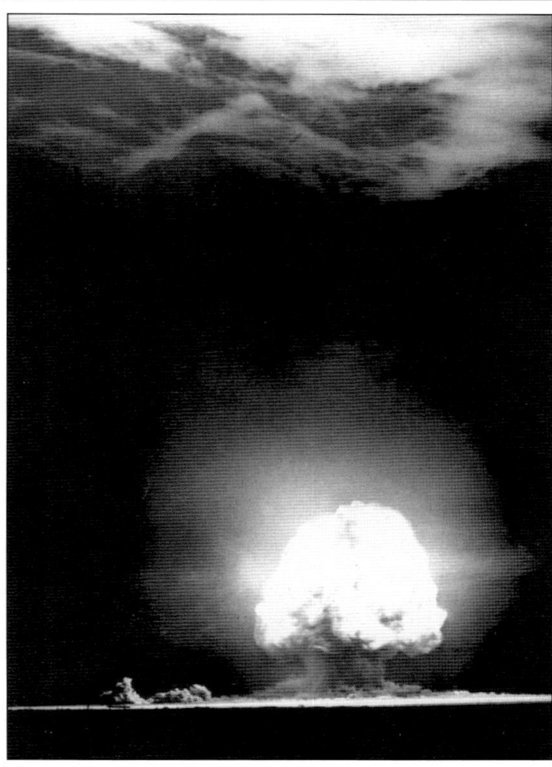

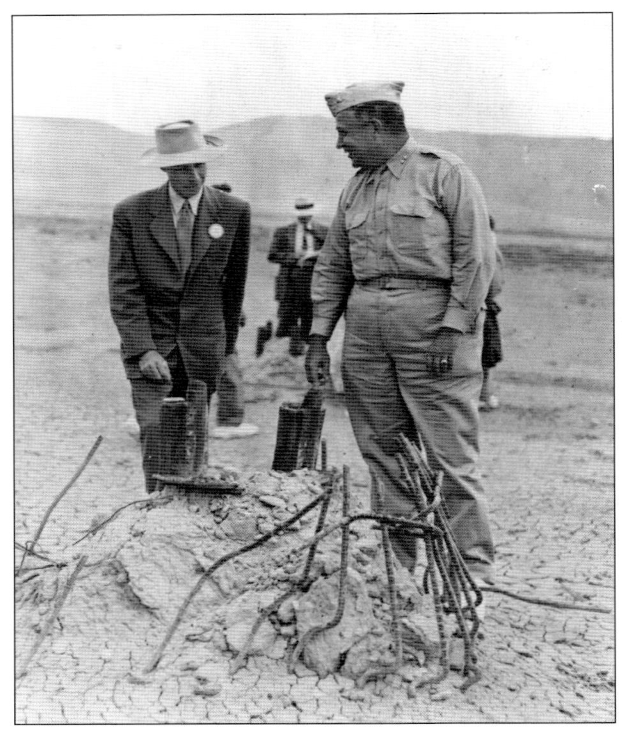

General Groves and Oppenheimer inspected all that remained of a 100-foot-high metal tower where the first atomic bomb had been tested at Trinity Site on July 16, 1945. The total destruction of two Japanese cities by atomic bombs developed in New Mexico finally ended World War II on August 15, 1945. The image to the left shows Oppenheimer and Groves inspecting the twisted remains of the tower that had held the device at ground zero. The image below memorializes that inspection with statues of Oppenheimer and Groves at Los Alamos. (Left, Los Alamos National Laboratory; below, Richard Melzer.)

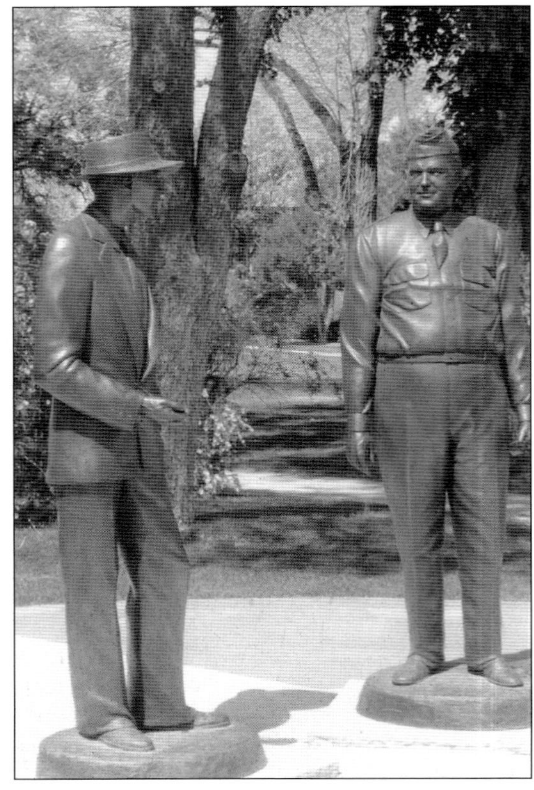

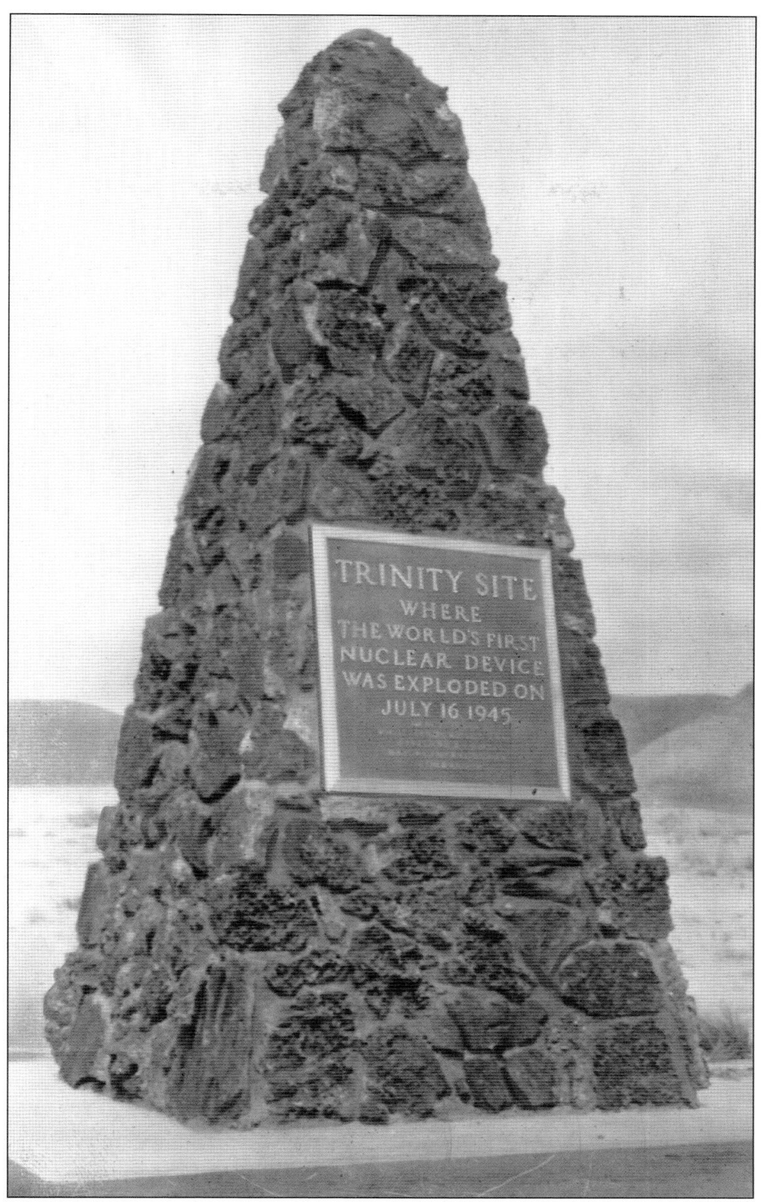

Trinity Site is south of the Stallion Gate on what is now the White Sands Missile Range. In the immediate aftermath of the Trinity test, individuals gathered pieces of the radioactive glass, called trinitite, formed from the sand by the extraordinary heat of the explosion. Some 75 years later, all the trinitite is gone, and there is essentially no residual radiation from the test explosion, so the site is open to visitors twice a year, during the first Saturday in April and the first Saturday in October. Thousands of travelers visit the site each year, often taking photographs of the obelisk erected at ground zero in 1965. The monument sits in the crater just over the location where the tower stood on July 16, 1945. A group of individuals who lived on ranches and in small communities downwind of the Trinity test were exposed to radiation from fallout from the detonation. Calling themselves the Tularosa Basin Downwinders, this group has agitated for appropriate government compensation for their physical and emotional distress. (US Department of Energy.)

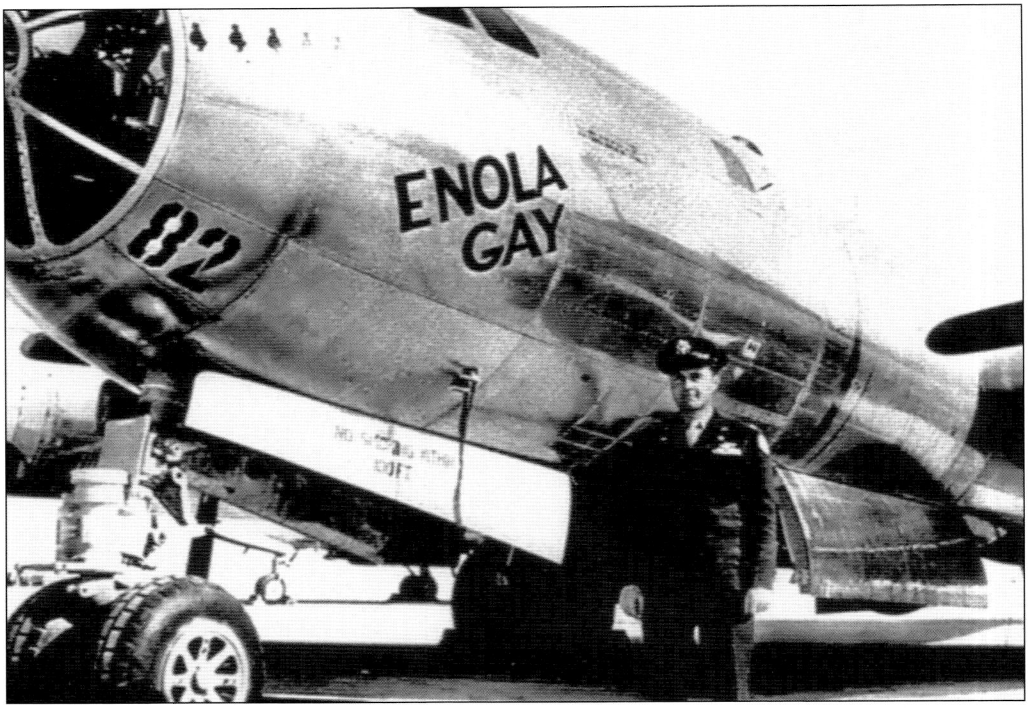

American bombers dropped leaflets warning the Japanese that unless they agreed to surrender, a terrible new weapon would be used against them. However, under the influence of his military advisors who were zealously committed to their historic samurai traditions, Emperor Hirohito refused. The Little Boy bomb had been delivered to the newly liberated island of Tinian. On August 6, 1945, Col. Paul Tibbetts (shown above) and his 11-man crew flew the *Enola Gay*, a B-29 named for Tibbetts's mother, to Japan and dropped the Little Boy on the city of Hiroshima, killing between 90,000 and 146,000 people. The terrible aftermath of that bombing is shown below. (Both, Los Alamos National Laboratory.)

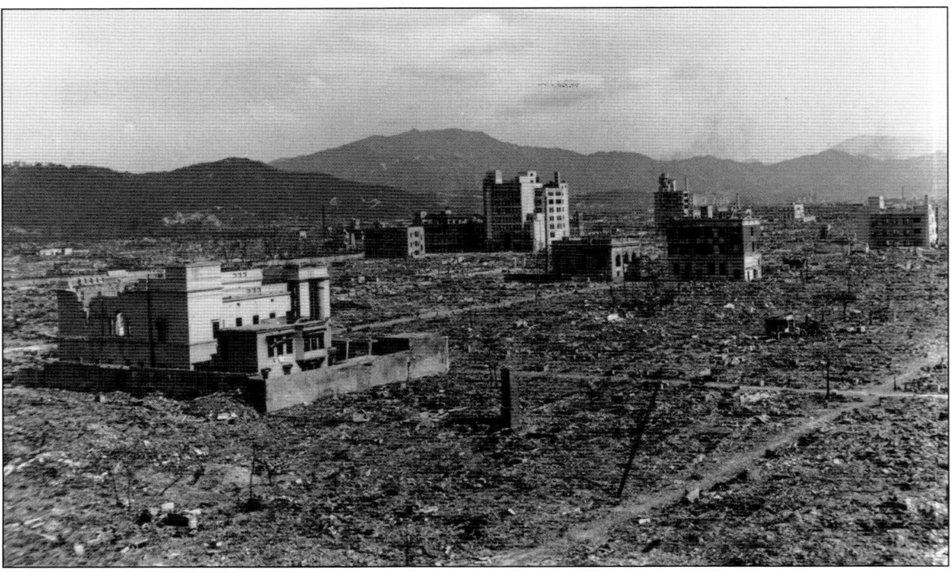

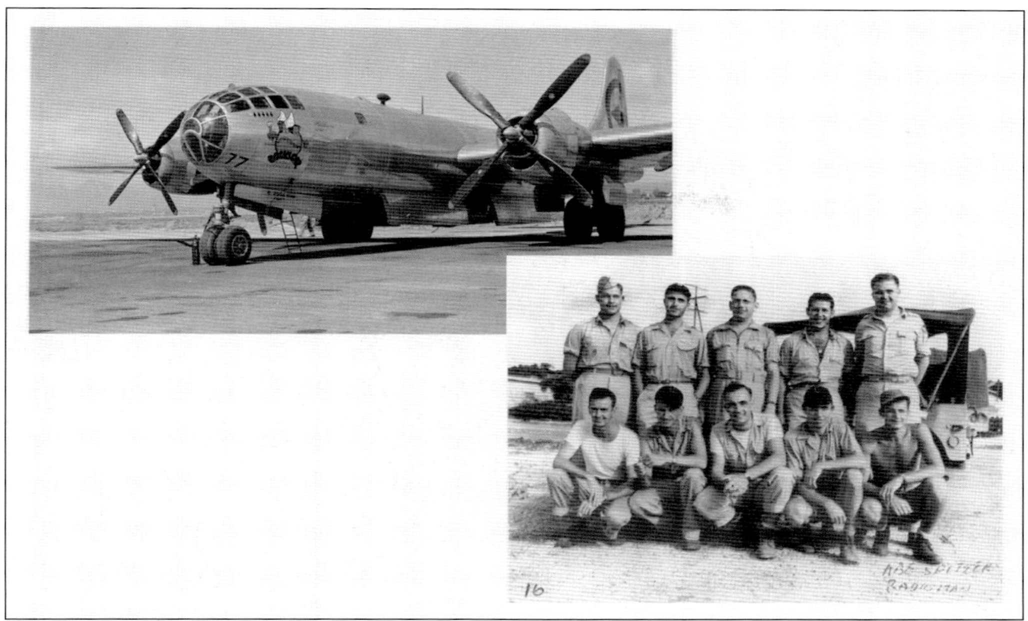

Three days later, on August 9, with the Japanese still refusing to capitulate, the 10,800-pound Fat Man was loaded onto a B-29 named *BocksCar*, piloted by Maj. Charles Sweeney (standing second from left above). The Japanese had intentionally covered Sweeney's primary target, Kokura, with a smokescreen from burning coal tar, so, with their fuel nearly depleted, Sweeney and his crew flew to their secondary target, Nagasaki, where the bomb was dropped, killing between 39,000 and 80,000 people. The plane and its crew barely made it back to Tinian, with their engines essentially running on fumes. The image below shows the utter devastation of Nagasaki. (Above left, Department of Energy; above right, Los Alamos National Laboratory; below, Los Alamos National Laboratory.)

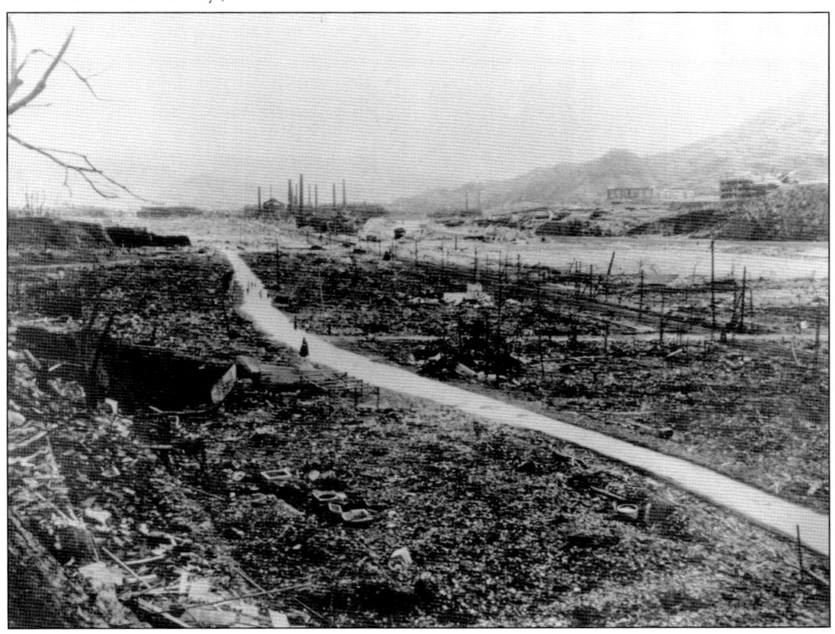

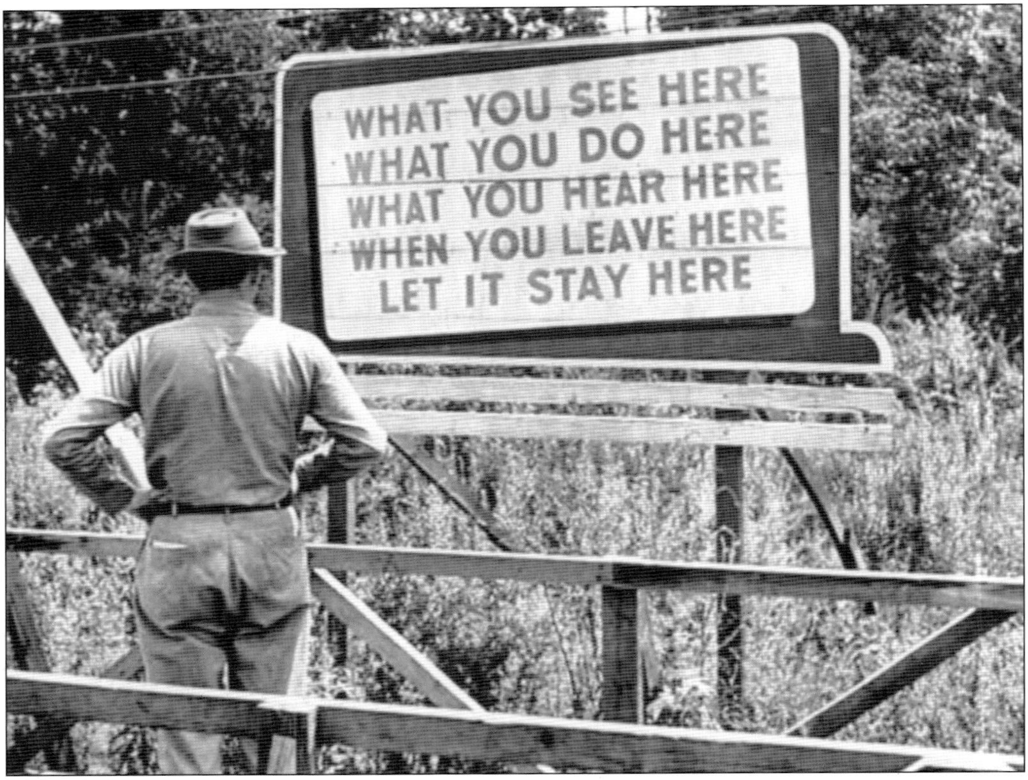

Despite stringent security and counterintelligence measures, Soviet sympathizers managed to get hired at Los Alamos. The Soviet spy network included nuclear physicist Klaus Fuchs (code name Charles) below left, physicist Ted Hall (code name Mlad) below right, machinist David Greenglass (code name Caliber or Bumblebee), and Pvt. Oscar Soberer (code name Godsend or Discovery). They were able to obtain security clearances, get access to highly classified information, and move it off-site and eventually to physicists in the Soviet Union. (All, Los Alamos National Laboratory.)

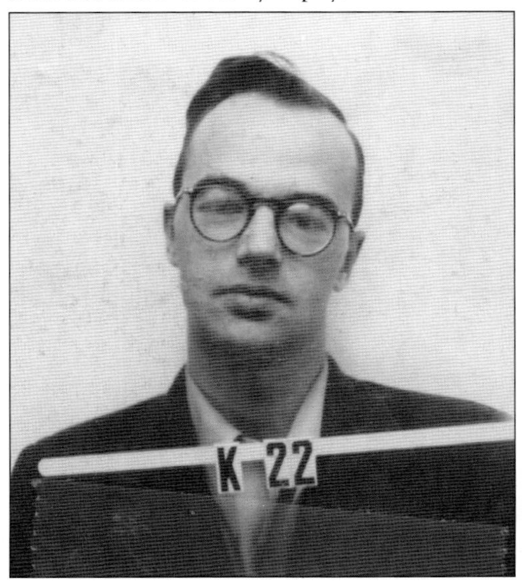

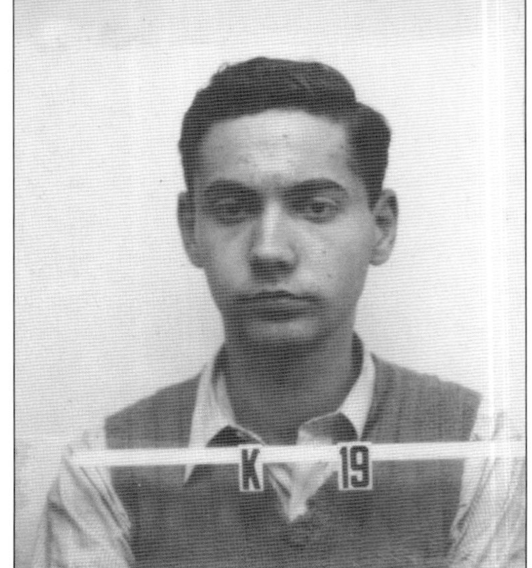

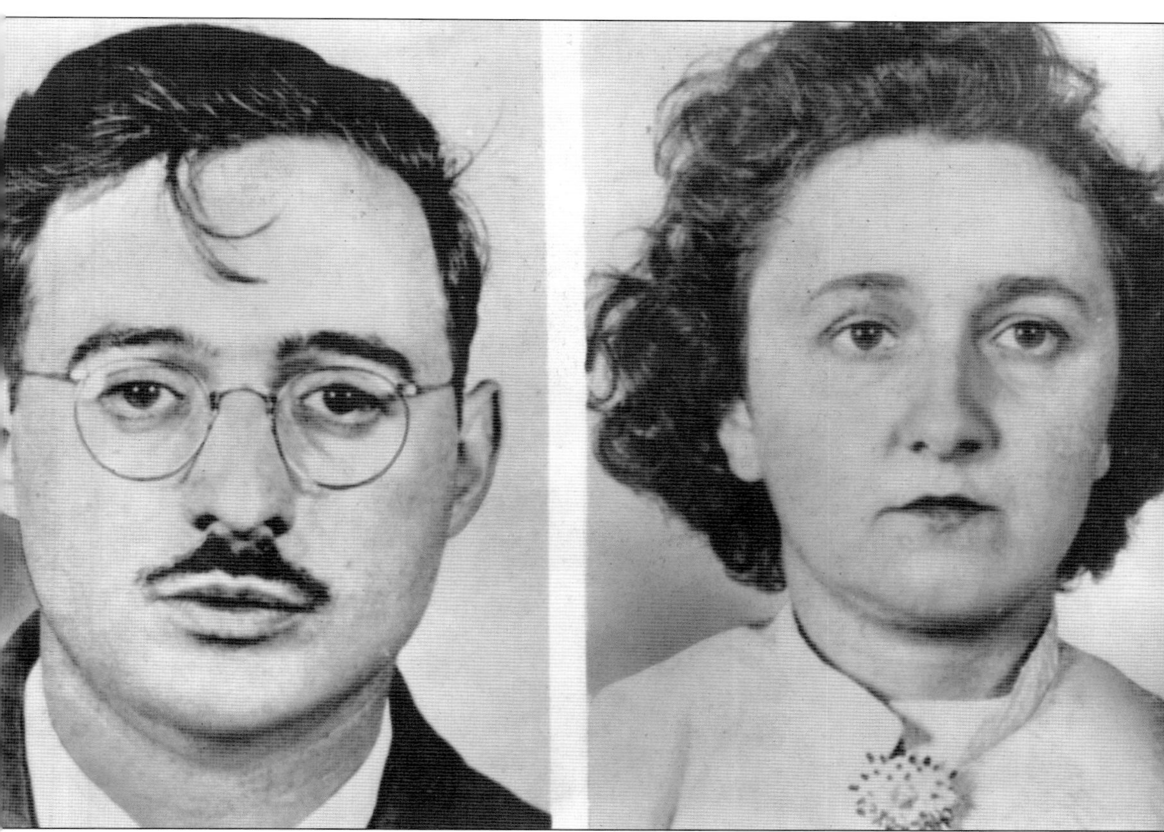

Although both Germany and Japan had begun nuclear weapon programs, only the Soviet Union developed a sophisticated espionage ring targeted at the American nuclear program. The ring had four spies embedded in the Los Alamos population (a fifth member, code-named Perseus, turned out to be part of a Soviet disinformation campaign and did not actually exist) and a carefully designed system for moving illicitly obtained secrets from Los Alamos to Soviet spy chief Lavrenti Beria in Moscow, who in turn passed the information to Igor Kurchatov, head of the Soviet nuclear weapon development program. Julius (code name Antenna) and Ethel Rosenberg, sister of the embedded machinist spy David Greenglass, provided one of the principal conduits for the material to pass to the Soviet Union. Found guilty of espionage, the Rosenbergs were executed in the electric chair at New York's Sing Sing prison on June 19, 1953. (Los Alamos National Laboratory.)

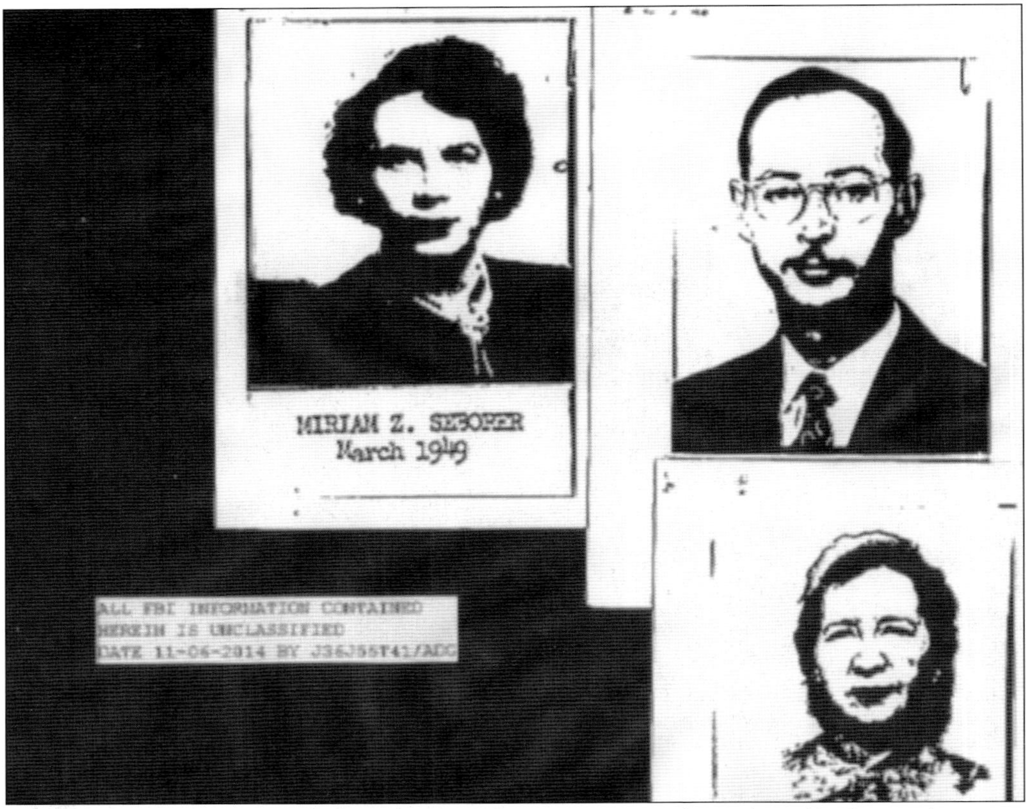

MIRIAM Z. SEBORER
March 1949

ALL FBI INFORMATION CONTAINED
HEREIN IS UNCLASSIFIED
DATE 11-06-2014 BY J36J55T41/ADC

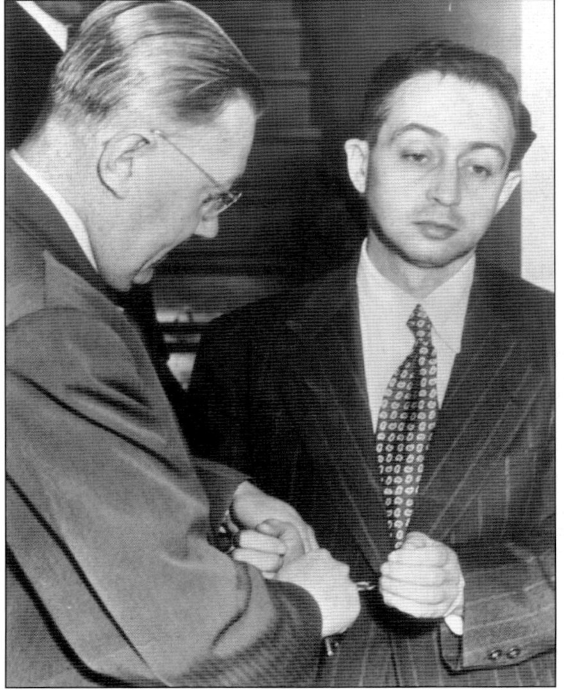

Oscar Seborer (FBI file shown above with his sister-in-law at upper left and her mother, Anna Zeitlin, at lower right) was another of the spies who obtained classified information from Los Alamos for the Soviet Union. He worked at Los Alamos from 1944 to 1946 and was present at the Trinity test as part of a seismological monitoring unit. Information from all of the "atomic spies" was passed to Julius Rosenberg in New York via couriers, including Harry Gold (code name Arno, left) and Seville Sax (code name Star), a college friend of Ted Hall. Fuchs (and perhaps Seborer) met Gold on more than one occasion at the Castillo Street Bridge on Paseo de Peralta in Santa Fe, while other clandestine meetings took place in Albuquerque. (Above, FBI; left, Los Alamos National Laboratory.)

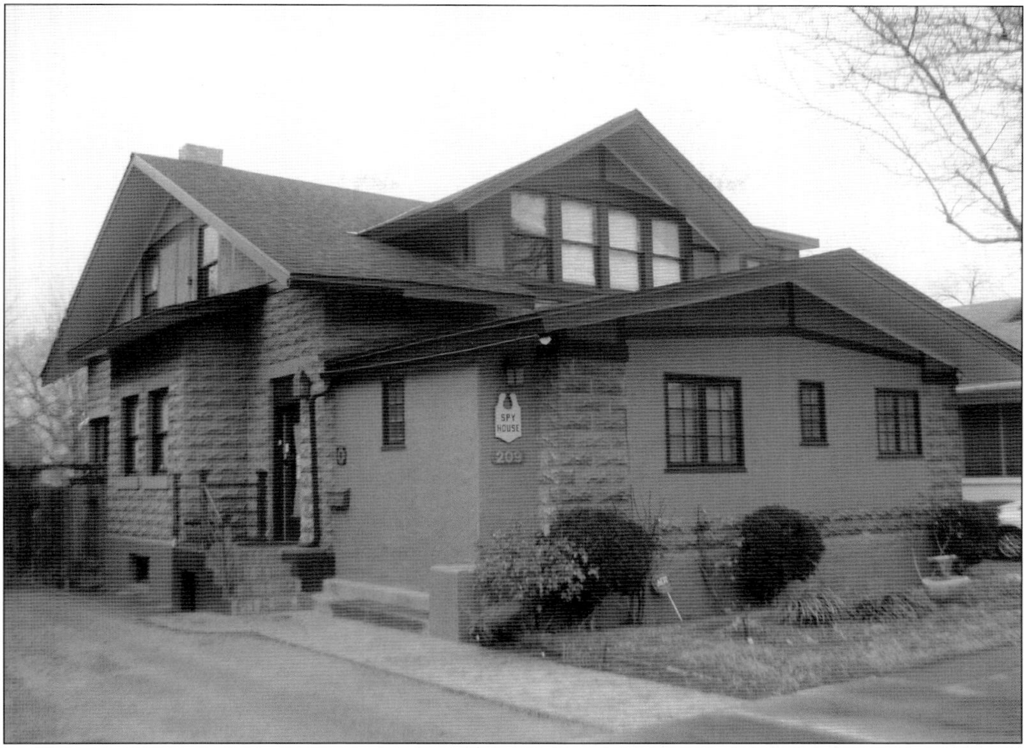

At least one of the clandestine meetings of the espionage ring took place at the Freeman boarding house on North High Street in Albuquerque (above). David Greenglass's wife, Ruth (code name Wasp), had rented a room at the boarding house while her husband worked at Los Alamos. Because he was "just a lowly machinist," he was allowed to come to Albuquerque for visits more frequently and with less oversight than many others at Site Y. Harry Gold, the courier, made contact with Greenglass (right) at the boardinghouse. The Freeman house is now a popular bed and breakfast known locally as the Spy House. Visitors can reserve room 4, which is where the clandestine meeting took place in June 1945. (Above, Richard Melzer; right, Los Alamos National Laboratory.)

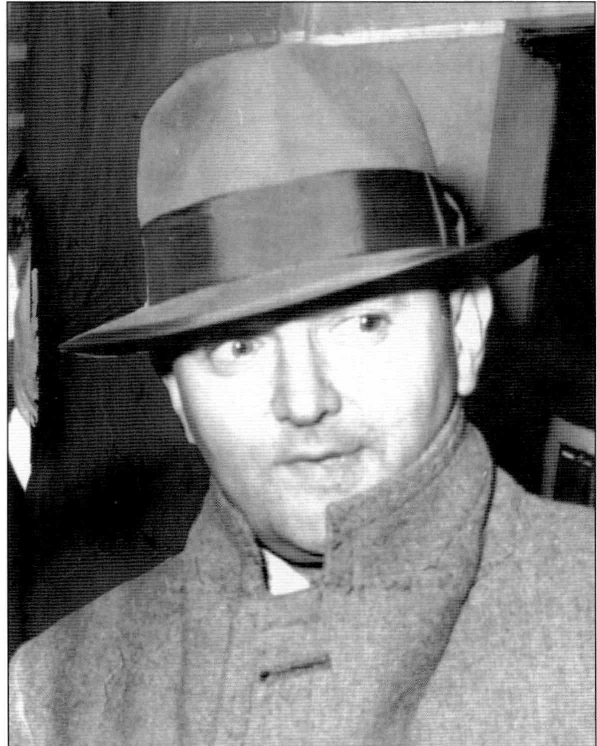

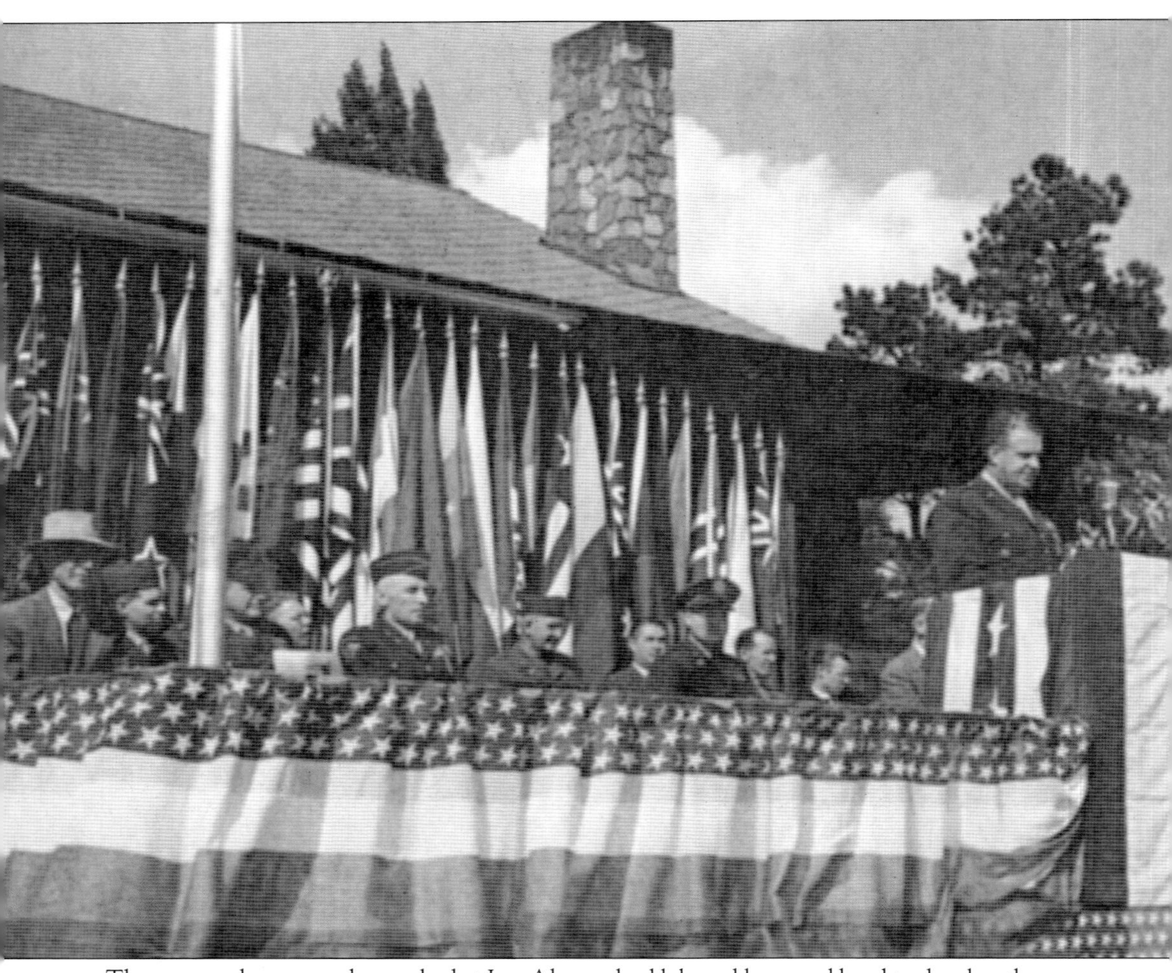

The men and women who worked at Los Alamos had labored long and hard to develop the weapon that shortened the war and saved tens of thousands of Allied and Japanese lives that would have likely been lost had an invasion of Japan been required. After years of enforced isolation, the veil of secrecy that had concealed the laboratory was finally lifted, with a ceremony to recognize and honor the scientists, engineers, and technicians of Site Y with the Army-Navy Award for Excellence. General Groves (at the podium), Robert Oppenheimer (in his usual porkpie hat on the left), and other distinguished military and civilian leaders spoke. Los Alamos, along with Sandia in Albuquerque and Lawrence Livermore in California, continued to serve as the nation's premier national security laboratories after the war, focusing on continued development of the country's nuclear weapons. (Los Alamos National Laboratory.)

Six

The Home Front Goes to War

As in all wars, World War II is best remembered for its major battles. But the battles on the front lines could not have been won without the matériel, support, and hard work of those who remained back home. If combat soldiers, sailors, marines, and airmen played the leading roles in the American victory in World War II, then the men and women back home played key supporting roles.

In general, New Mexicans played their supporting roles well, responding with energy and enthusiasm. New Mexicans produced important raw materials, from coal to crops, transporting them on miles of railroad tracks and highways. Asked to buy war bonds to help finance the war, New Mexicans responded by buying more than their fair share per capita. Faced with shortages in essential wartime materials, most New Mexicans cooperated, using government-issued ration books, decreasing consumption, and increasing the production of crops and livestock whenever possible.

Many New Mexicans worked in war-related jobs in-state. But others migrated to higher-paying jobs on the West Coast, helping there but creating an acute labor shortage at home. Many women filled essential jobs on the railroads, on farms, and on ranches. Mexican laborers, known as braceros, entered the United States to assist as well.

New Mexico's men and women in the armed forces were welcomed home when on leave. Families organized parties, while communities gave dances, and facilities like Carlsbad Caverns organized special days for them.

When able, New Mexicans aided Jews who escaped from Nazi Germany and helped American POWs via an organization called the Bataan Relief Organization. Thousands of wounded men and women received good care at Bruns Army Hospital in Santa Fe. Many New Mexicans, as discussed in chapter five, assisted in the development of the atomic bomb in the Manhattan Project, centered in Los Alamos and tested at Trinity Site.

Little of what New Mexicans did on the home front was ever recognized with commendations or statues. But their help must not be forgotten if New Mexico's story in World War II is to be accurate, fair, and complete.

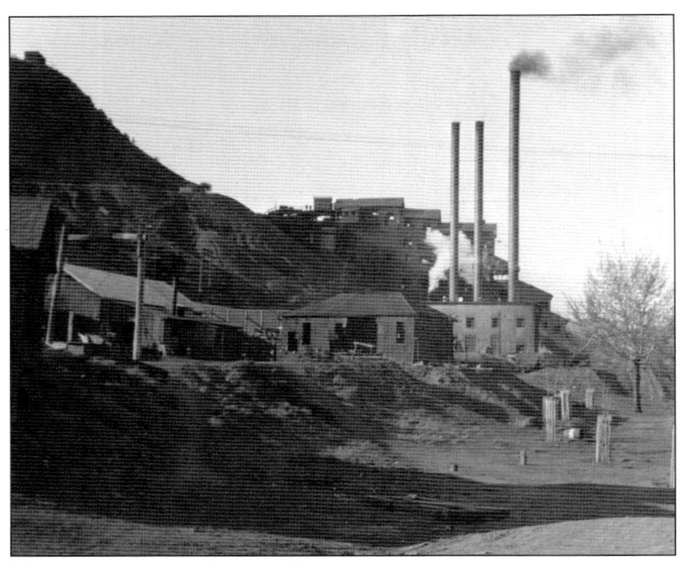

Wartime demands led to record production in New Mexico's coal camps, including Gamerco, Dawson, and Madrid (pictured). Madrid's proximity helped decision-makers choose Santa Fe as the location of Bruns Army Hospital and Los Alamos as the location of the site for Site Y of the Manhattan Project. Ironically, atomic scientists who developed man's most advanced form of energy relied on one of the most basic forms of energy, coal, to complete their labors. (Richard Melzer.)

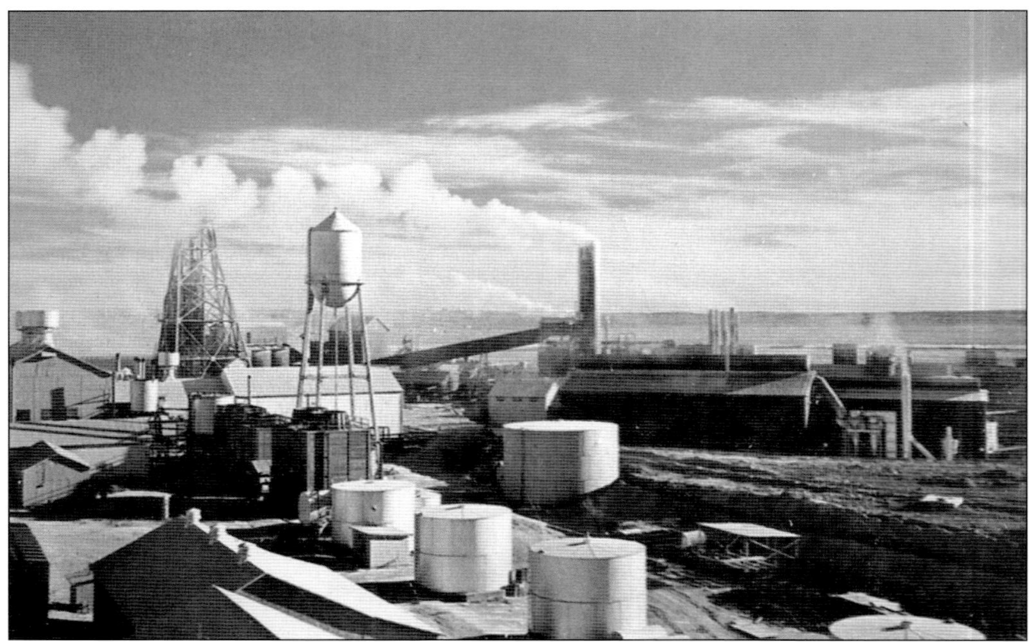

New Mexico provided other important raw materials, including crude oil, natural gas, silver, lead, zinc, copper, and potash. Many of these critical wartime resources experienced increased production during the war. Oil production, for example, increased from 31.5 million barrels in 1942 to 39.5 barrels in 1944. New Mexico led all states in the production of potash, used to produce high explosives. A potash plant near Carlsbad is pictured here. (Richard Melzer.)

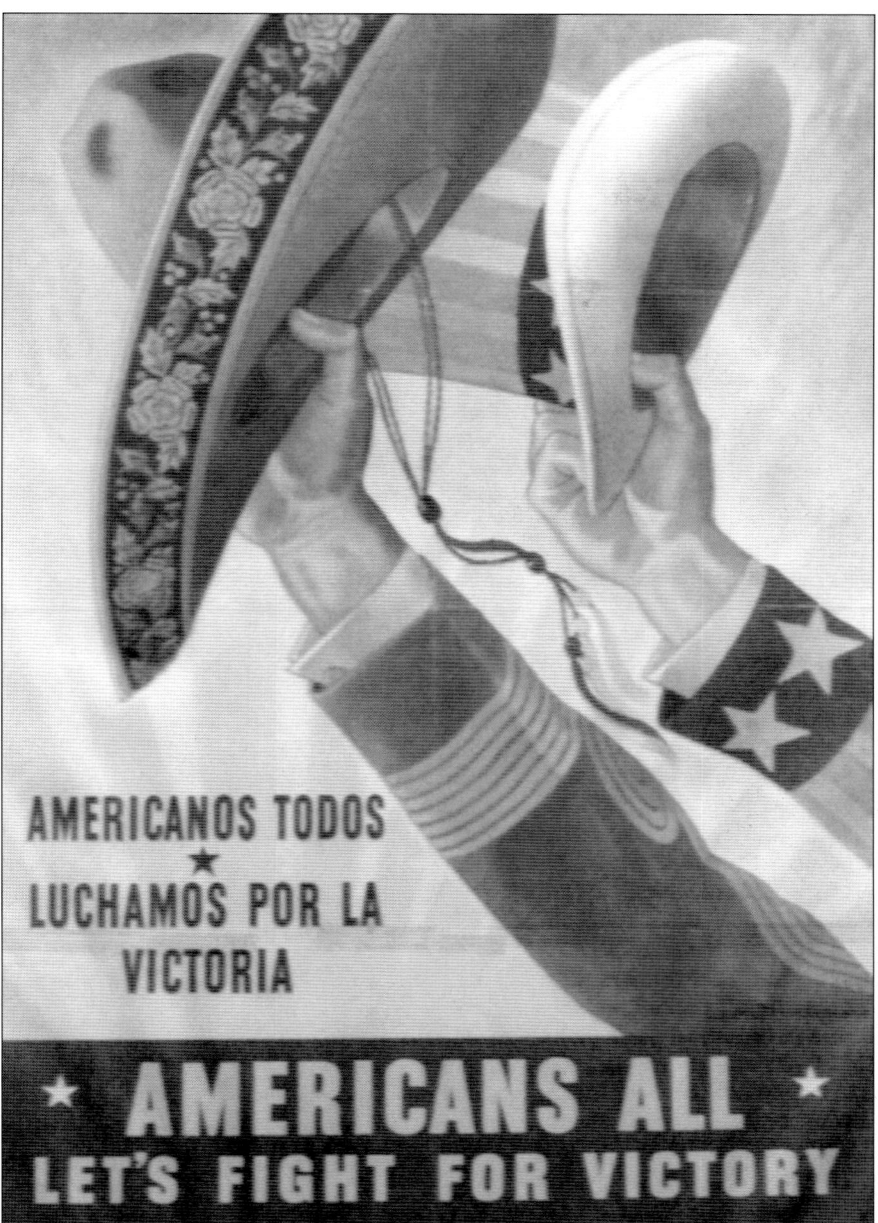

While New Mexico's agricultural production soared, the state lacked sufficient workers to harvest its crops and perform other essential labor. Turning south to help solve this problem, the United States signed an agreement with Mexico that allowed Mexican laborers to cross the border with guarantees of adequate working conditions and wages. Whole families were enticed to participate in the program with posters like the one shown here. Known as braceros, thousands of Mexican nationals helped on farms, ranches, railroads, and mines across the Southwest. Unfortunately, the terms of the agreement were not well enforced, leaving many Mexicans vulnerable to unfair treatment. The program nevertheless lasted from early in the war until 1964. As in World War I and other periods of American history, Mexican laborers were recruited only to be exploited, degraded, abused, and often deported. (Margaret Espinosa McDonald.)

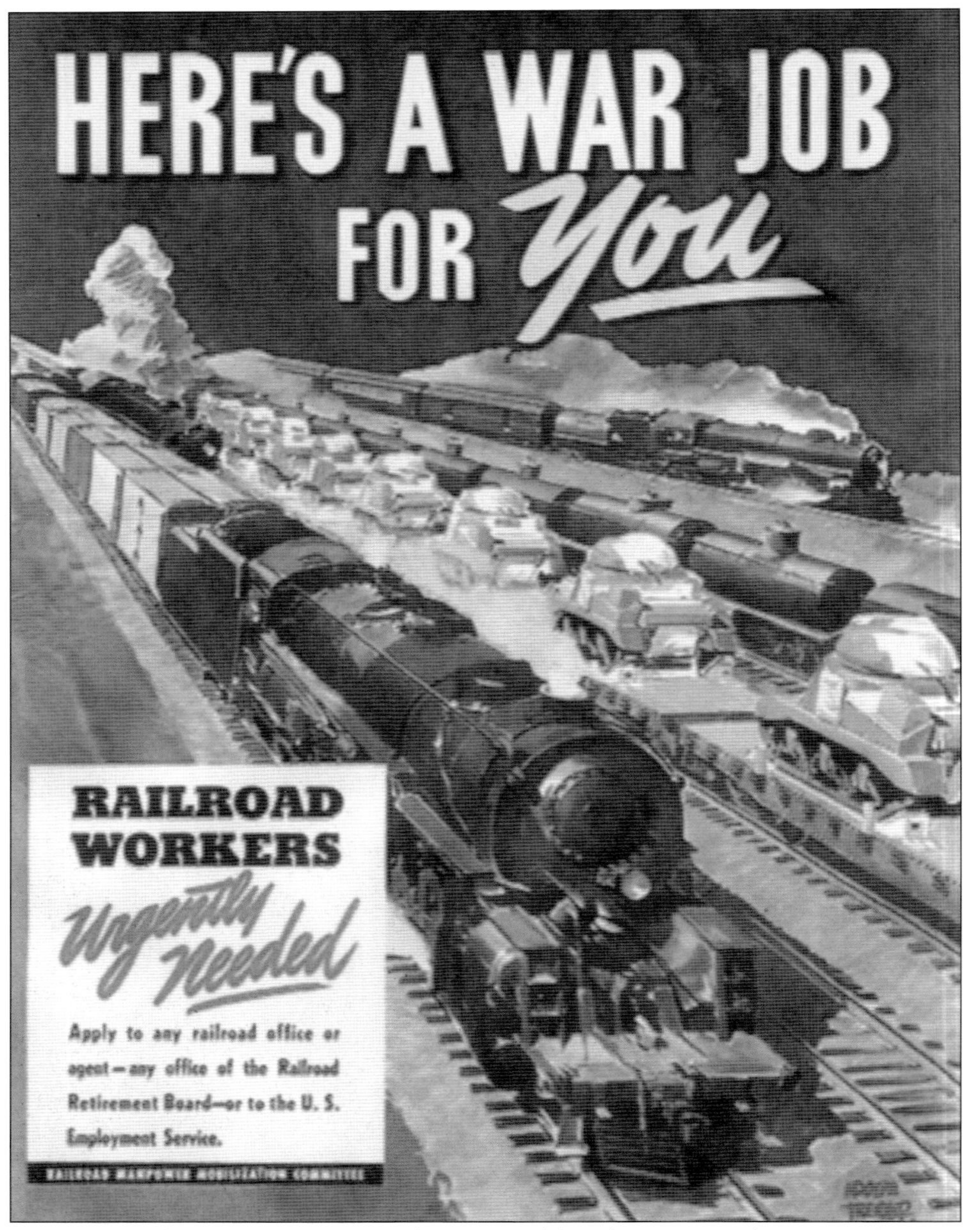

A major reason why New Mexico suffered a wartime labor shortage was that many of its citizens served in the military, and many others were attracted to good-paying jobs elsewhere, especially on the West Coast. New Mexicans who moved West often encouraged relatives and friends to follow in a wartime serial migration. Newspaper ads enticed New Mexicans to railroad jobs in towns like Barstow, California. Others found employment at shipyards in cities like Oakland and Portland or at aircraft plants in Los Angeles and Seattle. Women who worked in these industries were nicknamed "Rosie the Riveters." Hispanic women were called "Rosita the Riveters." Some of these workers returned to New Mexico after the war. Others remained on the coast, although they always considered New Mexico their cultural home. Many visited New Mexico, especially during fiestas, and returned to the state years later in retirement. (Railroad Retirement Board.)

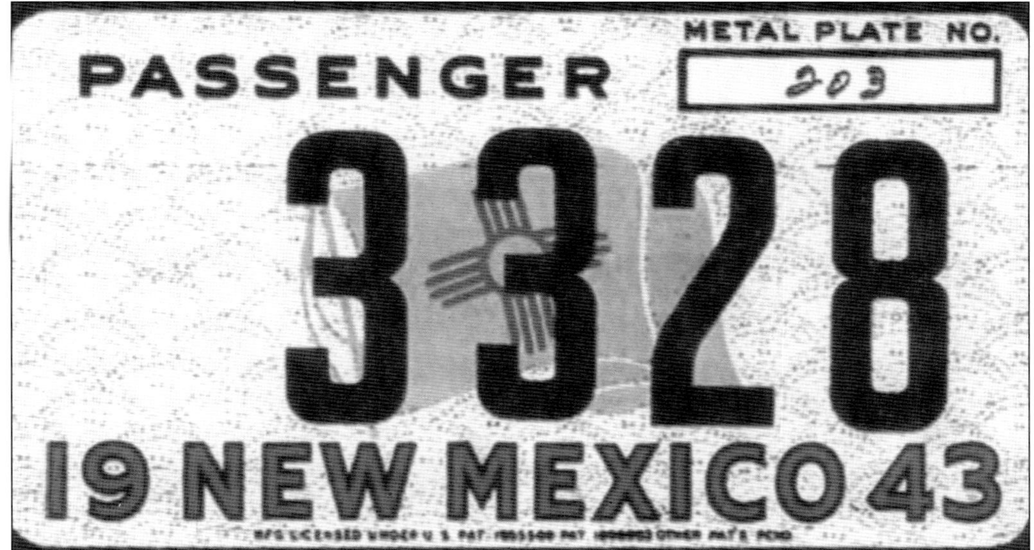

The war had hardly begun when many essential war materials became scarce based on increased demand and, sometimes, hoarding. Gasoline, metal, rubber, silk, sugar, and coffee were among the important items in short supply. As an example of dealing with the shortage of metal, New Mexico did not issue new license plates in 1943; instead, the state issued license stickers (above) that were glued to the inside of vehicle windshields. To deal with other shortages, the federal government rationed many goods, allocating ration books with stamps to limit purchases. Most New Mexicans cooperated, using ration books or choosing alternatives (like molasses for sugar) or growing victory gardens, as many had in World War I. Others traveled to Mexico to buy scarce goods or purchased them illegally on the black market. (Both, Richard Melzer.)

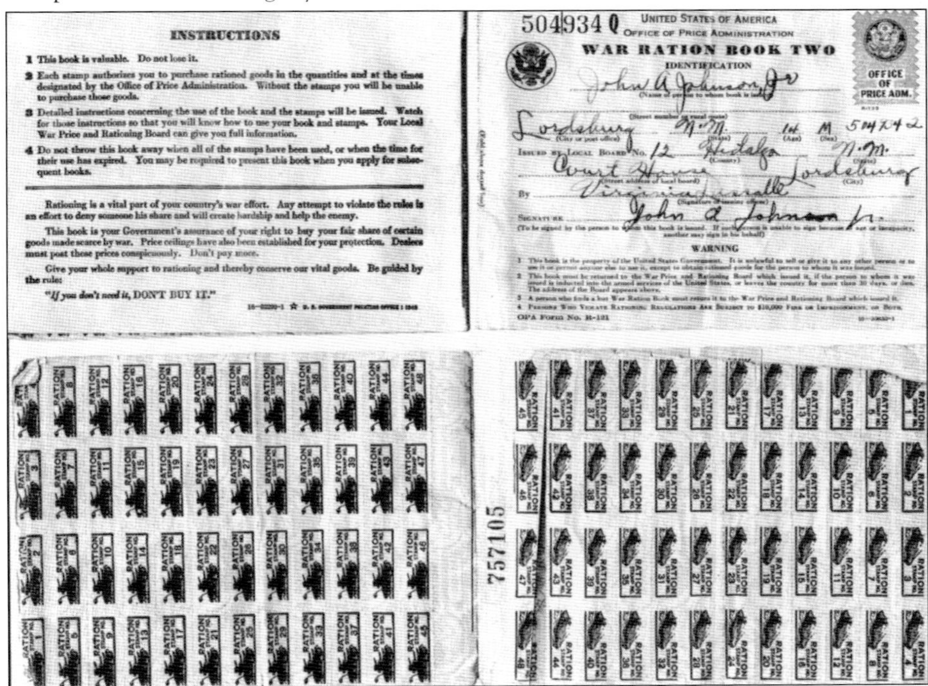

INSTRUCTIONS

1 This book is valuable. Do not lose it.

2 Each stamp authorizes you to purchase rationed goods in the quantities and at the times designated by the Office of Price Administration. Without the stamps you will be unable to purchase those goods.

3 Detailed instructions concerning the use of the book and the stamps will be issued. Watch for those instructions so that you will know how to use your book and stamps. Your Local War Price and Rationing Board can give you full information.

4 Do not throw this book away when all of the stamps have been used, or when the time for their use has expired. You may be required to present this book when you apply for subsequent books.

Rationing is a vital part of your country's war effort. Any attempt to violate the rules is an effort to deny someone his share and will create hardship and help the enemy.

This book is your Government's assurance of your right to buy your fair share of certain goods made scarce by war. Price ceilings have also been established for your protection. Dealers must post these prices conspicuously. Don't pay more.

Give your whole support to rationing and thereby conserve our vital goods. Be guided by the rule:

"If you don't need it, DON'T BUY IT."

504934 Q

UNITED STATES OF AMERICA
OFFICE OF PRICE ADMINISTRATION

WAR RATION BOOK TWO

IDENTIFICATION

John A Johnson Jr
(Name of person to whom book is issued)

(Street number or rural route)

Lordsburg (City or post office) N.M. (State) 14 (Age) M (Sex) 504242

ISSUED BY LOCAL BOARD No. 12 Hidalgo (County) N.M. (State)

Court House (Street address of local board) Lordsburg (City)

By Virginia [illegible] (Signature of issuing officer)

SIGNATURE John A Johnson Jr.

(To be signed by the person to whom this book is issued. If such person is unable to sign because of age or incapacity, another may sign in his behalf)

OFFICE OF PRICE ADM.

WARNING

1 This book is the property of the United States Government. It is unlawful to sell or give it to any other person or to use it or permit anyone else to use it, except to obtain rationed goods for the person to whom it was issued.

2 This book must be returned to the War Price and Rationing Board which issued it, if the person to whom it was issued is inducted into the armed services of the United States, or leaves the country for more than 30 days, or dies. The address of the Board appears above.

3 A person who finds a lost War Ration Book must return it to the War Price and Rationing Board which issued it.

4 PERSONS WHO VIOLATE RATIONING REGULATIONS ARE SUBJECT TO $10,000 FINE OR IMPRISONMENT, OR BOTH.

OPA Form No. R-121

757105

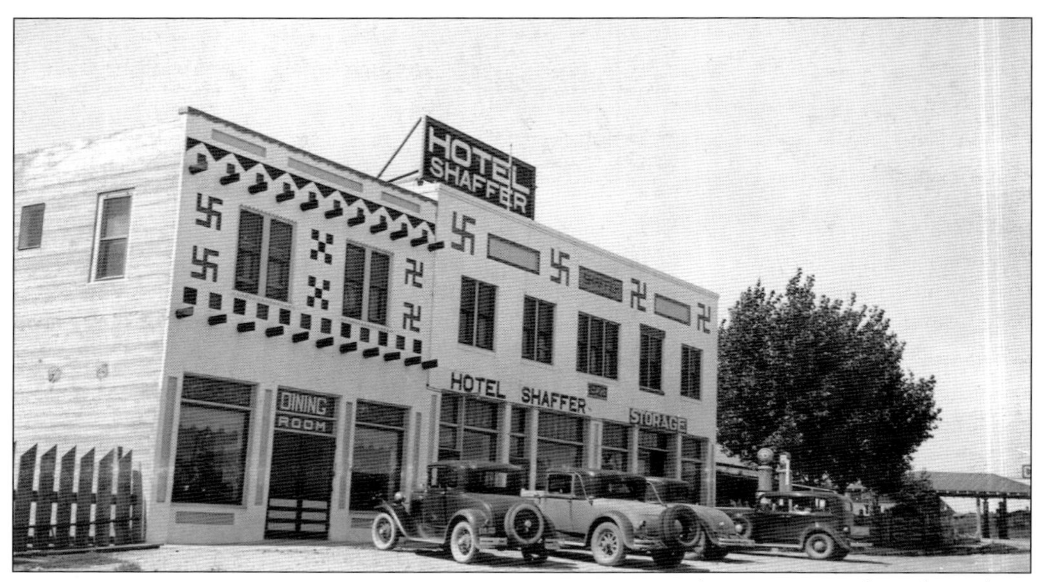

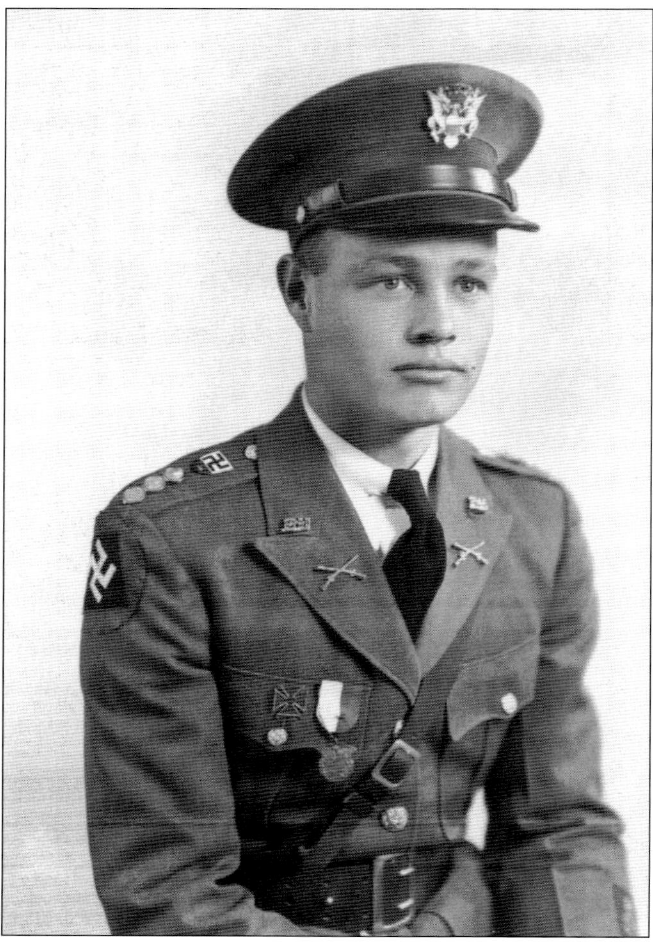

A stranger traveling through New Mexico might have been taken aback by the swastikas on various artifacts and buildings in the state. Swastikas could be found on hotels like the Shaffer Hotel in Mountainair (above), on Navajo blankets, and even on ROTC shoulder patches at New Mexico A&M (left). Strangers might well have thought that any person who displayed swastikas must have been Nazi sympathizers. Many did not realize that swastikas had deep cultural meaning in New Mexico long before the rise of Adolf Hitler. Rather than being a racist symbol of evil and hate, swastikas in the Southwest were symbols of peace and well-being, especially among tribes like the Navajo and Hopi. Realizing that many people might misinterpret their swastikas, most New Mexicans removed them during the war. (Above, Richard Melzer; left, New Mexico State University.)

Although it is normally identified as a hot, arid state with far more desert than farm or ranch land, New Mexico contributed a surprising variety of agricultural products to the war effort. By World War II, Torrance County had become known as the Pinto Bean Capital of the nation. Cotton grew in abundance in the Mesilla Valley. Carrots were a prosperous crop near Grants. Although not as important as in New Mexico's early history, sheep ranchers still produced meat and wool. Having become the dominant livestock in the state by the late 19th century, cattle roamed the vast ranges of southern and eastern New Mexico. (Right, Richard Melzer; below, B.G. Burr.)

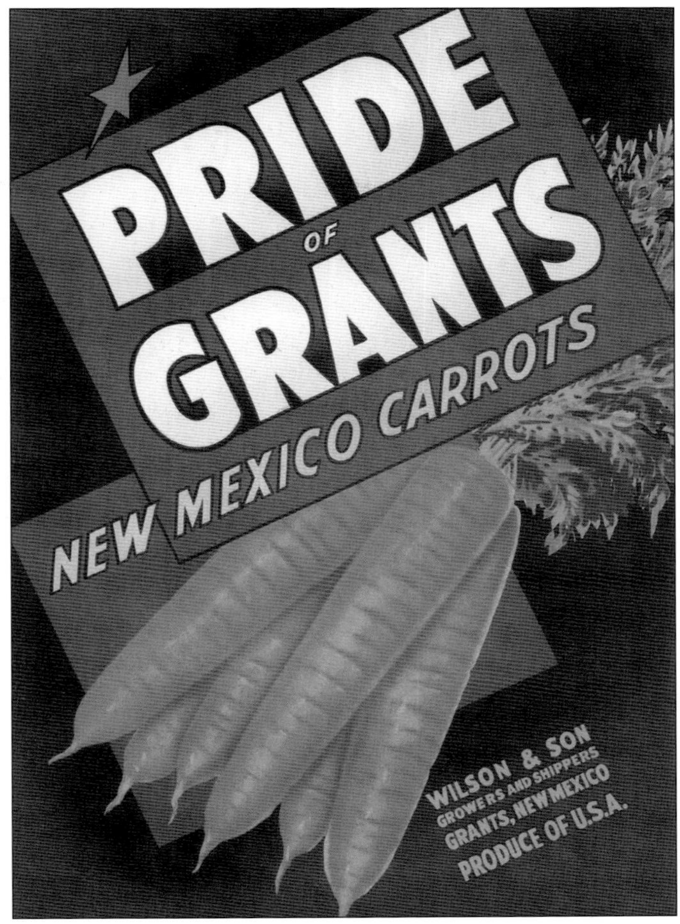

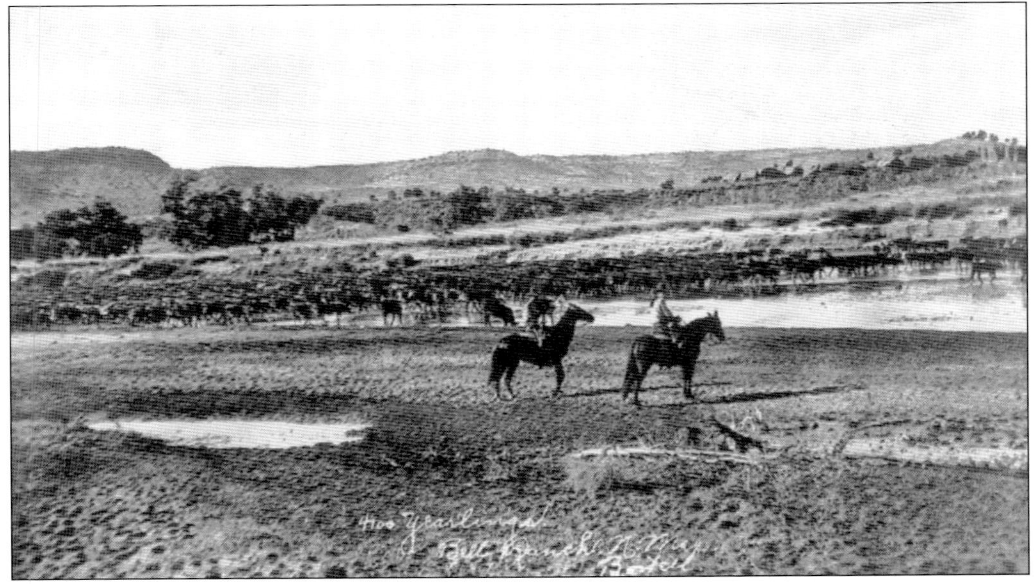

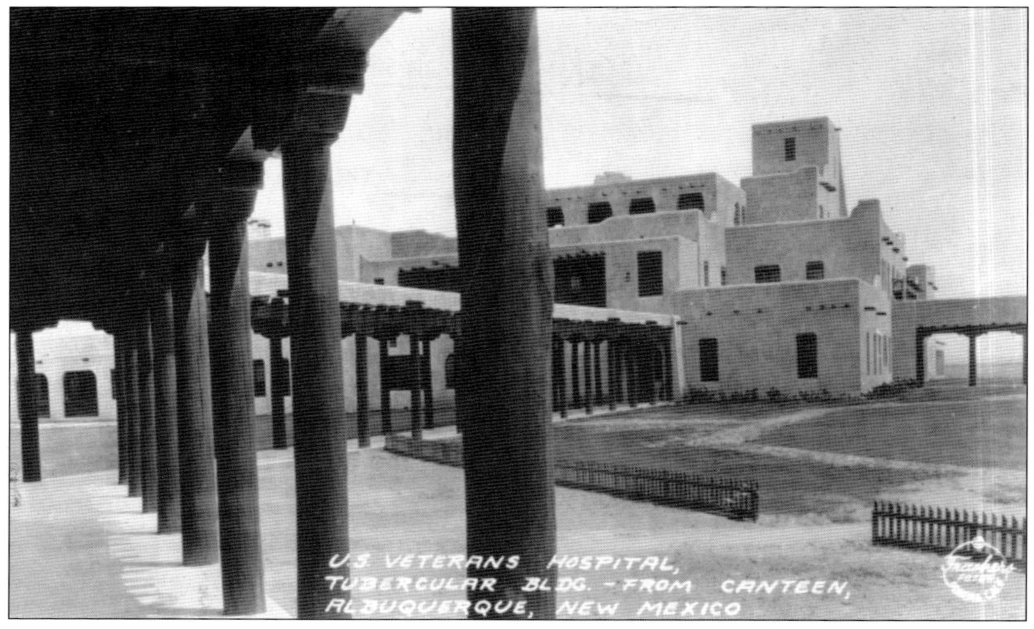

Responding to the medical needs of veterans from earlier wars, the Veterans Administration built a 262-bed hospital in southeastern Albuquerque in mid-1932. Military hospitals at Ft. Bayard and Ft. Stanton treated veterans with tuberculosis. These hospitals continued to function during World War II, but additional facilities were needed for returning casualties. The Army responded by constructing Bruns General Hospital on Cerrillos Road in Santa Fe. The 2,000-bed unit, dedicated in September 1943, was named to honor Col. Earl Bruns, a pioneering New Mexico tuberculosis physician. At its peak in 1945, Bruns Hospital treated 2,200 patients, including many liberated survivors of the Bataan Death March. Closed in 1946, the hospital's buildings were distributed throughout New Mexico, including to the state tuberculosis hospital near Socorro and the UNM campus in Albuquerque. The remaining buildings were used at what became the College of Santa Fe. (Both, Richard Melzer.)

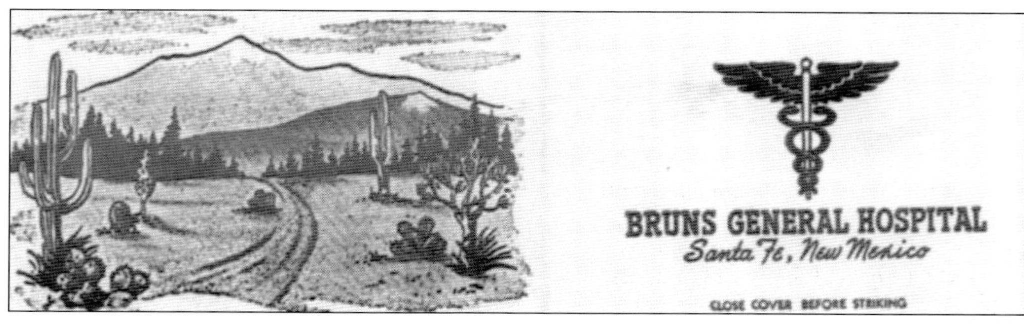

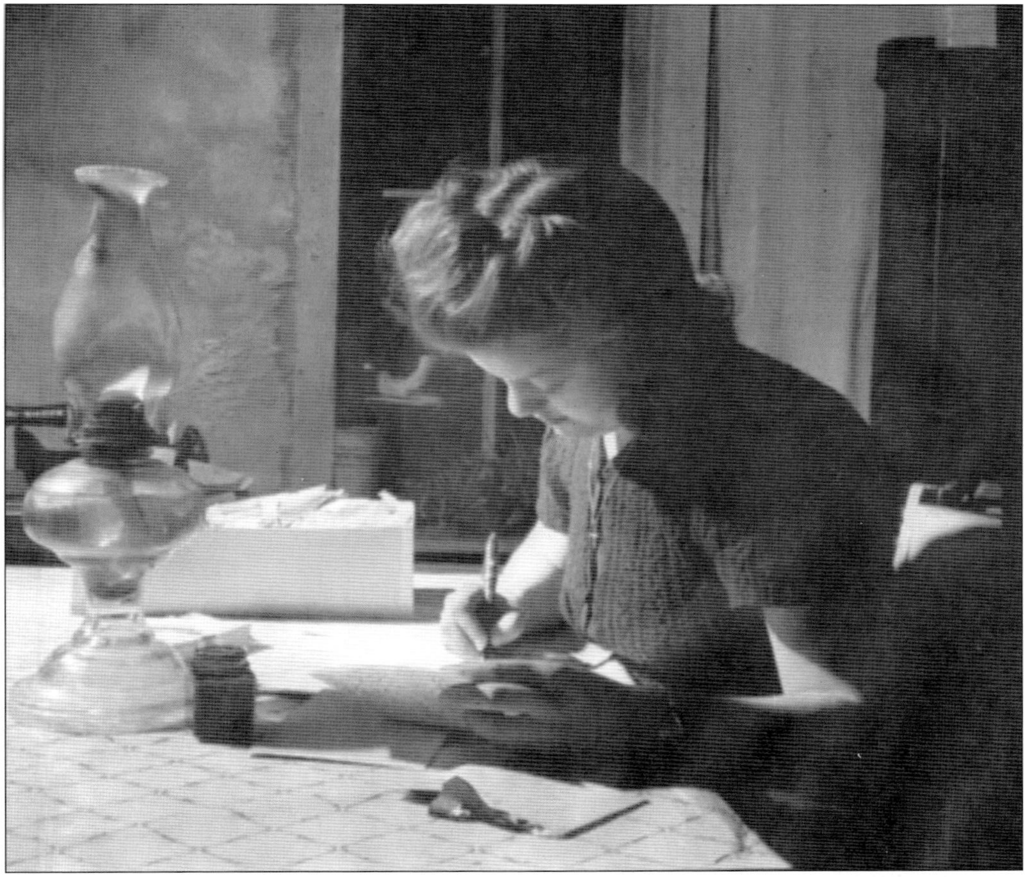

In World War II, as in all wars, letters were essential to maintaining morale. Soldiers craved news from home to remain connected to their loved ones and previous lives. Meanwhile, loved ones like Mary Mutz of the Moreno Valley (above) eagerly sought news from abroad to alleviate their fears. Tons of mail were sent, taking precious space on supply ships. To solve this problem, the military used V-Mail. Correspondents wrote on small sheets, which were then microfilmed, transported, and printed on arrival. Using this method, 37 bags of mail could be reduced to one. The record number of letters sent by a New Mexican probably belongs to New Mexico A&M engineering dean Daniel Jett, pictured at right with some of his students. Jett sent over a thousand letters and newsletters to his former students serving around the world. (Above, Library of Congress; right, New Mexico State University.)

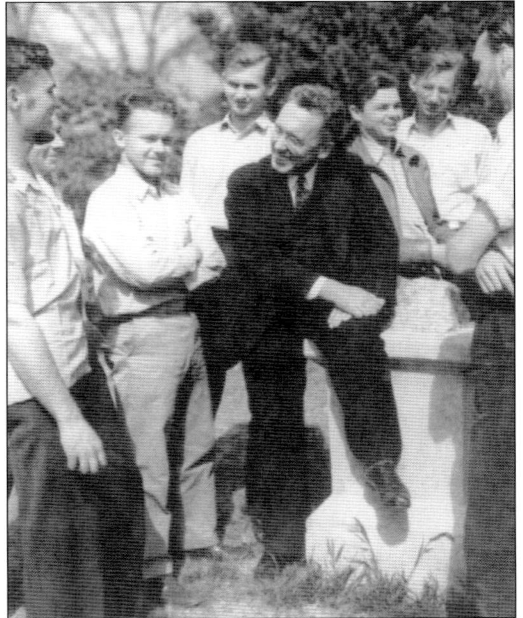

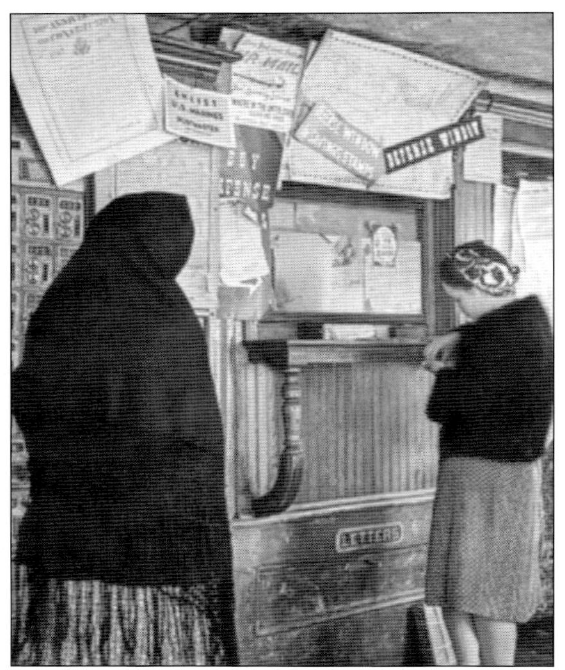

The United States financed almost half of the enormous cost of World War II through the sale of war bonds. Like all states, New Mexico was given quotas for war bond sales. New Mexicans consistently met or surpassed these goals, purchasing various amounts at locations like post offices, as the two women in Questa in the photograph at left are doing. Although banks, large corporations, and, to a lesser extent, small businesses purchased the majority of bonds, individuals also purchased a significant amount. More than a hundred patriotic volunteers sold war bonds door-to-door in Santa Fe. The patients and medical personnel at Bruns Hospital bought thousands of dollars of bonds. Even children purchased bonds, buying stamps for as little as a dime each. Large signs on railroad boxcars served as mobile billboards for the bond drive (below). (Both, Library of Congress.)

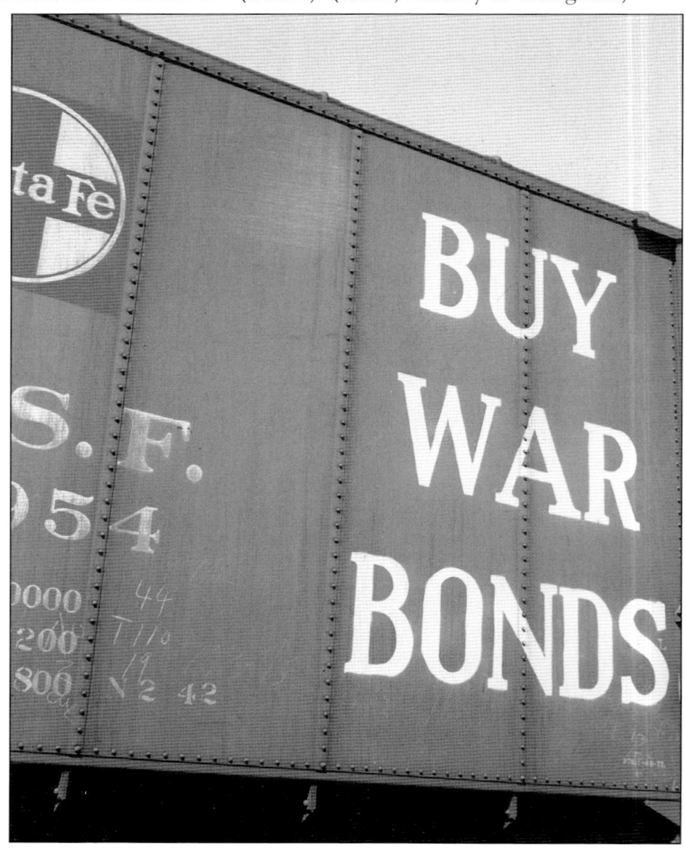

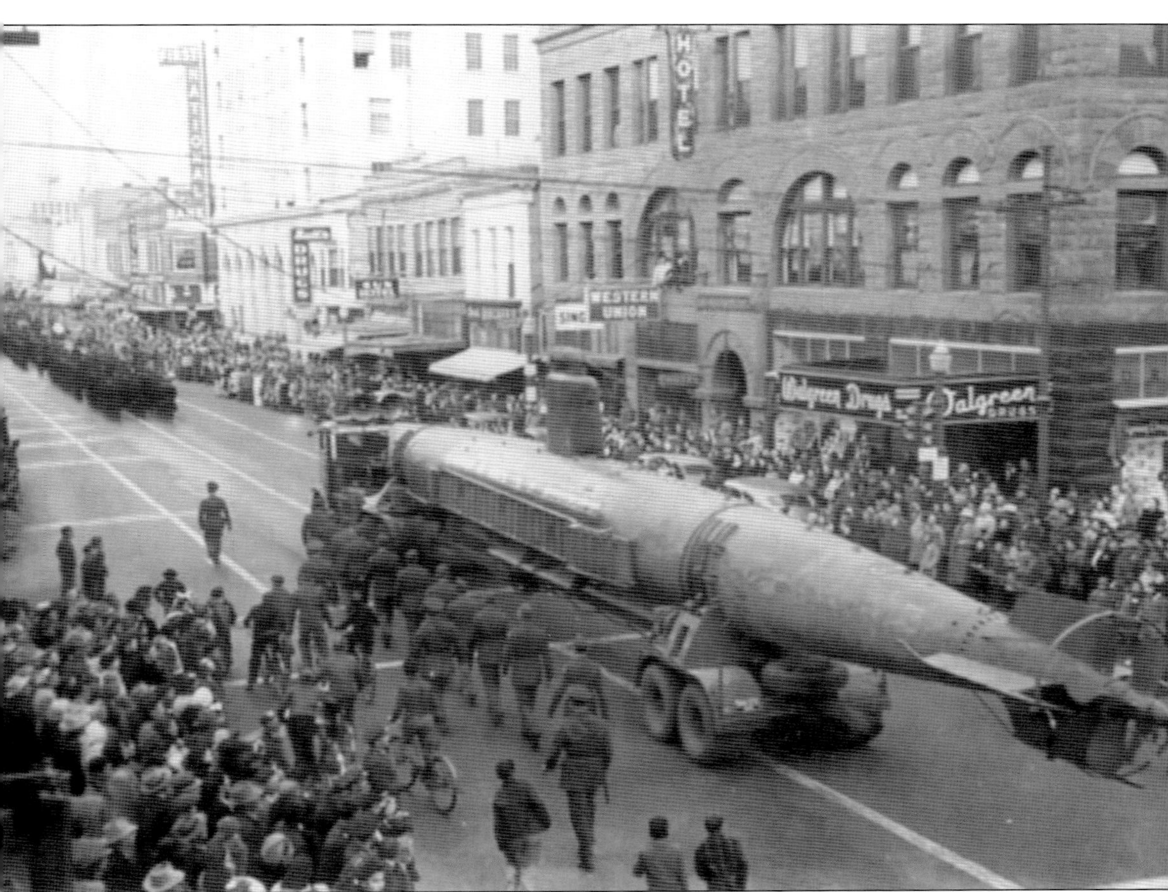

New Mexicans were encouraged to buy war bonds in many ways. The government offered to name a new bomber whatever a group selected if they sold $30,000 worth of bonds. New Mexicans, led by the Bataan Relief Organization, sold the required amount of bonds and proudly named a new plane the *Spirit of Bataan*. Uniquely, a two-man Japanese submarine captured at Pearl Harbor was displayed in small towns like Belen and larger cities like Albuquerque. Five thousand citizens bought over $100,000 worth of bonds at the Las Cruces event. In Albuquerque, the sub traveled down Central Avenue in the largest parade ever staged in the city. The ship's tour through New Mexico helped generate $700,000 in bond sales. (Albuquerque Museum, PA1982.118.19.)

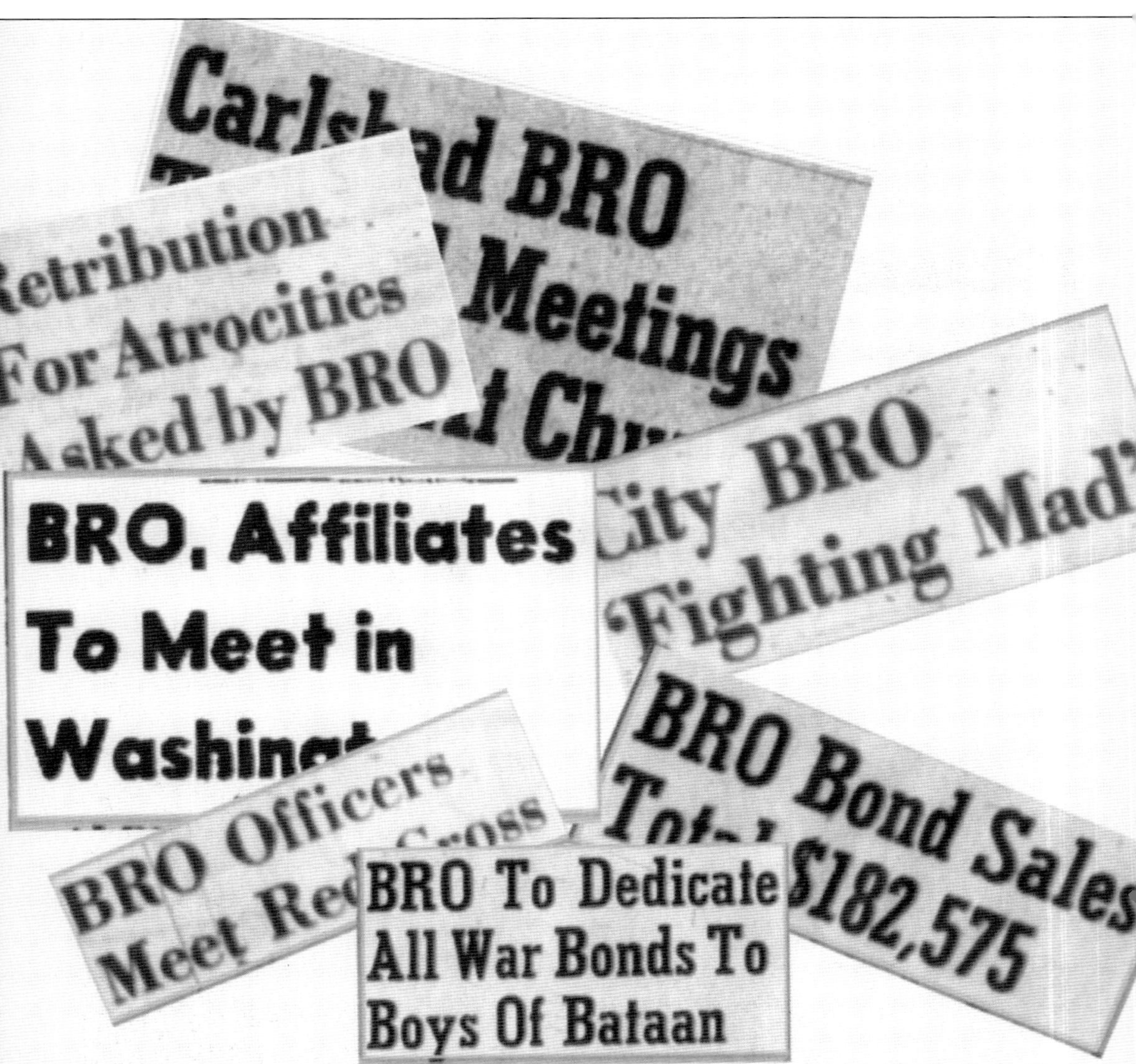

As described in chapter one, Allied forces, including 1,806 New Mexicans, surrendered to the Japanese on the Bataan Peninsula on April 9, 1942. Within days, worried families back home organized the Bataan Relief Organization (BRO). Members worked feverishly to learn the fate of their loved ones, even listening to Japanese radio broadcasts for any small bit of information they could glean. Working through organizations like the Red Cross, the BRO sent supplies, helped sell war bonds, and facilitated whatever mail could be sent to or received from the POWs. A BRO bulletin shared the latest information on the POWs' condition. While the BRO helped the POWs in every way possible, it also served as an important way in which the families themselves remained active, believing that they were contributing to efforts to save their loved ones and possibly shorten their nightmarish captivity. (John Taylor.)

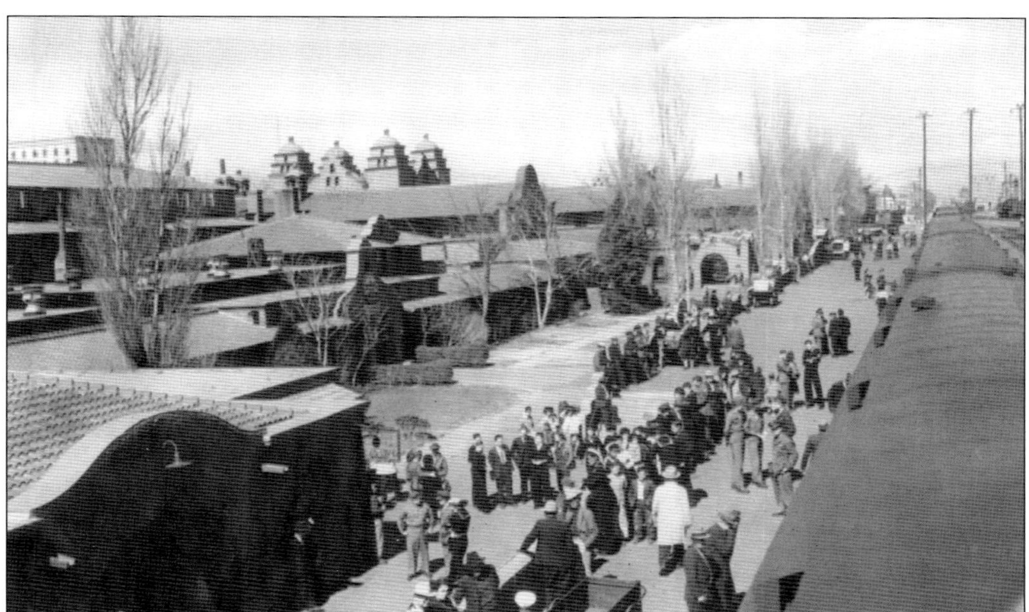

Thousands of servicemen and servicewomen traveled through New Mexico en route to military assignments in all directions. Most traveled by train, stopping in railroad towns where they were greeted by generous local residents who shared items like food, magazines, and, in the case of some willing young women, their addresses. Harvey Girls served thousands of box lunches prepared at large sandwich-making operations in Harvey House restaurants in Clovis, Albuquerque (shown here), and Gallup. (Albuquerque Museum, No. 1982.180.226.)

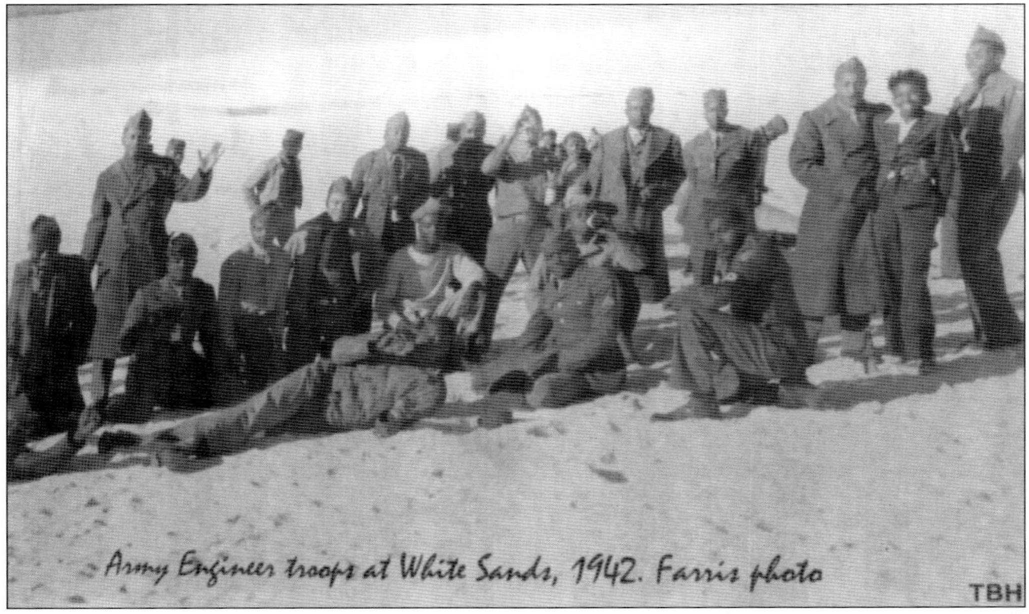

White Sands National Monument in southeastern New Mexico opened its gates to service personnel. Servicemen were also welcome at Carlsbad Caverns. This particular group of engineers, on leave from nearby Alamogordo Army Airfield, consisted solely of African Americans, two of whom are female. US military units were still segregated during World War II. (Farris Photography.)

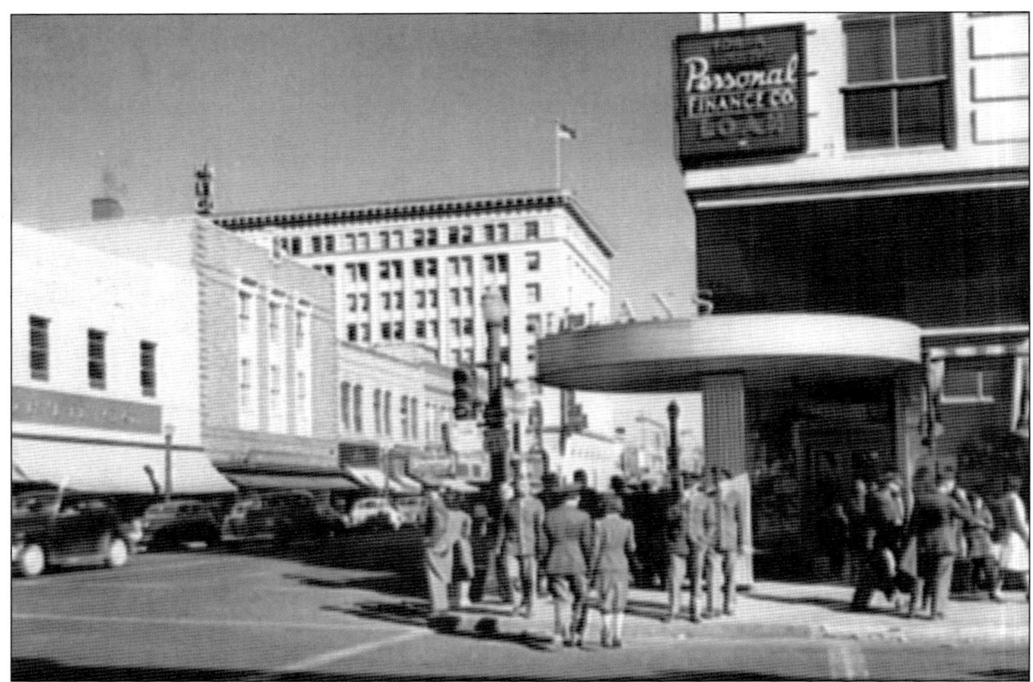

Having finished their stateside training, servicemen and women usually received leave to visit home before being shipped out, often to overseas assignments. Others came home during their service, especially if their assignments were in installations near New Mexico. Their homecomings were always cause for joy and celebration. They visited favorite haunts such as Central Avenue in Albuquerque (above). Small towns like Penasco often welcomed their soldiers home with parties and dances (below). Native Americans received special attention: ceremonies, prayers, and blessings were performed to assure a son's safety as he left home or to purify him once he returned. (Both, Library of Congress.)

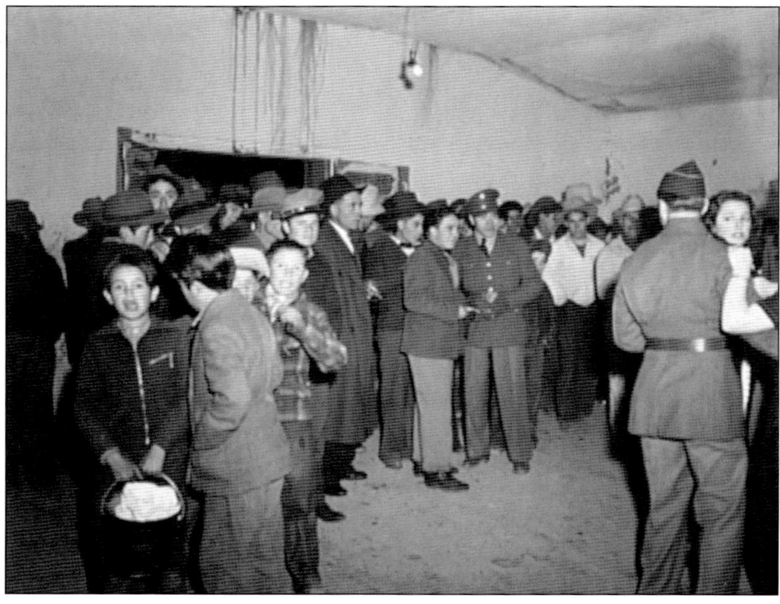

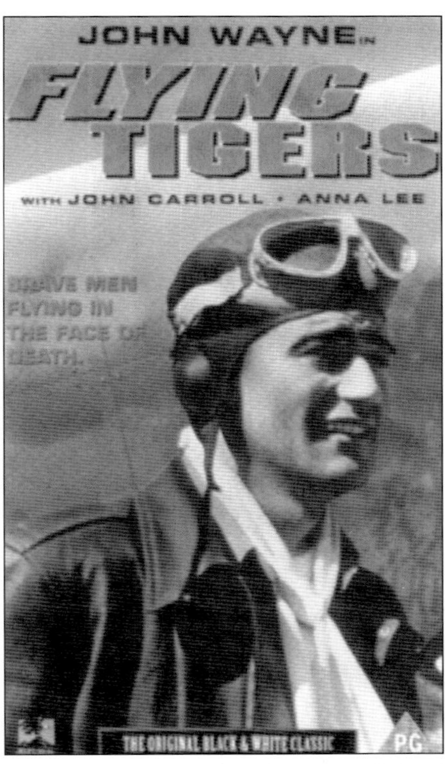

By the early 1940s, New Mexico had begun to be a favorite location for Hollywood movie makers. Four war movies were made in the state during World War II, including *Flying Tigers* (1942). The movie starred John Wayne, although most of the shots taken in New Mexico were of the state's beautiful sky rather than of Wayne himself. Nominated for three Academy Awards, *Sundown* (1941) was filmed on Acoma pueblo's high mesa. Acoma was transformed into a 40-tent village in British East Africa. A short railroad had to be built to the top of the mesa to transport the film's actors, crew, equipment, elephants, camels, ostriches, and zebras. Two years later, *The Desert Song* became the first musical shot in New Mexico. A fourth film, *Bombardier*, was shot at Kirtland Air Base in Albuquerque. (Both, Richard Melzer.)

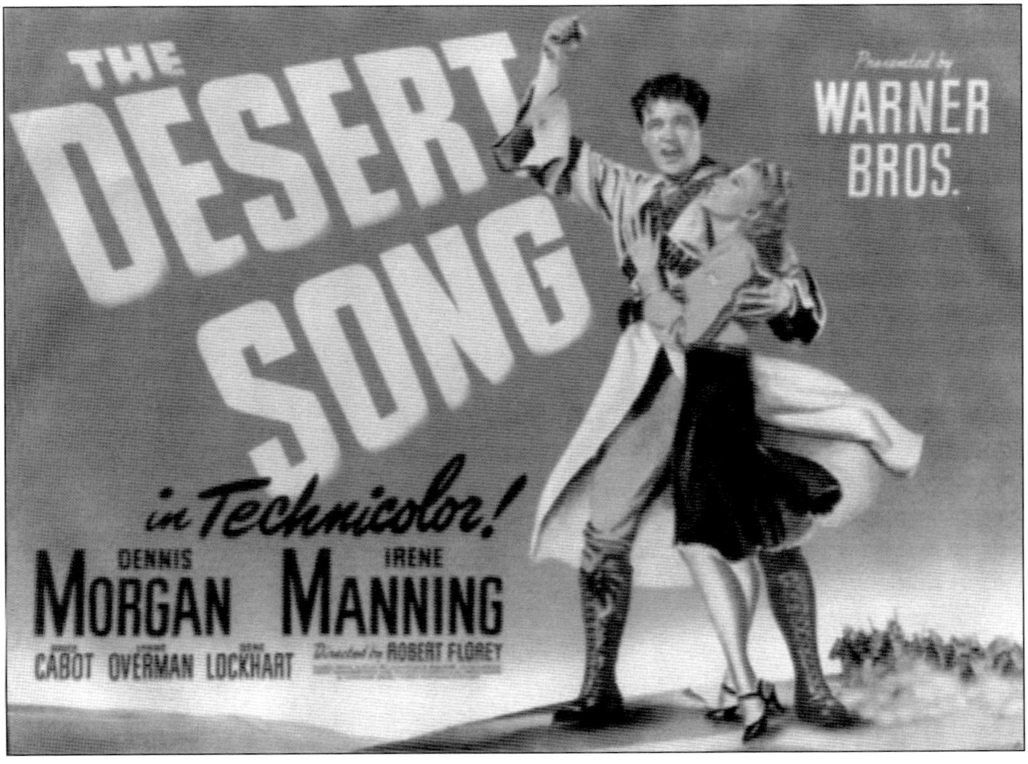

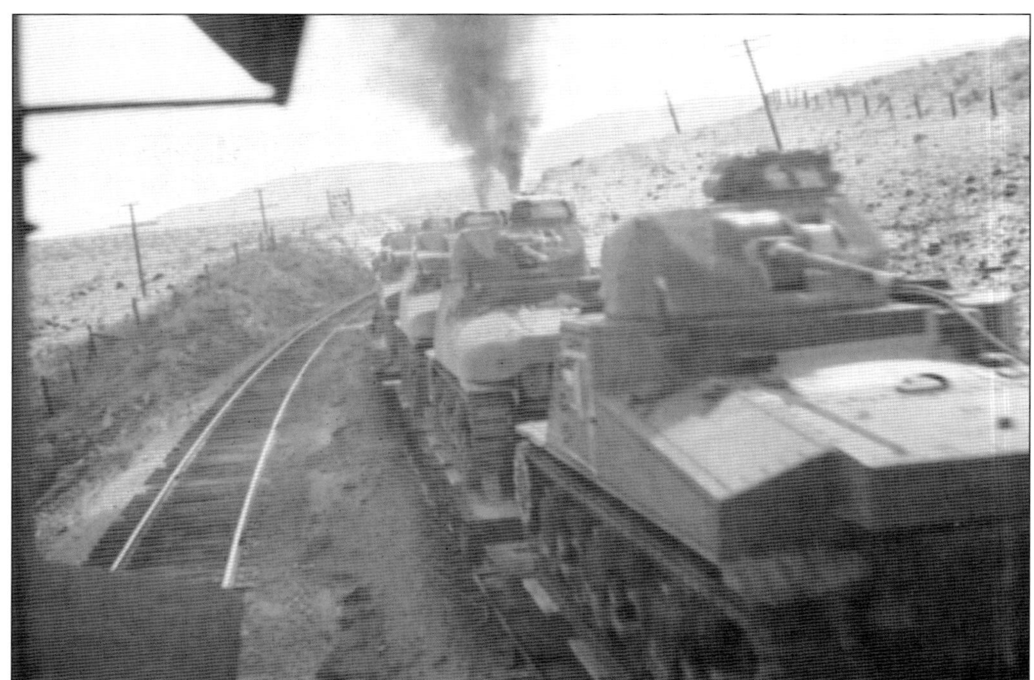

Railroads were critical in transporting troops and supplies throughout the country during World War II. The Atchison, Topeka, & Santa Fe Railway, with tracks laid north-to-south and east-to-west through New Mexico, was particularly vital to the nation's transcontinental infrastructure and national security. Women, Native Americans, and Mexican immigrants joined railroad crews, often for the first time in New Mexico history. Securing the tracks was important from the first day of the war when guards were posted at strategic points, including on railroad bridges and at Abo Pass entering the Rio Grande Valley. As railroad traffic increased, so did the odds of accidents. In one near disaster, a train filled with Red Cross nurses derailed west of Clovis. Incredibly, no one was seriously hurt. (Both, Library of Congress.)

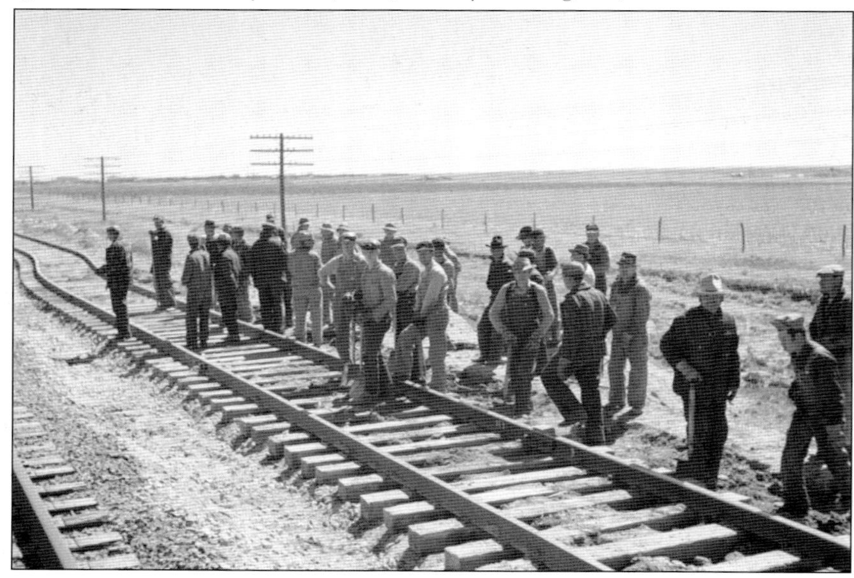

Despite the Santa Fe Railway's best efforts, serious calamities did occur. The worst happened on November 30, 1944, when a freight train carrying 165 five-hundred-pound bombs derailed near the small village of Tolar. A fire broke out, burning for about 30 minutes before 36 carloads of bombs ignited and exploded. Felt as far away as Clovis, the explosion nearly wiped Tolar's 11 buildings off the map. Amazingly, only one person was killed when he was hit by flying debris. Few residents were in town because many had gone to Clovis to see the popular movie *Gone with the Wind* about the Civil War. Few realized that as they watched the movie, their own town had gone with the wind—a casualty of another terrible war. (Both, Riley Switch.)

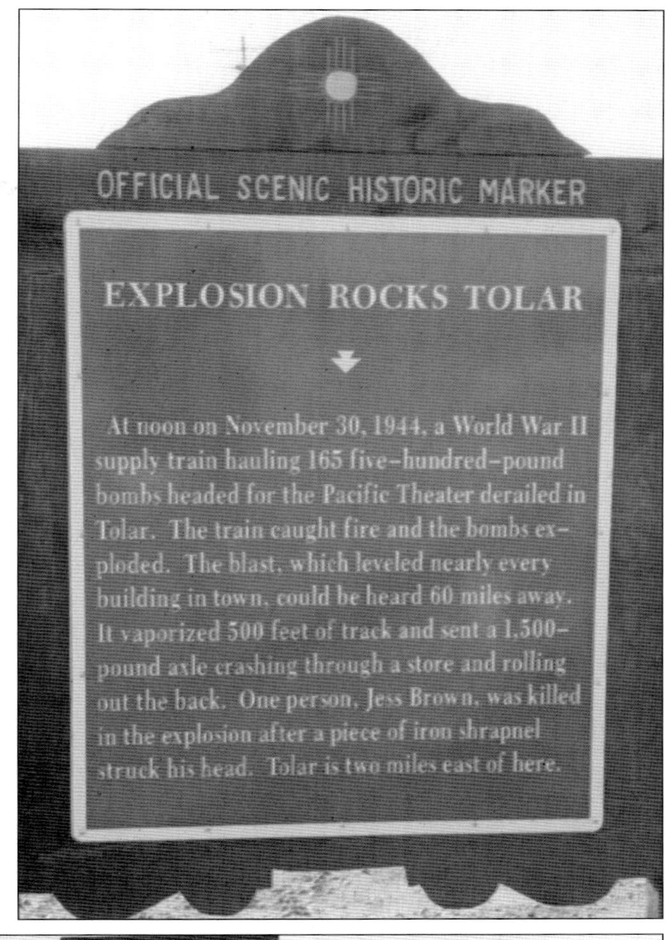

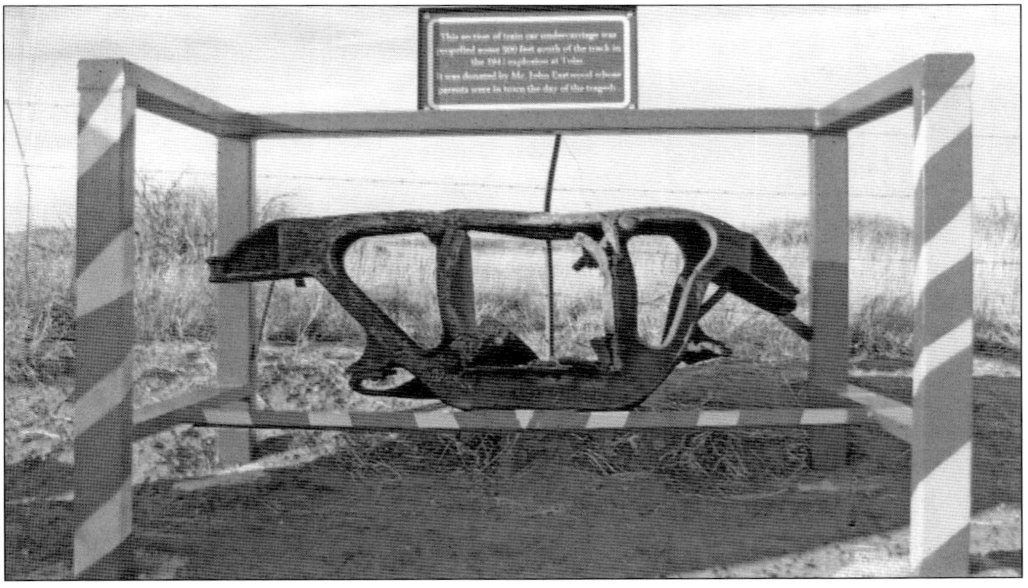

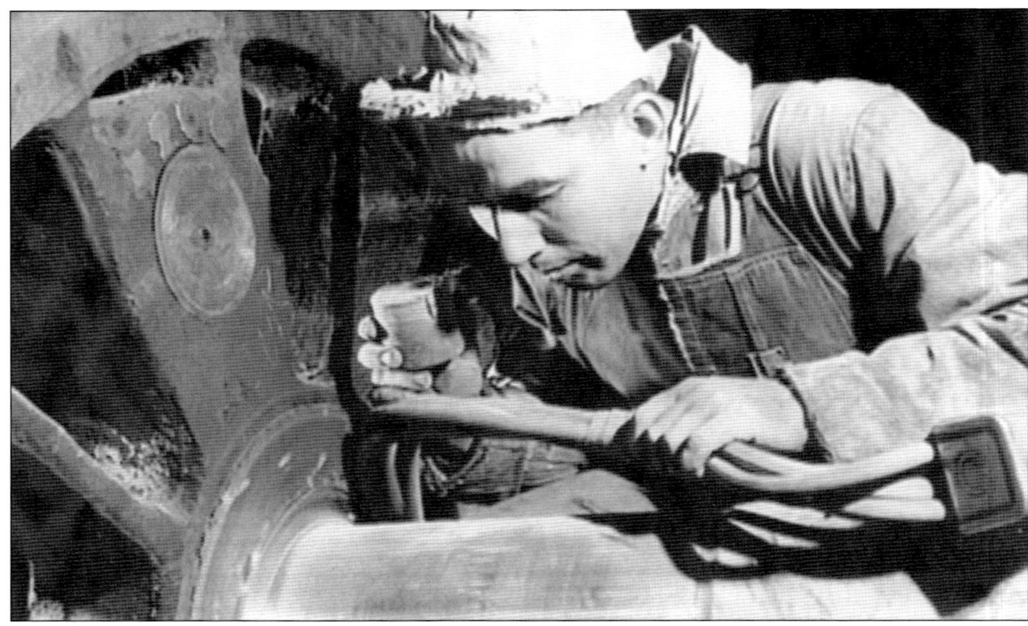

The Santa Fe Railway's shops in Albuquerque were the railroad's largest shop west of the Mississippi River. Always essential to the railroad's smooth operation, these shops became even more vital to the upkeep of locomotives and rolling stock during the war. About 40 locomotives were overhauled per month. The shops, south of the Albuquerque depot in the largely Hispanic Barelas neighborhood, hired many additional workers to keep up with the increased workload; the workforce increased 400 percent. The railroad solidified its position as the number one employer and most important sector of Albuquerque's economy. In the photograph above, a worker tests a wheel in the Albuquerque shops during a typical nine-hour shift. The photograph below shows two women who worked as potash car cleaners in the Clovis yards. (Both, Library of Congress.)

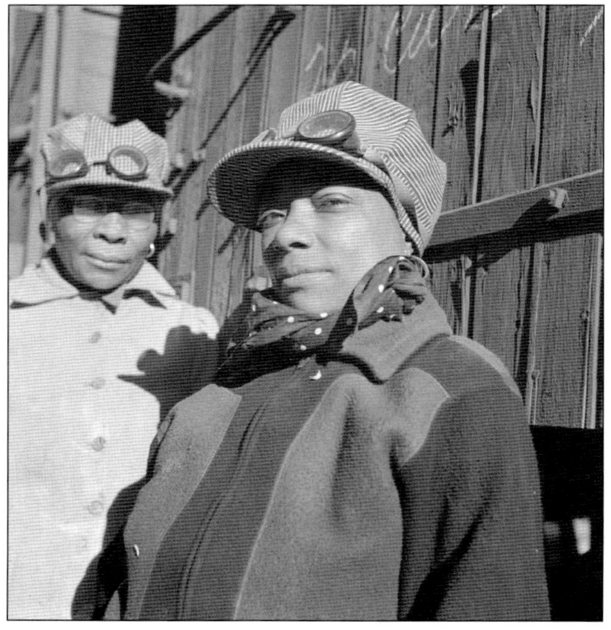

Of all of Adolf Hitler's atrocities, the mass murder of over six million humans in the Holocaust was the most brutal. Although small, the Jewish population of New Mexico worked hard to help defeat Hitler. Fundraisers were held, war bonds were sold, and 44 members of Albuquerque's Congregation Albert's 88 families served in the military. The congregation's Rabbi Solomon Starrels (far right below) conducted services at Bruns Army Hospital and at Los Alamos, where many scientists and their families were Jewish. Starrels's board reportedly grew angry when he left on Saturdays without disclosing his destination. Of course, he could not divulge his whereabouts without compromising the Manhattan Project's secrecy. Jewish families also did all they could to help fellow Jews flee to New Mexico from Europe, avoiding almost certain death in German concentration camps. (Both, Congregation Albert.)

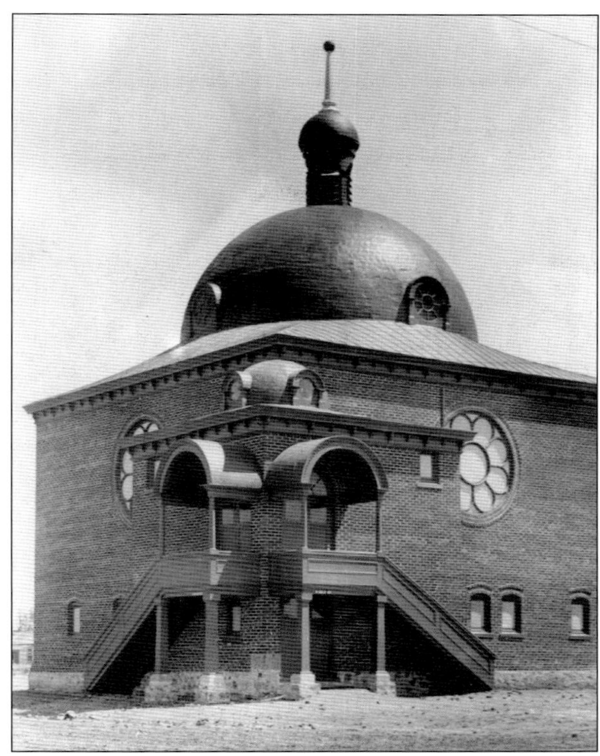

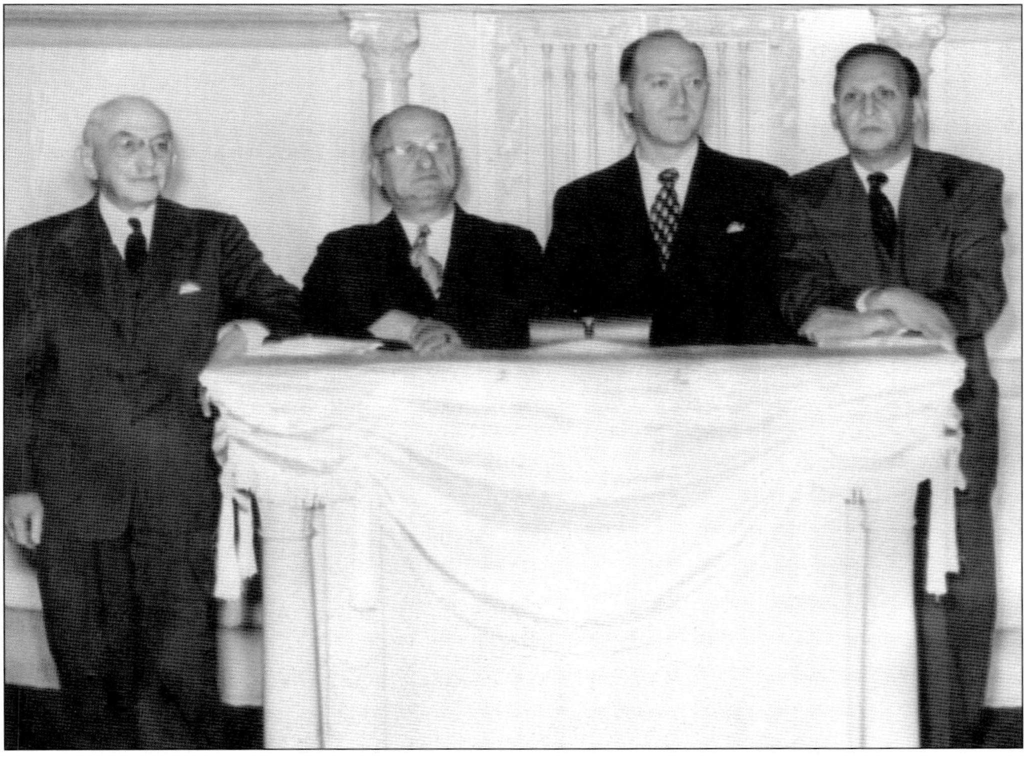

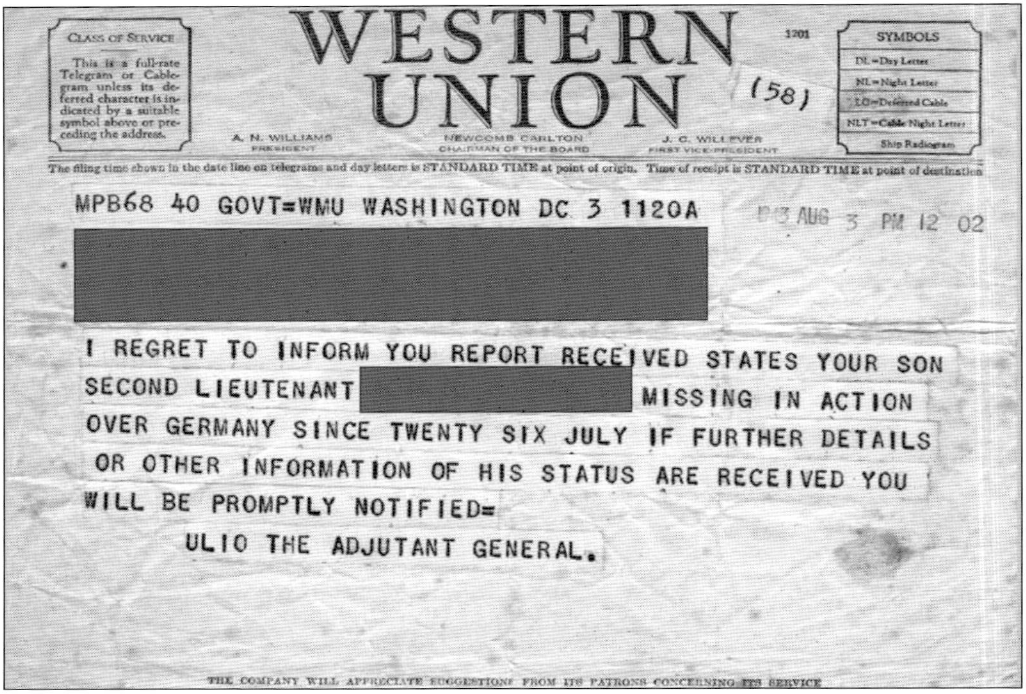

CLASS OF SERVICE

This is a full-rate Telegram or Cablegram unless its deferred character is indicated by a suitable symbol above or preceding the address.

WESTERN UNION

1201

SYMBOLS

DL = Day Letter

NL = Night Letter

LC = Deferred Cable

NLT = Cable Night Letter

Ship Radiogram

(58)

A. N. WILLIAMS, PRESIDENT — NEWCOMB CARLTON, CHAIRMAN OF THE BOARD — J. C. WILLEVER, FIRST VICE-PRESIDENT

The filing time shown in the date line on telegrams and day letters is STANDARD TIME at point of origin. Time of receipt is STANDARD TIME at point of destination

MPB68 40 GOVT=WMU WASHINGTON DC 3 1120A

1943 AUG 3 PM 12 02

I REGRET TO INFORM YOU REPORT RECEIVED STATES YOUR SON SECOND LIEUTENANT MISSING IN ACTION OVER GERMANY SINCE TWENTY SIX JULY IF FURTHER DETAILS OR OTHER INFORMATION OF HIS STATUS ARE RECEIVED YOU WILL BE PROMPTLY NOTIFIED=

ULIO THE ADJUTANT GENERAL.

THE COMPANY WILL APPRECIATE SUGGESTIONS FROM ITS PATRONS CONCERNING ITS SERVICE

Over 49,500 New Mexicans served in the Army, Army Air Corps, Navy, Marines, and Coast Guard during World War II. Proud parents displayed banners with blue stars to indicate the number of family members fighting in the war. Mothers who showed these small banners in their windows were known as Blue Star Mothers. Tragically, 2,263 New Mexicans died in the conflict, including many, like brothers Jose and Macedonio Duran of San Felipe Pueblo, who were buried in American cemeteries overseas. Their heartbroken families often received the dreaded news in Western Union telegrams, like the one shown above with names removed. These families displayed banners with gold stars sewn over their previous blue stars. Mothers whose sons or daughters paid the ultimate price for their country were known as Gold Star Mothers. (Above, David Doughty; below, John Taylor.)

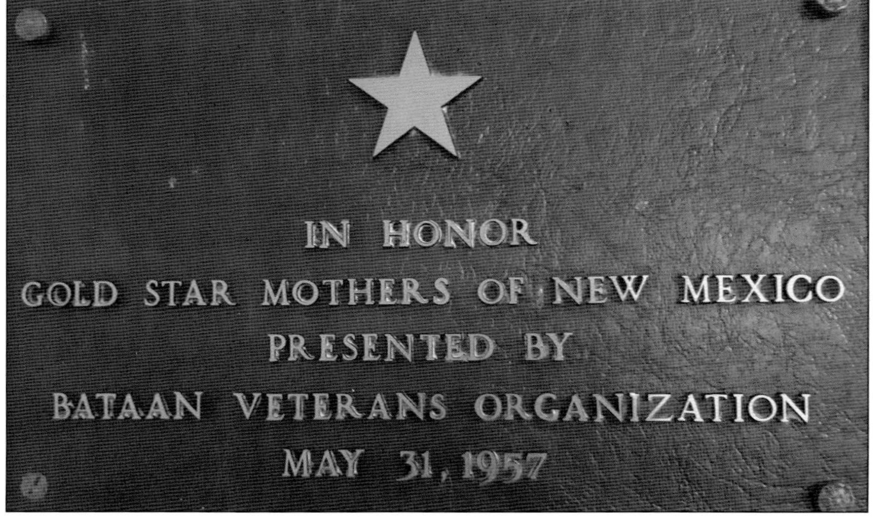

Seven

NEW MEXICO'S HEROES

War, both on the fighting front and the home front, involves individuals—the men and women who compose the armies, the workers, the communities. This chapter examines a few of the thousands of individual New Mexicans who merit special attention as heroes.

Eight New Mexicans won the nation's highest honor for gallantry, the Medal of Honor—five of them posthumously. Sandy Bonnyman died in the fierce assault on Tarawa in the Pacific. Joseph Martinez died in the frigid Aleutians. Harold Moon died defending against 200 Japanese soldiers in the Philippines. Jose Valdez died fighting a German tank in France. Kenneth Walker died in a plane crash on Rabaul in the South Pacific.

Ernie Pyle and cartoonist Bill Maudlin are noted for their work as war correspondents. Pyle spent most of his time on the front lines with the GIs in the trenches and was known as the soldiers' correspondent. Mauldin was famous for his cartoon soldiers Willie and Joe. These grizzled men represented every soldier who had lived in a foxhole and eaten C-rations while fighting for his life.

Women were heroes, too. Some flew planes from factories to the training or deployment sites; others were nurses or worked in industrial facilities such as the Santa Fe shops in Albuquerque. Several women were involved in the Manhattan Project, not only in clerical positions, but as scientists and engineers. In addition, many were leaders of bond drives, grew victory gardens, and kept the home fires burning while their fathers, husbands, sons, and brothers were fighting overseas.

Sen. Dennis Chavez worked tirelessly to ensure that critical supplies such as petroleum and scarce metals were available from our Latin American neighbors. Two religious leaders, Fray Angelico Chavez and Fr. Albert Braun, served as battlefield chaplains during the war, returning after the conflict to become, respectively, a famous historian and the main builder of the Catholic church on the Mescalero reservation.

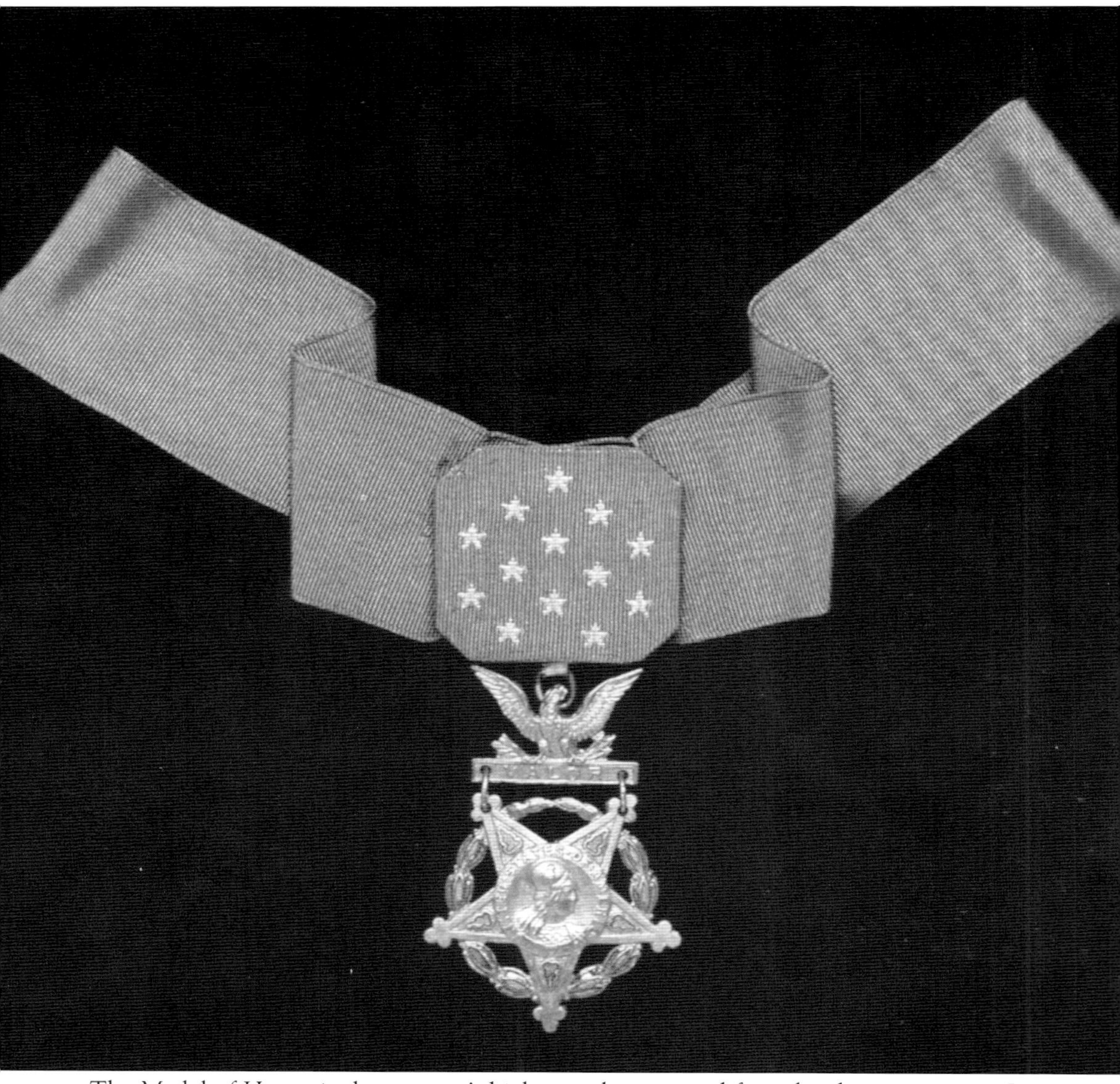

The Medal of Honor is the country's highest military award for valor during wartime. It was introduced during the Civil War and is awarded by the president in the name of Congress. For that reason, the medal is often referred to, erroneously, as the "Congressional Medal of Honor." There are three slightly different versions of the medal for the Army, Navy, and Air Force. The medal is awarded "for conspicuous gallantry and intrepidity at the risk of life above and beyond the call of duty." Since the award was instituted in 1861, there have been over 3,500 recipients. More than 620 have been awarded posthumously. Sixteen men with strong New Mexico connections have been given this award, eight of them for their gallantry during World War II. They are described here in alphabetical order. (Ned Forney.)

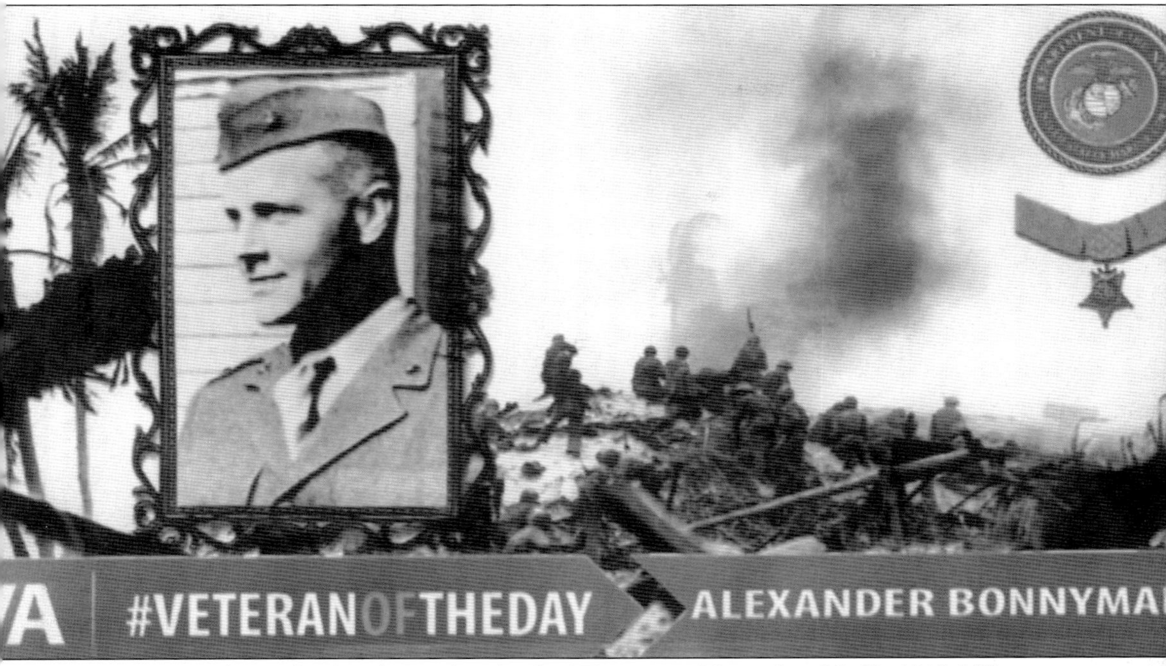

During an assault on the South Pacific island of Tarawa on November 20–22, 1943, US troops were trapped by fire from Japanese shore batteries. Again and again, First Lt. Alexander "Sandy" Bonnyman Jr. organized and led the men across an open pier to the beach and later led them in organized attacks against the Japanese artillery sites. The next day, he crawled ahead of the lines and laid demolition charges at the entrance of a Japanese stronghold. He then led an assault on the bastion. He was killed fighting to keep the Japanese from retaking the position. His citation reads, "By his dauntless fighting spirit, unrelenting aggressiveness, and forceful leadership throughout three days of unremitting, violent battle, First Lieutenant Bonnyman had inspired his men to heroic effort." A prepositioning ship, MV *1st Lieutenant Alexander Bonnyman* (T-AK-3003), was named in his honor. (US Department of Veterans Affairs.)

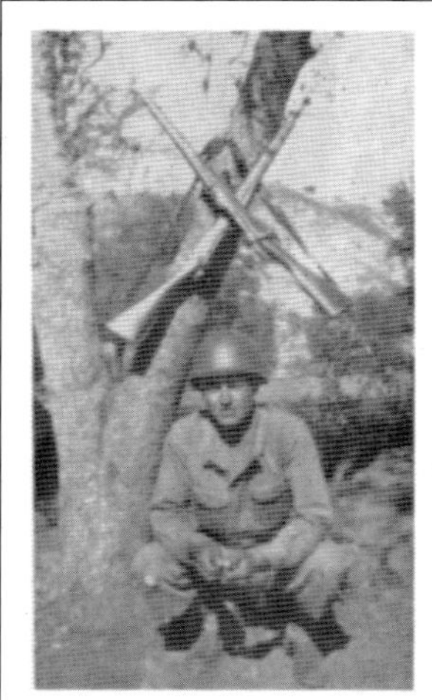
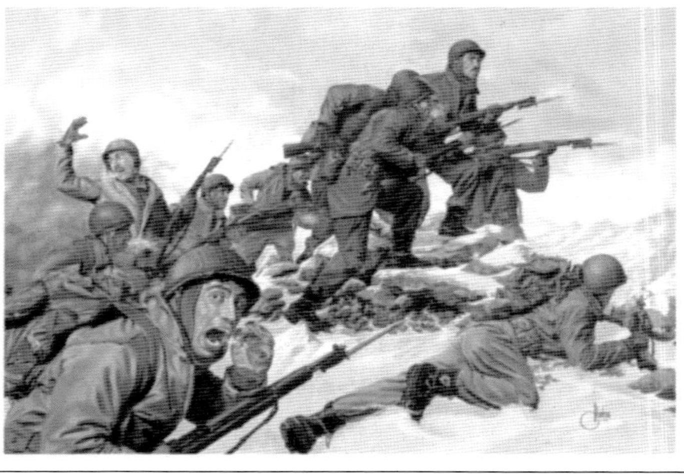

Pvt. Joseph Martinez, a Taos native, is the only American to be awarded the Medal of Honor for action on US soil during World War II. On May 26, 1943, in the Aleutians, Martinez kept going under withering machine-gun fire. He was mortally wounded fighting at the top of a pass, but cleared the way for his fellow soldiers to take the pass. (City of Greeley Museum.)

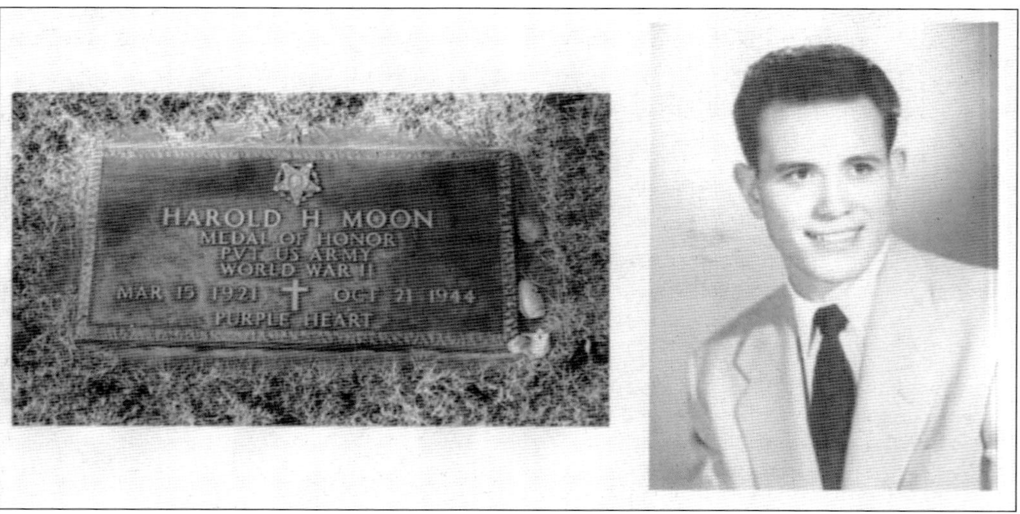

Pvt. Harold Herman Moon Jr. was the first Albuquerquean to receive the Medal of Honor. During a fight in the Philippines, "an entire Japanese platoon charged with fixed bayonets. In a final display of bravery, he stood up to throw a grenade. He was hit and instantly killed. Nearly 200 dead Japanese were found within 100 yards of his foxhole." (Left, Richard Melzer; right, Albuquerque Veterans' Memorial.)

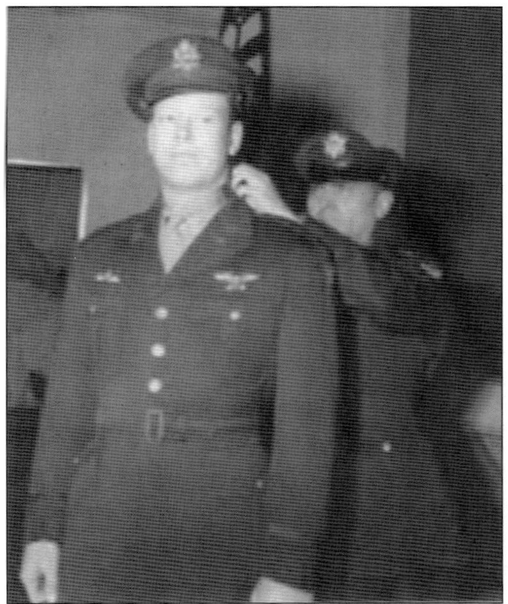

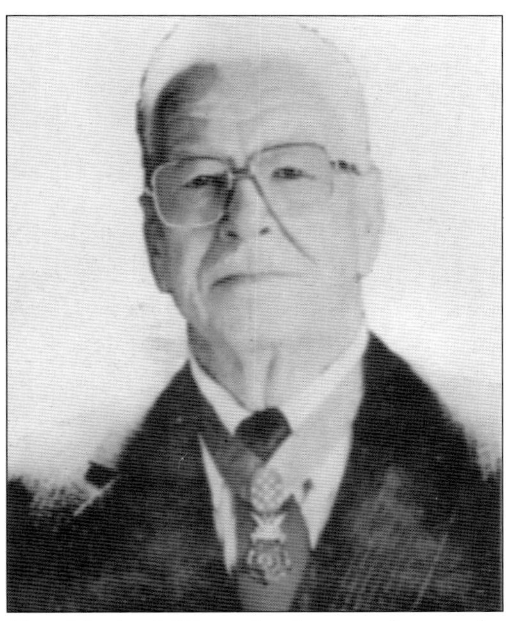

Second Lt. John Cary "Red" Morgan is the only New Mexico Military Institute graduate to be awarded the Medal of Honor. When his B-17 was attacked by German fighters. Both the pilot and the co-pilot, Morgan, were injured. For two hours, he held position, flying with one hand, fighting off the hallucinating pilot with the other. His heroism is depicted in the movie *12 O'Clock High*. (Both, New Mexico Military Institute.)

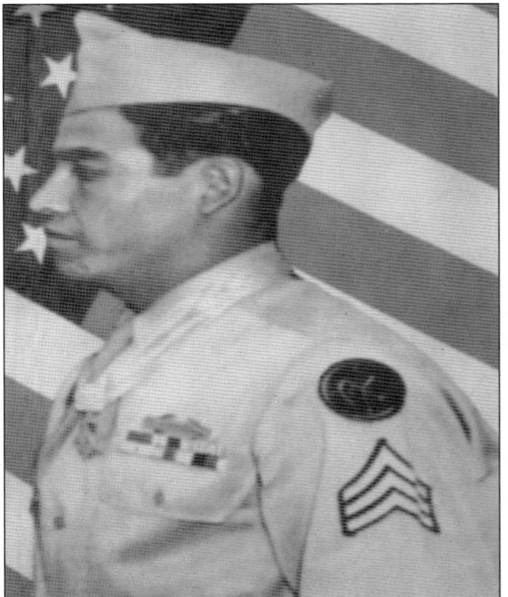

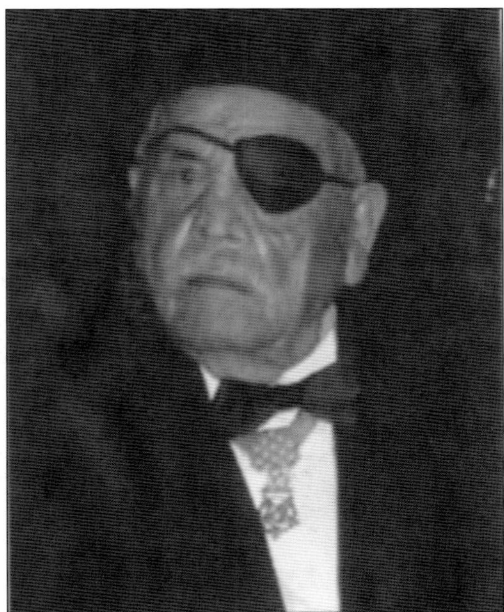

Private First Class Alejandro Ruiz, a native of Loving, was nominated for his actions while on Okinawa. While pinned down under a machine-gun and grenade attack from the camouflaged enemy, Ruiz leaped through grenades and rifle fire, running to a pillbox and firing into one opening after another. "His heroic conduct, in the face of overwhelming odds, saved the lives of many comrades," according to the citation. (Both, Albuquerque Veterans' Memorial.)

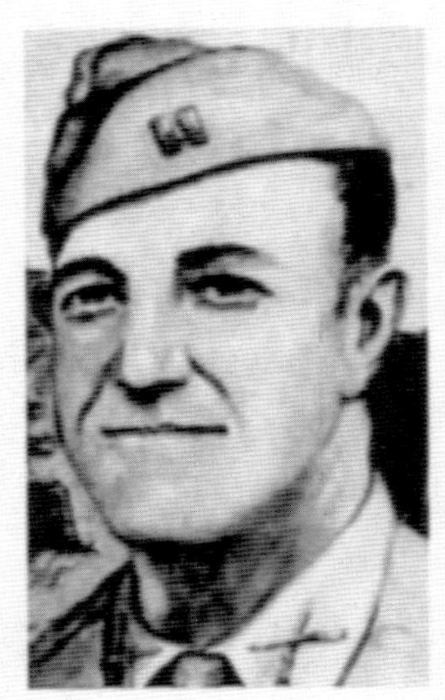

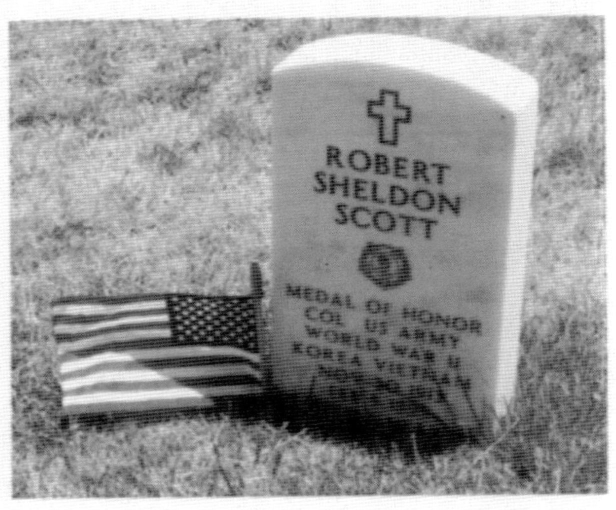

UNM graduate Capt. Robert Sheldon Scott is pictured here. On July 29, 1943, Scott singlehandedly advanced to within 75 yards of a critical hilltop near an airstrip on New Georgia in the Solomon Islands. Scott threw grenades repeatedly until the enemy fell back. His actions inspired other troops to charge forward and take the hill, allowing US forces to capture the airstrip four days later. (Both, Richard Melzer.)

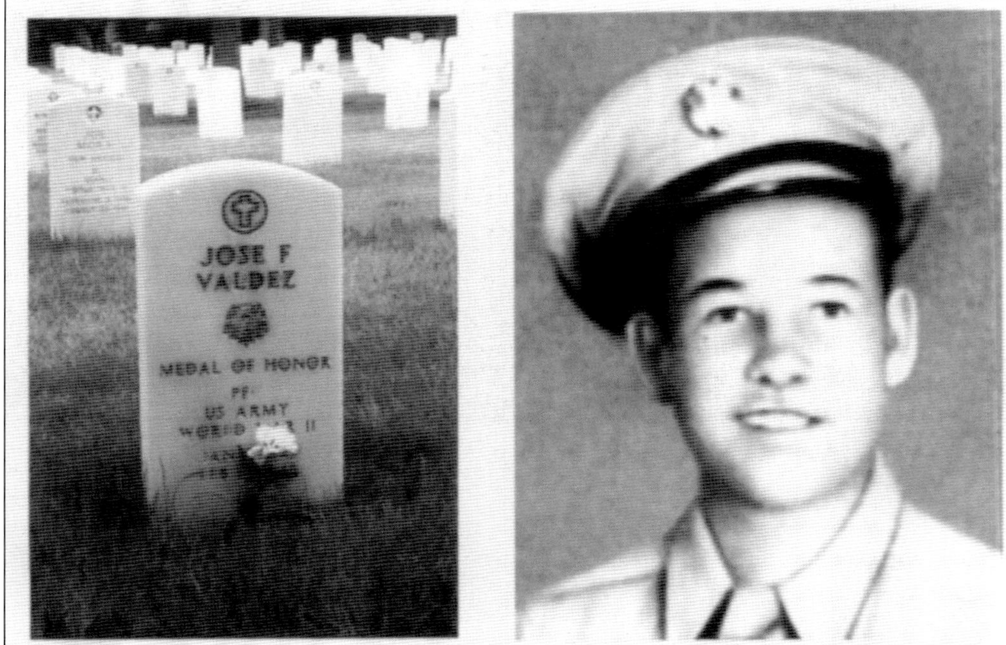

Pvt. Jose Valdez, born in Gobernador, New Mexico, was on duty near Rosenkrantz, France. Valdez was credited with helping a patrol reach safety under withering fire from two companies of German infantrymen. He continued firing while mortally wounded until the others reached safety, then called in artillery and mortar fire. A US Army transport ship, the USS *Private Jose F. Valdez* (T-AG-169), was named in his honor. (Left, Richard Melzer; right, US Navy.)

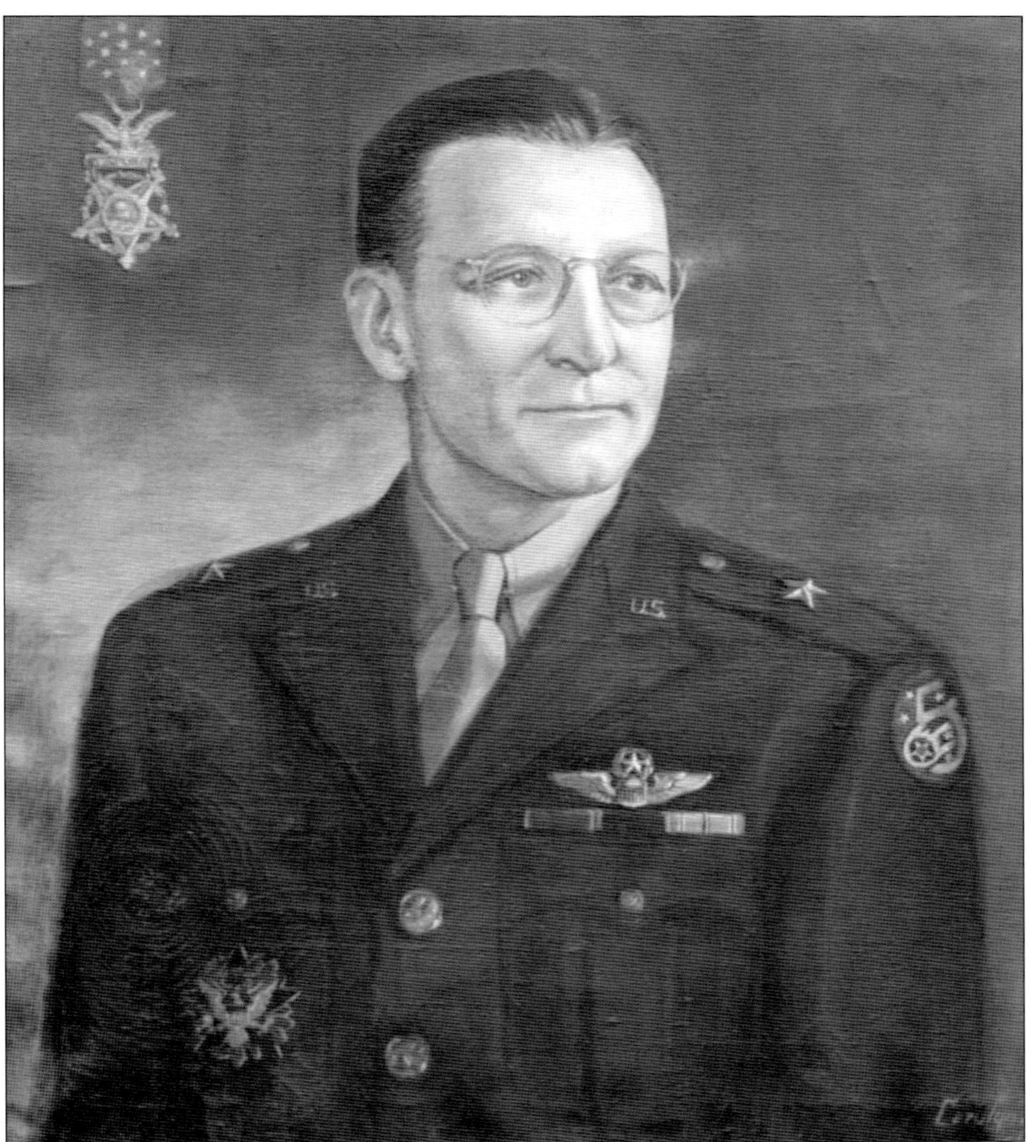

Brig. Gen. Kenneth Newton Walker was born in Cerrillos, New Mexico. His posthumous Medal of Honor citation reads, "For conspicuous leadership above and beyond the call of duty involving personal valor and intrepidity at an extreme hazard to life. As commander of the V Bomber Command during the period from 5 September 1942, to 5 January 1943, Brigadier General Walker repeatedly accompanied his units on bombing missions deep into enemy-held territory. From the lessons personally gained under combat conditions, he developed a highly efficient technique for bombing when opposed by enemy fighter airplanes and by antiaircraft fire. On 5 January 1943, in the face of extremely heavy antiaircraft fire and determined opposition by enemy fighters, he led an effective daylight bombing attack against the shipping in the harbor at Rabaul, New Britain, which resulted in direct hits on 9 enemy vessels. During this action his airplane was disabled and forced down by the attack of an overwhelming number of enemy fighters." Walker Air Force Base in Roswell (now Roswell International Airport) is named in his honor. (Walker Air Force Base Museum.)

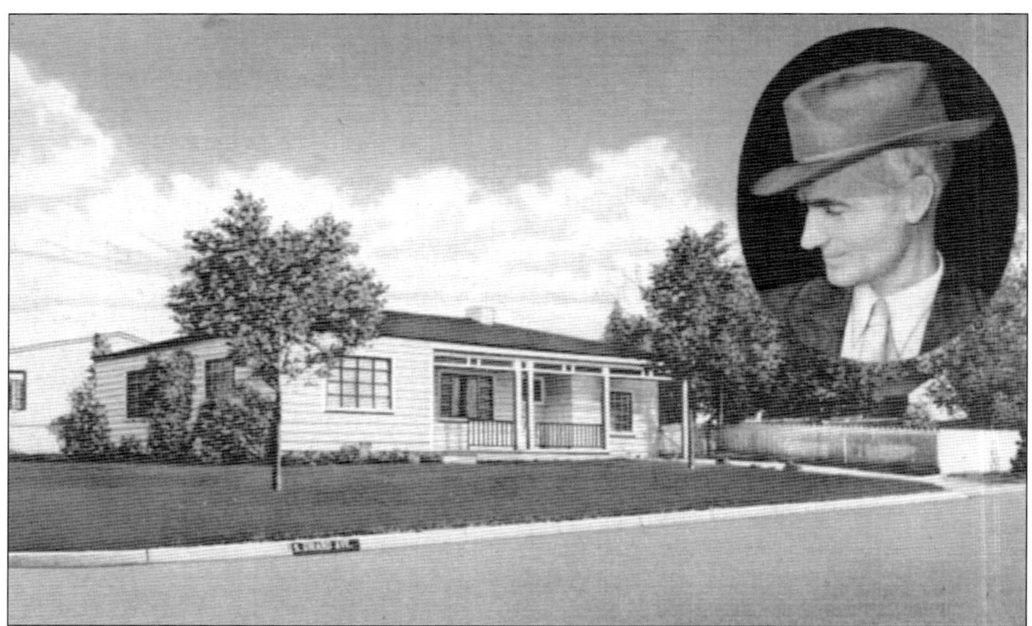

Ernie Pyle was the most famous American war correspondent of World War II. After years as a traveling reporter, Pyle and his wife, Jerry, built a small house in Albuquerque because they considered New Mexico their favorite state. Once the war began, Jerry stayed in Albuquerque while Ernie traveled overseas. Serving as a civilian correspondent, he lived among GIs like those shown below. His daily newspaper columns about individual soldiers told readers of actual conditions on the front lines in Africa and Europe. Some of the men he interviewed were fellow New Mexicans. Each person he interviewed received a Zippo lighter as a gift from Pyle and the Zippo Lighter Company. Pyle wrote so much about the average GI that his columns were compiled as whole books, including *Brave Men* (1944). He won a Pulitzer Prize that same year. (Above, Richard Melzer; below, B.G. Burr.)

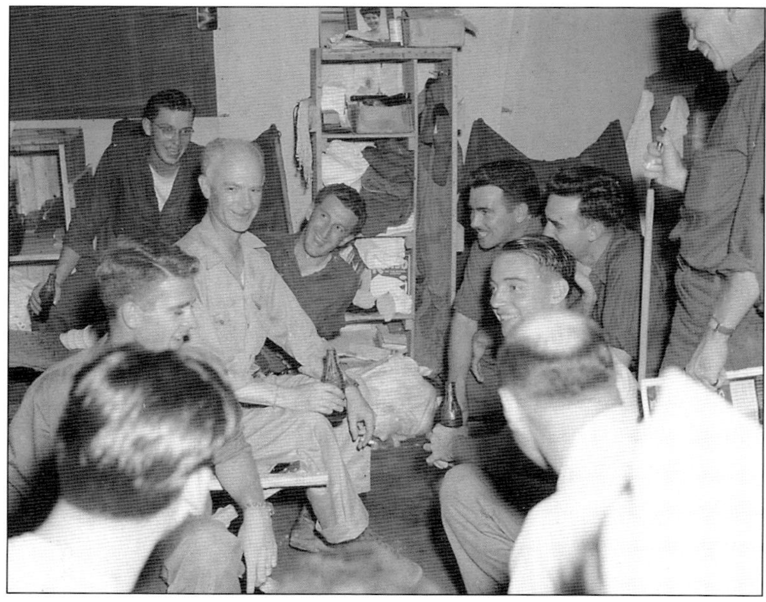

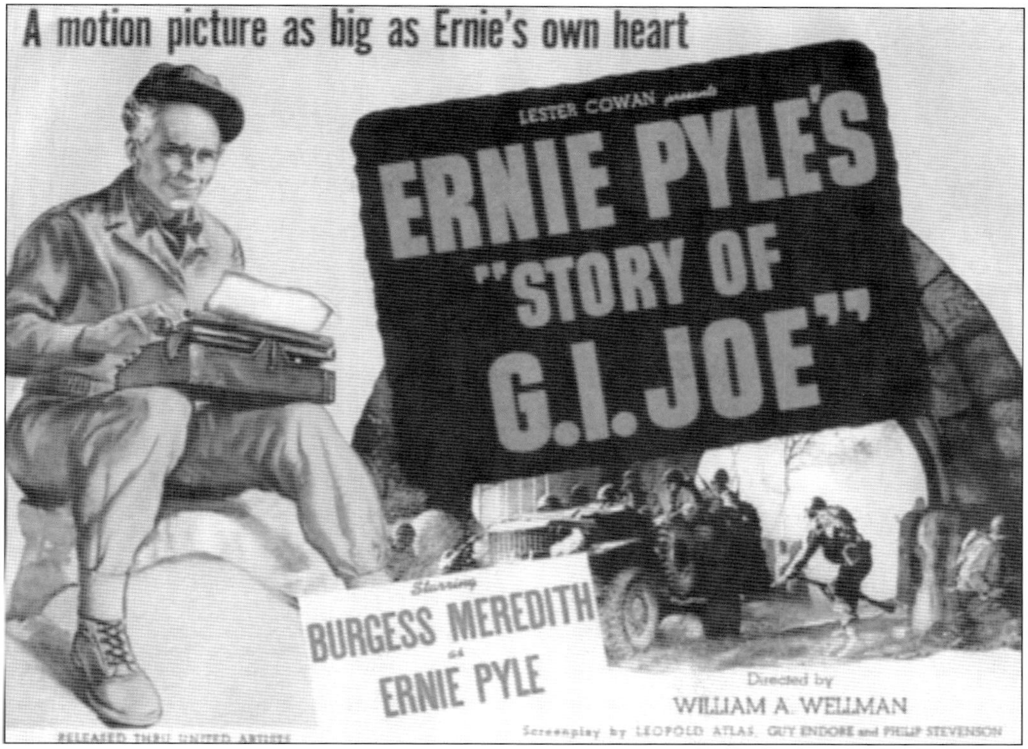

A motion picture as big as Ernie's own heart

LESTER COWAN presents

ERNIE PYLE'S "STORY OF G.I. JOE"

Starring

BURGESS MEREDITH

as

ERNIE PYLE

Directed by

WILLIAM A. WELLMAN

Screenplay by LEOPOLD ATLAS, GUY ENDORE and PHILIP STEVENSON

RELEASED THRU UNITED ARTISTS

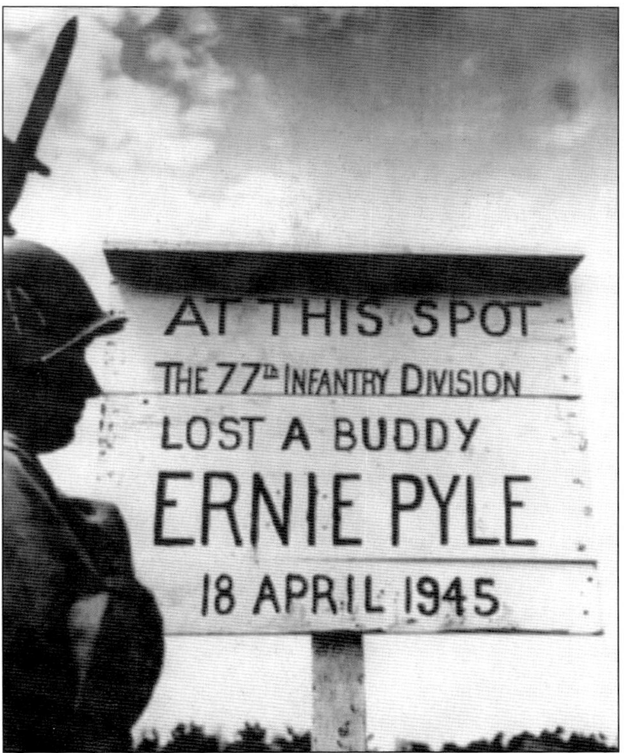

After covering the European front, Pyle returned home to Albuquerque, where he received an honorary degree from UNM. Soon, Eleanor Roosevelt and others convinced Pyle to cover the war in the Pacific to help raise morale among those serving there and back home. Before departing, Pyle helped with the production of *The Story of GI Joe*, a movie based on his wartime experiences. Once in the Pacific, Pyle interviewed average fighting men, just as he had done in Europe. Tragically, Pyle was killed by a Japanese sniper on the tiny island of Ie Shima on April 18, 1945. He was initially buried near where he died (right). He was later reinterred in the national cemetery in Hawaii, an honor few civilians receive. The Pyles' house later became the Albuquerque Public Library's first branch library. (Above, B.G. Burr; right, Library of Congress.)

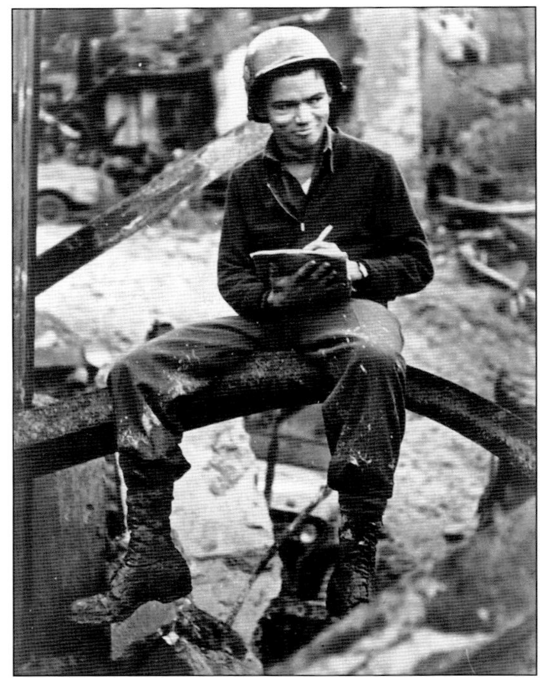

Bill Mauldin was the most famous cartoonist of World War II. Born into a poor family in Mountain Park, New Mexico, he enlisted in the Army and soon began drawing cartoons for Army newspapers, including *Stars and Stripes*. At first, his often-satirical cartoons angered his superior officers, but they soon realized that his work was good for soldiers' morale. His cartoons became so popular that they also began to appear in hundreds of newspapers in the United States, including the *Albuquerque Tribune*. Mauldin's cartoons and Ernie Pyle's columns often appeared side-by-side in the same newspapers. The two New Mexicans became good friends. (Both, Richard Melzer.)

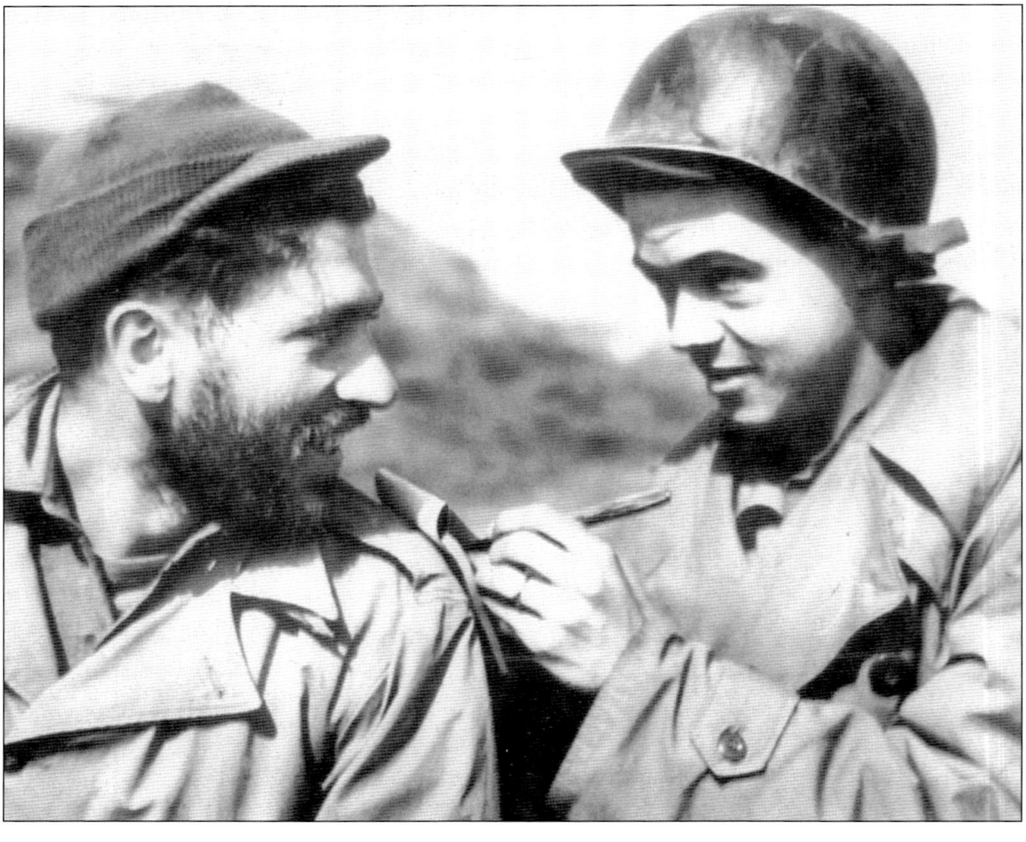

Bill Mauldin's cartoons featured two GIs in particular: Willie and Joe. With a dry sense of satire, Willie and Joe commented on the many problems soldiers faced in combat. In a way, Mauldin drew the average GI just as Ernie Pyle wrote about them. Both journalists had their pictures on the cover of *Time* magazine, although Mauldin was represented by his famous character, Willie. Like Pyle, Mauldin compiled his work in books and received a Pulitzer Prize. Both New Mexicans had US stamps dedicated in their honor. One of Mauldin's favorite cartoons shows a GI sadly shooting his broken Jeep just as he might have shot his wounded horse. Mauldin survived the war, living much of his post-war civilian life in Santa Fe. He is shown below in 1986. (Right, *Stars and Stripes*; below, Richard Melzer.)

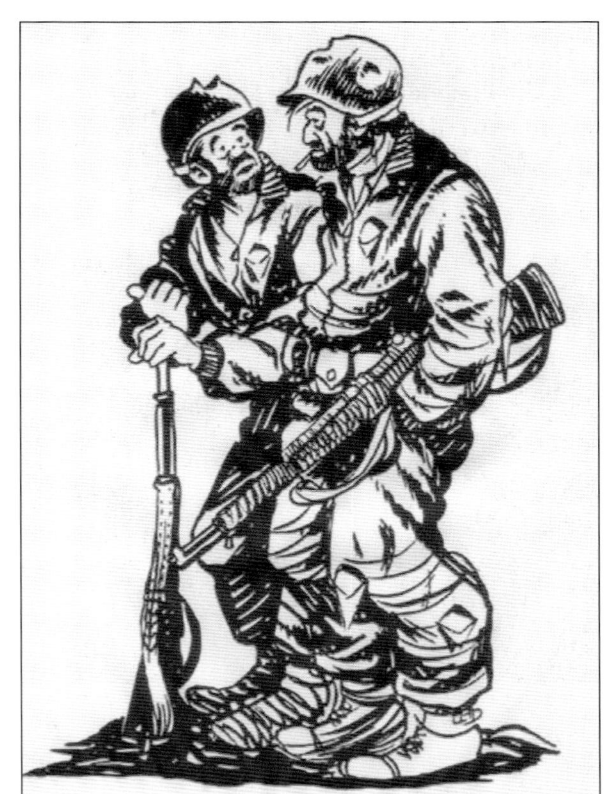

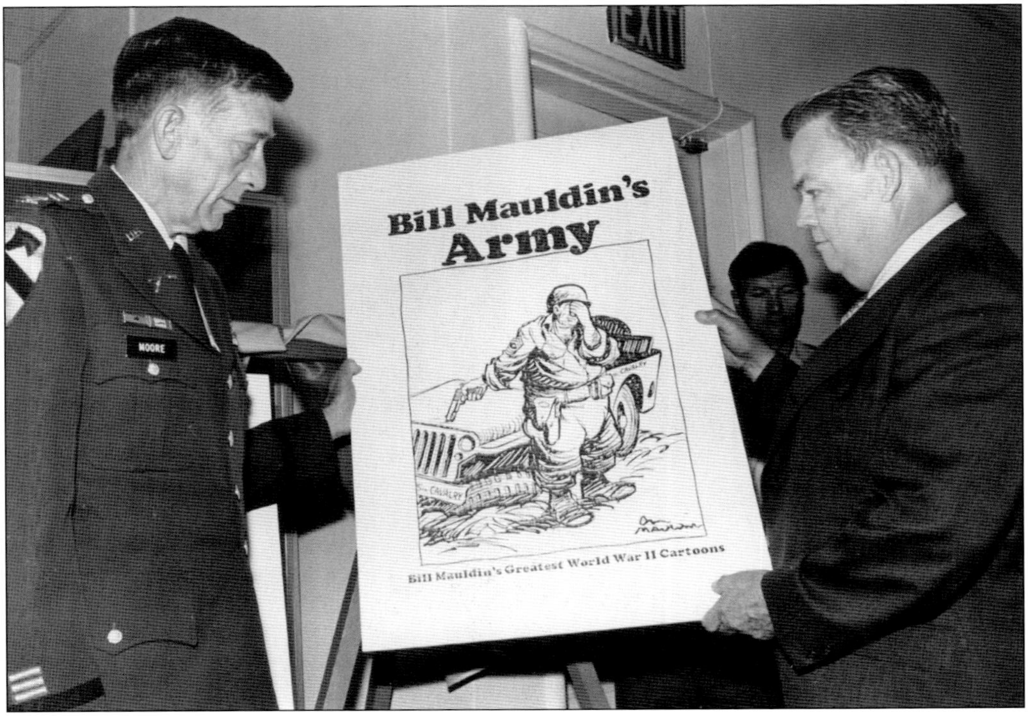

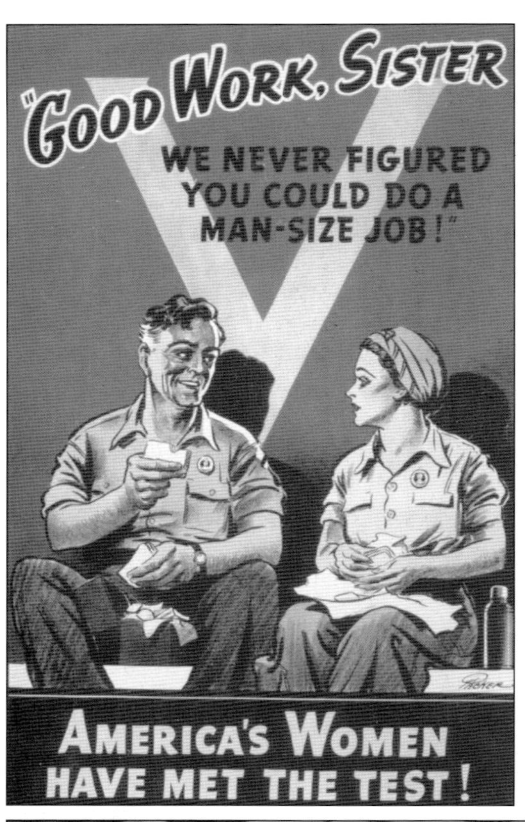

Many groups experienced new opportunities during World War II in New Mexico. Women shared in these opportunities, assuming social and economic responsibilities normally dominated by the men who were serving their country in the armed forces. With thousands of husbands gone to war or to wartime industries, women often became the heads of households in cities, on farms, and on ranches. Although New Mexico was not a manufacturing center, women worked in the Santa Fe Railroad yards laboring alongside men who were unable to enlist. In addition, they worked in light industries, as shown below. (Both, Richard Melzer.)

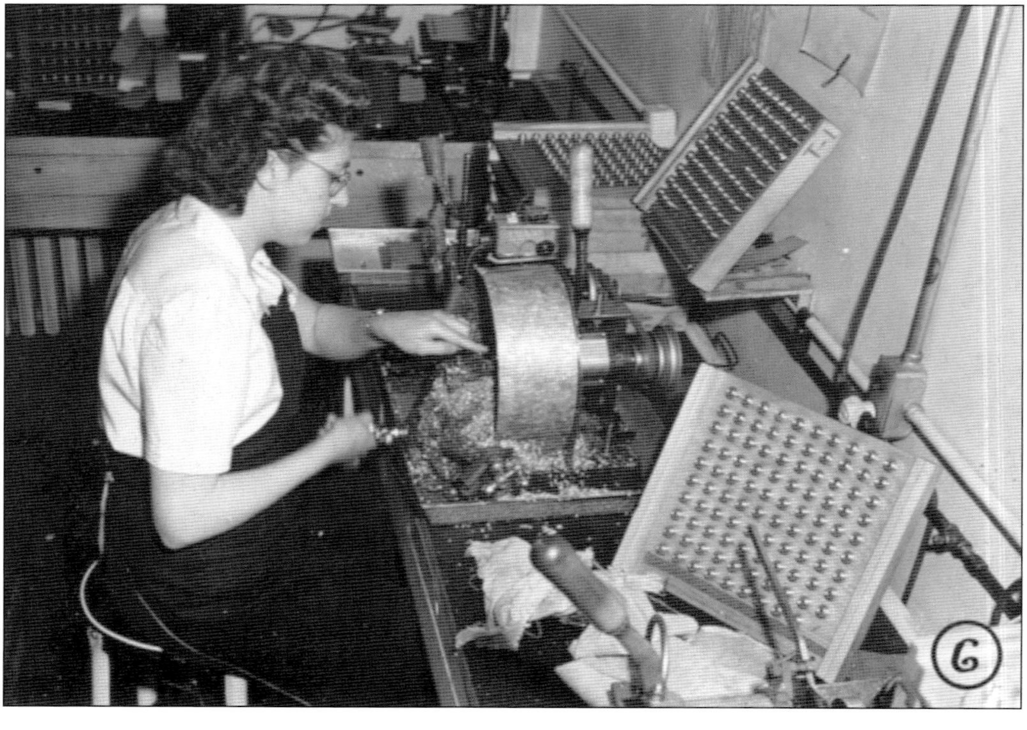

Many women volunteered to join branches of the military, including the Women's Army Auxiliary Corps (WAACs) and the Women Accepted for Voluntary Emergency Service (WAVES). Not yet given combat roles, most women in the armed forces worked in clerical jobs, as nurses in medical facilities like Bruns Hospital, and as technical assistants, scientists, and engineers for the Manhattan Project. Many New Mexico women served in other states and overseas. (Richard Melzer.)

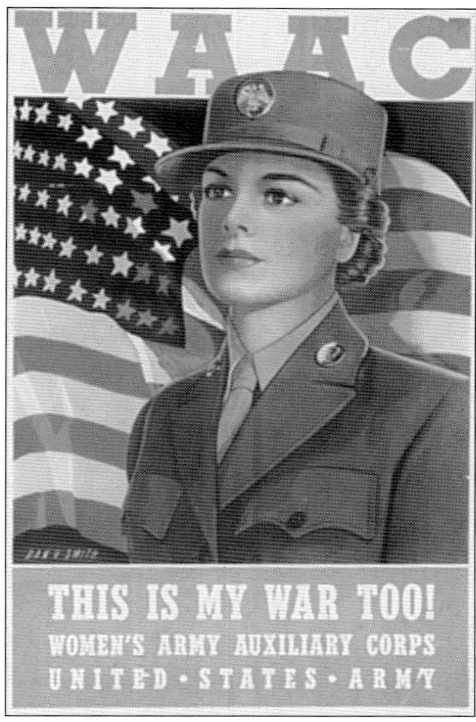

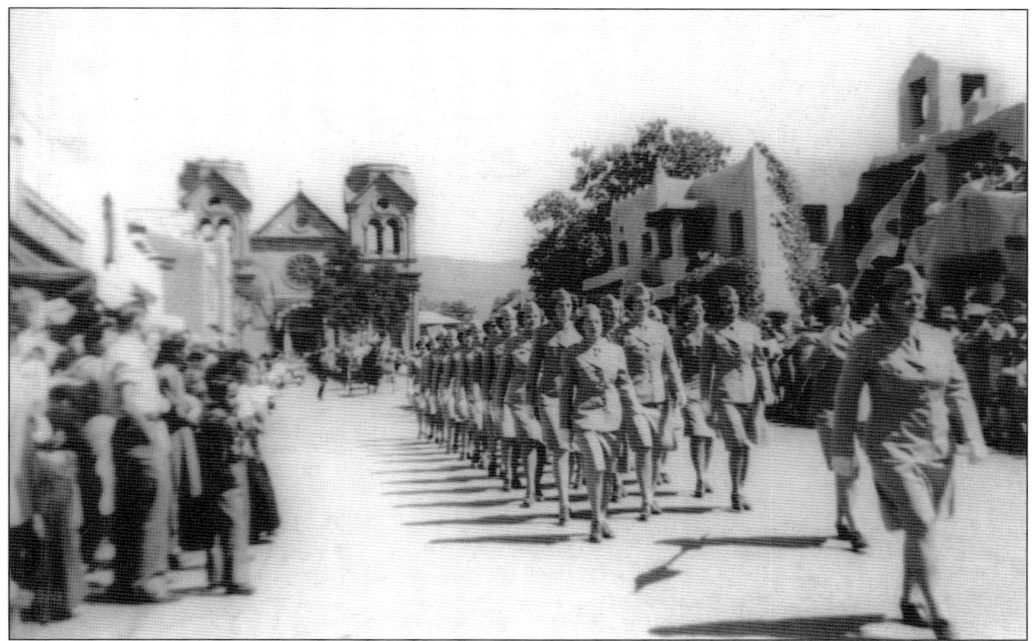

New Mexico women were recruited to become WAACs with the offer of some unusual benefits. Known as the Coronado Platoon, women in this program were promised that they would be sworn in together in a patriotic ceremony in Carlsbad Caverns, accompanied by the singing of "Rock of Ages." They would also receive their basic training together in Florida. The 63 women seen here marching in Santa Fe joined the platoon from 17 towns in New Mexico. (Museum of New Mexico, HP.2020.7.1.)

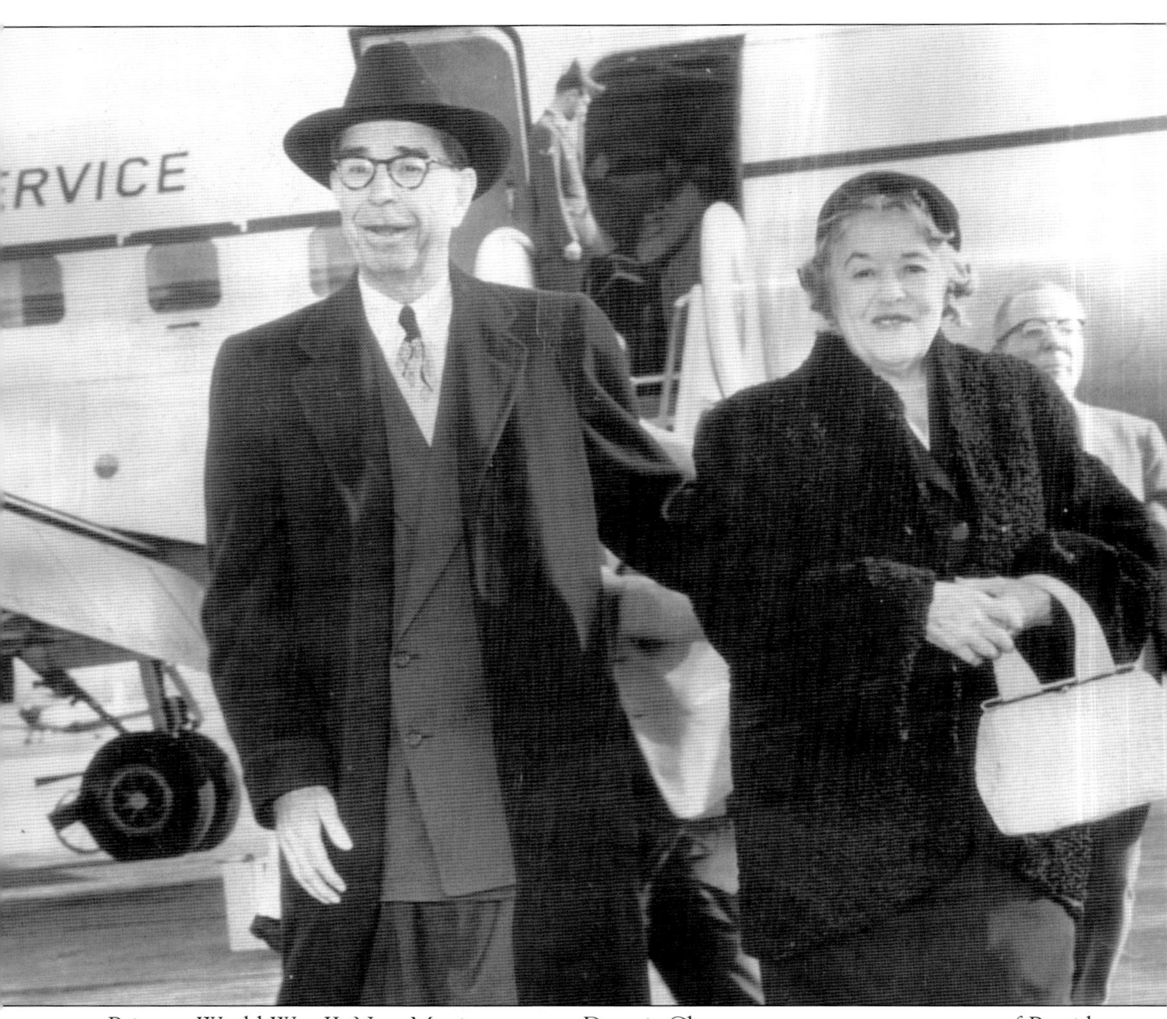

Prior to World War II, New Mexico senator Dennis Chavez was a strong supporter of President Roosevelt's Good Neighbor Policy in Latin America. Although he initially opposed US participation in the war because he felt that it would decrease US aid to Latin America, he became a wholehearted supporter of the Allied cause after Pearl Harbor. In particular, he worked tirelessly to ensure that the United States acquired valuable resources and supplies from several Latin American nations. Due to his efforts, the United States received such critical strategic materials as crude oil from Venezuela, copper and nitrates from Chile, tin from Bolivia, quartz crystals and manganese from Brazil, and cadmium and mercury from Mexico. It was widely acknowledged that Chavez's work to procure these supplies helped the United States and its allies win the war. (Richard Melzer.)

Fray Angelico Chavez was the first native New Mexican to be ordained as a Franciscan priest. He attended the US Army's chaplaincy school and was assigned as a chaplain to the 77th Infantry Division. He was present at the division's landings on Guam and Leyte. After the war, Chavez became a renowned historian and served as the archivist for the Archdiocese of Santa Fe. The state history library is named in his honor. (Richard Melzer.)

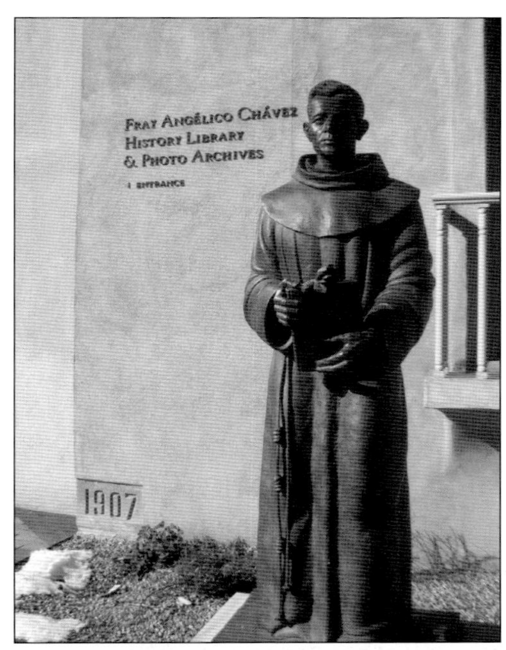

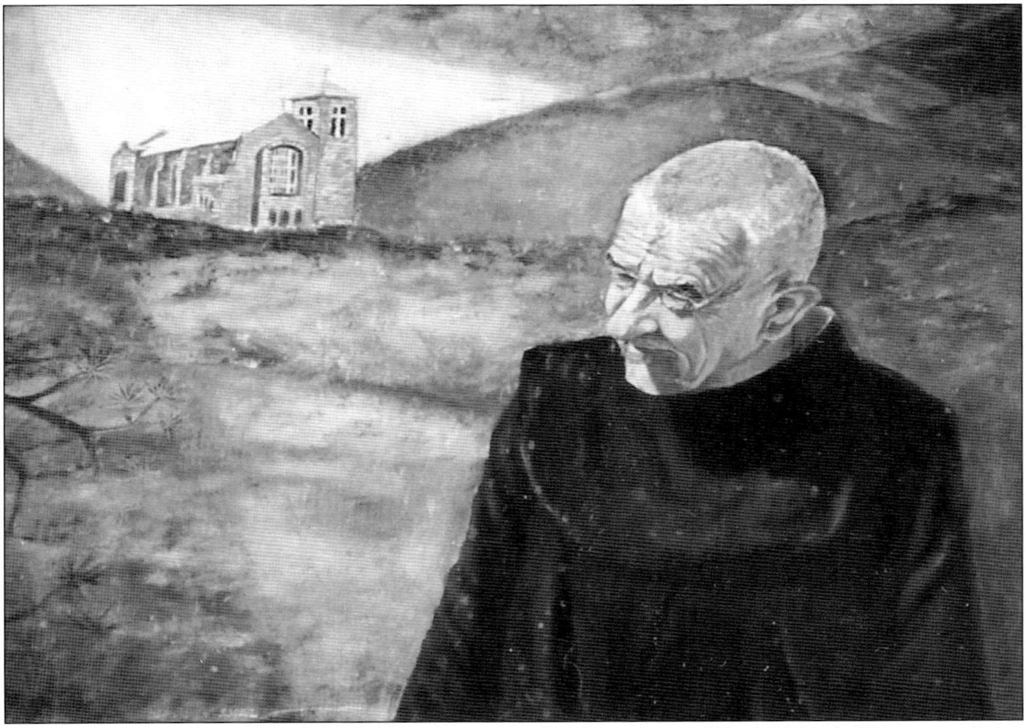

Fr. Albert Braun was wounded while serving as a chaplain during World War I. He rejoined the chaplain corps and was assigned to the 92nd Coast Artillery during World War II. Captured in the Philippines, he endured the Bataan Death March and subsequent imprisonment. He received a Purple Heart, two Silver Stars, and the Legion of Merit. Braun almost singlehandedly built the mission church on the Mescalero Apache reservation. (St. Joseph Apache Mission.)

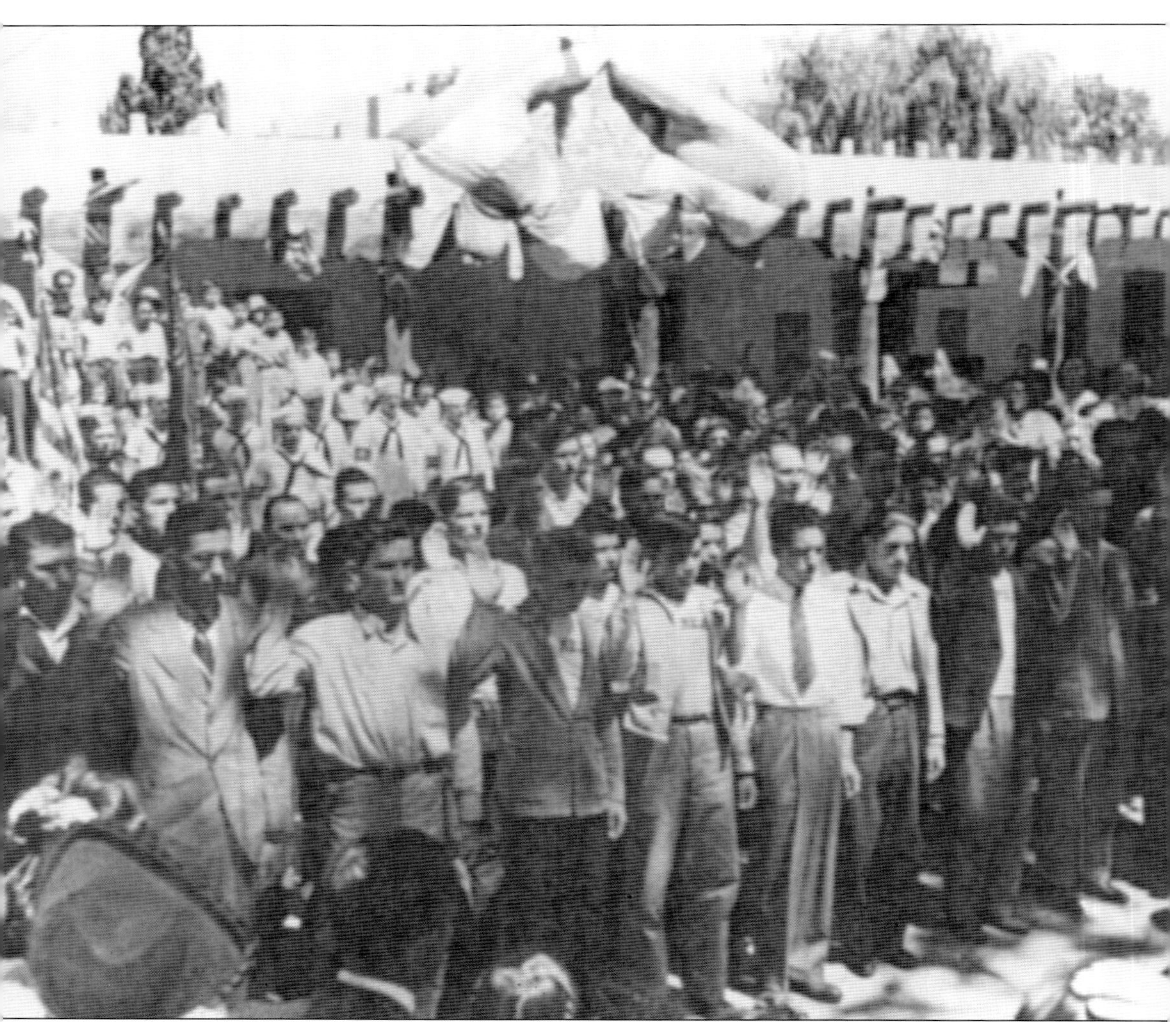

In this chapter, many individual heroes have been identified, from Medal of Honor recipients to columnist Ernie Pyle and cartoonist Bill Mauldin. But every New Mexican who served during World War II deserves to be remembered as a hero. With a population of 531,818 as of 1940, a total of 49,579 New Mexicans volunteered or were drafted into the military, giving New Mexico the distinction of having the highest percentage of servicemen and servicewomen per capita of any state in the country. These men and women, some of whom are pictured here enlisting, represented every segment of New Mexico's diverse population, including Hispanics, Native Americans, blacks, whites, Japanese Americans, Jews, and the descendants of recent European immigrants. New Mexicans served in every branch of the armed forces. With the highest casualty rate of any state in the United States, more than 2,200 New Mexicans paid the ultimate price for their country, dying in battle, in captivity, or from disease. Thousands are buried overseas or in New Mexico's national cemeteries in Santa Fe and Fort Bayard. (Albuquerque Museum, HP.2007.20.410.)

Eight

Prisoner of War Camps

The United States maintained 686 prisoner of war camps during World War II. With the exception of three states, each state in the country had at least one. Two camps were established in southern New Mexico, near Roswell and Lordsburg. Nineteen smaller branch camps were opened in or near towns and cities like Albuquerque and Las Cruces. A unique camp for German merchant marines captured off a sunken passenger ship, the SS *Columbus*, was established at Fort Stanton.

New Mexico was an ideal location for POW camps for several reasons. First, the state was isolated and far from either coast, making escape or rescue attempts difficult. Next, New Mexico's mild climate, especially in the southern portion of the state, meant less of a need for fuel to heat facilities during winter months. New Mexico was also an ideal location for these camps because the state suffered a serious labor shortage on its farms and ranches. Mexican immigrants in the bracero program helped solve this problem, but the shortage persisted as the war dragged on. POWs were usually used as field hands but, in keeping with Article 27 of the Geneva Conventions of 1929, were never required to work at jobs considered unhealthy, dangerous, or humiliating. POW letters home reflect the men's longing for loved ones in Germany and Italy, but without serious complaints regarding camp conditions. Usually treated well, some POWs returned after the war to visit or permanently reside in New Mexico.

Few POWs attempted to escape. Of those who did, most were captured and returned to their camps. One exception, an escapee from Las Cruces, was finally captured in Mexico City in 1954. Georg Gaerthner remained on the lam even longer. Escaping from a camp near Deming in September 1945, Gaerthner changed his name to Dennis Whiles, got married, worked for years, received Social Security benefits, and lived in both California and Colorado before surrendering to the FBI in 1985. He became known as "Hitler's last soldier in America," the title of a book about his years as a fugitive.

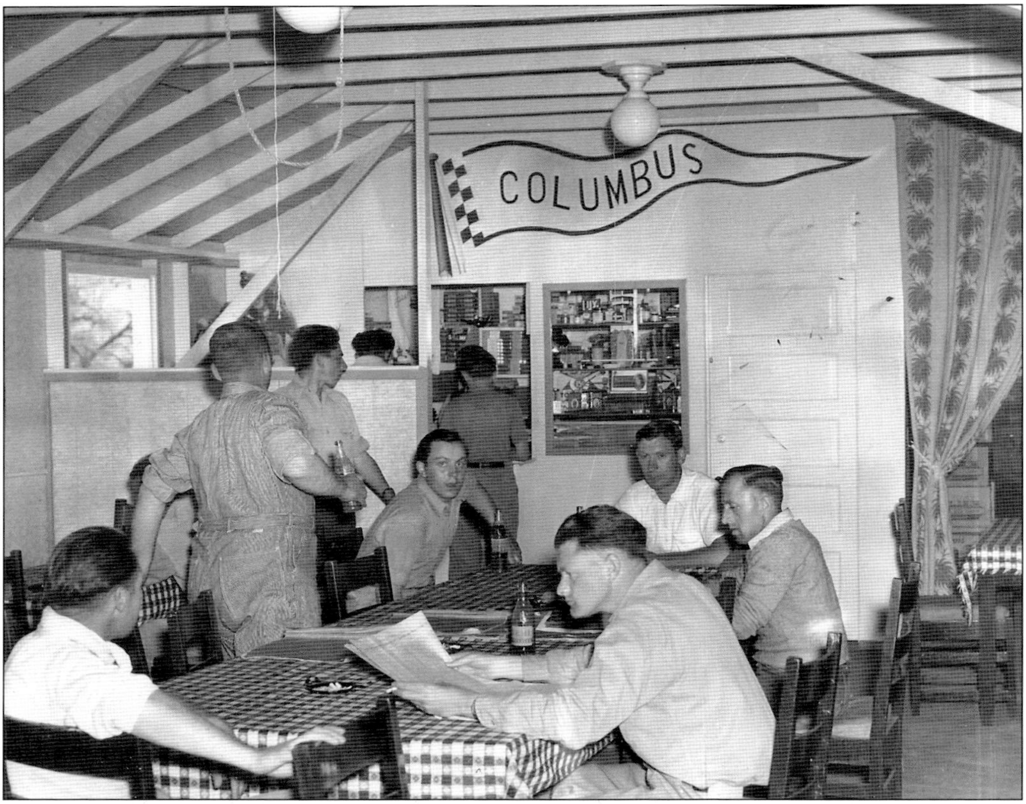

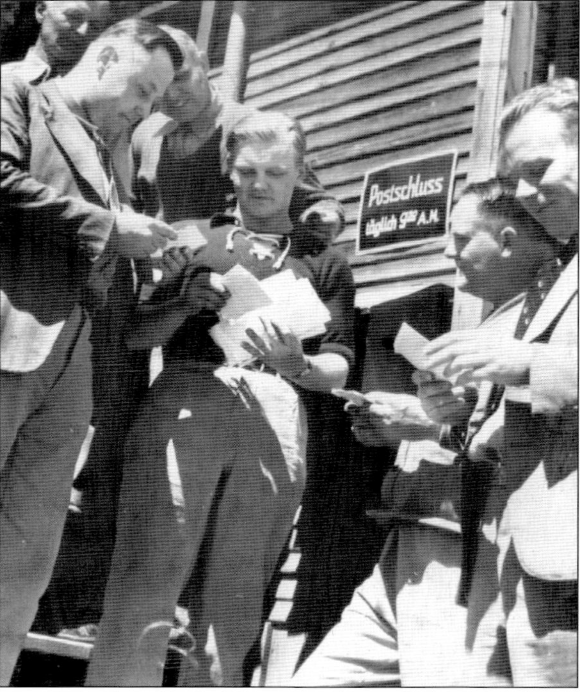

Crew members of the German passenger ship SS *Columbus* sank their vessel rather than surrender it to the British navy in 1939. The US Navy rescued these 401 crewmen but refused to allow their return to Germany for fear they would join the military. Instead, the United States detained the men, although, as civilians, they were technically not POWs until the United States entered the war in late 1941. The German crew was detained at a former CCC camp at Fort Stanton, an old military fort built during the Indian wars of the 19th century. These photographs show the men reading and relaxing in the camp's canteen and receiving mail from Germany at mail call. (Both, Richard Melzer.)

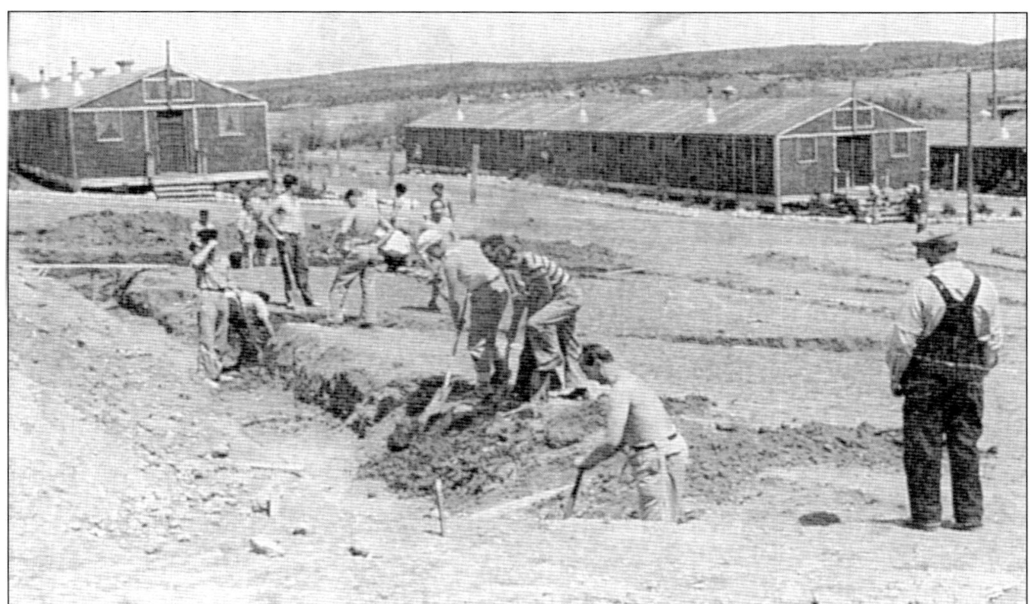

The men of the *Columbus* were not required to work on the farms and ranches that surrounded their camp. They nevertheless stayed active, improving their community by building a large swimming pool, planting gardens, and creating a golf course. Four died: two from natural causes, one in a fight, and one by suicide. They were buried in a corner of the Fort Stanton cemetery. (Richard Melzer.)

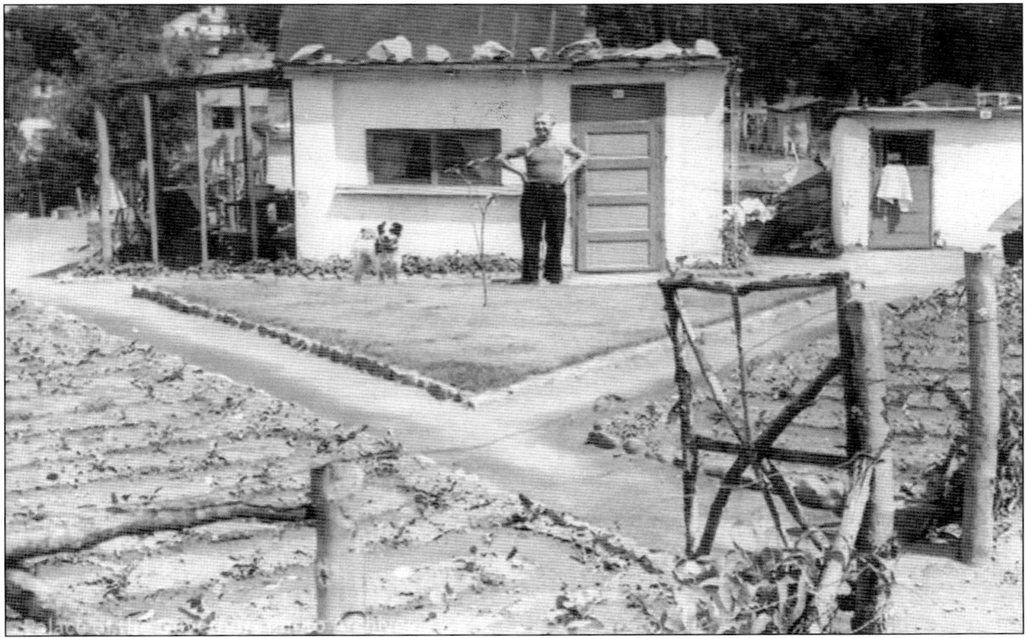

Captured crew members of the *Columbus* also landscaped their camp, as shown here. In 1941, they held their own Olympics. Nazis among them celebrated Adolf Hitler's birthday. Few attempted to escape; when they did, it was usually at night to visit local bars in Capitan. Relations with the residents of Capitan were so good that the Germans presented a large engraved stone to the nearby community. (Richard Melzer.)

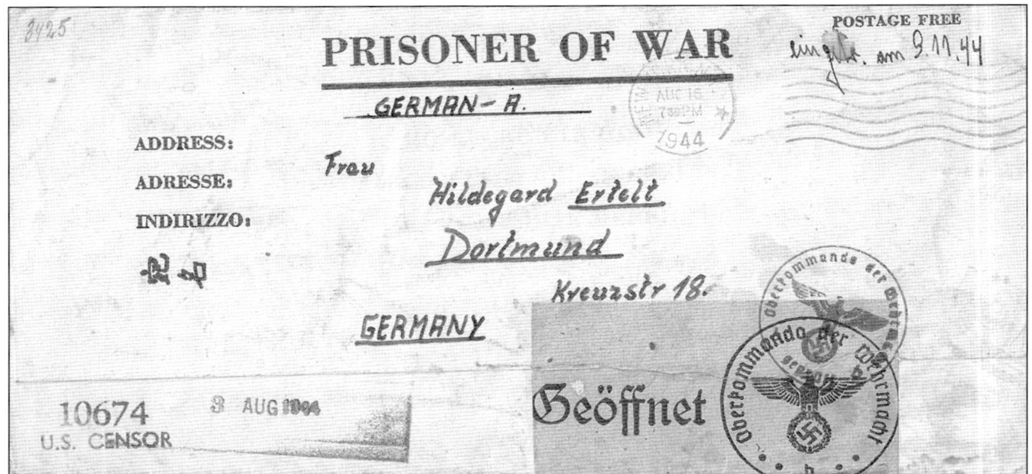

A German POW camp was opened 14 miles southeast of Roswell in 1943. One of the first and largest camps in the United States, it had originally been a CCC camp in the 1930s. Housing Germans from Rommel's Afrika Corps, the POW facility was isolated from any large community and most ranches. Isolation helped breed antagonism, with rumors spreading among ranchers that the German prisoners received special privileges, including access to rationed goods. Some prisoners expressed their displeasure with their incarceration by creating an iron cross (below), symbolizing German nationalism, with rocks at a worksite in Roswell. Outraged local residents poured concrete over the cross, but the concrete washed away, and the image resurfaced in Spring River Park. Erected in 1996, a monument in the park now honors POWs and MIAs from all wars and all nations. (Above, University of New Mexico/Center for Southwest Research; below, Richard Melzer.)

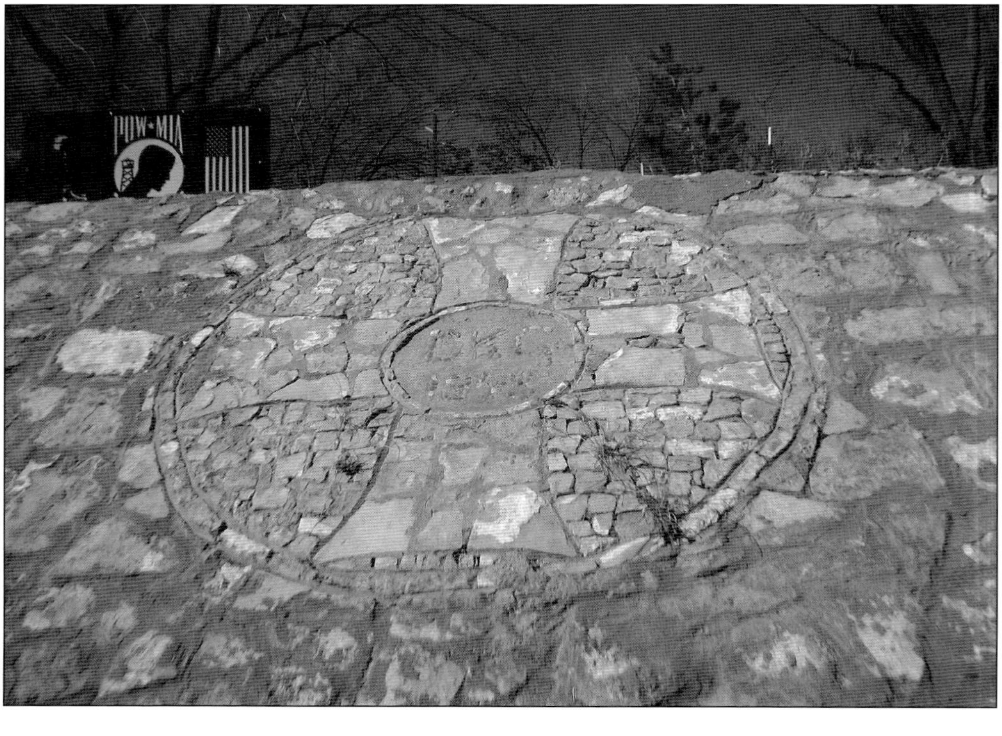

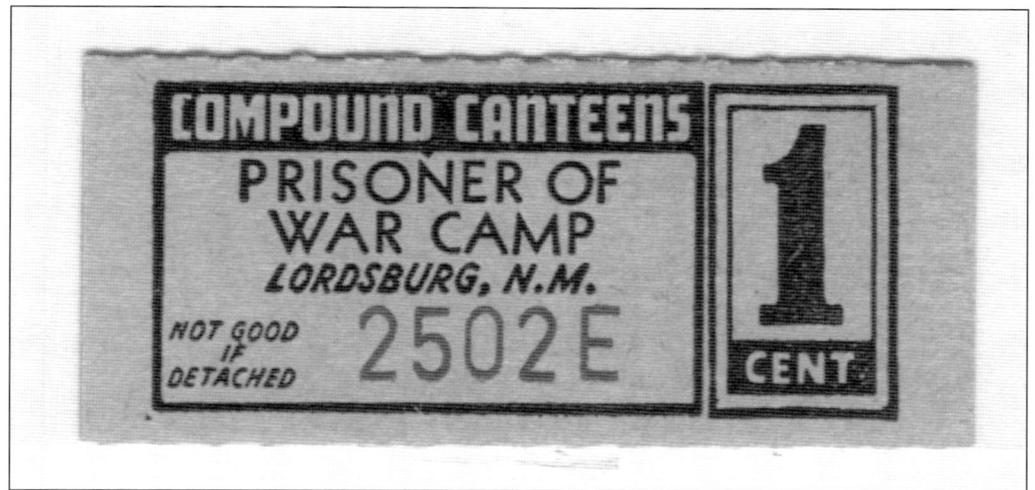

The US military also established a German POW camp outside Lordsburg. The location had the advantage of lying close to the Southern Pacific Railroad's tracks, facilitating transportation to and from the camp. Unlike other camps in New Mexico, the Lordsburg camp later held Italian prisoners, although not both groups at the same time. By war's end, 5,500 Germans and 3,000 Italians had been imprisoned at Lordsburg. (Richard Melzer.)

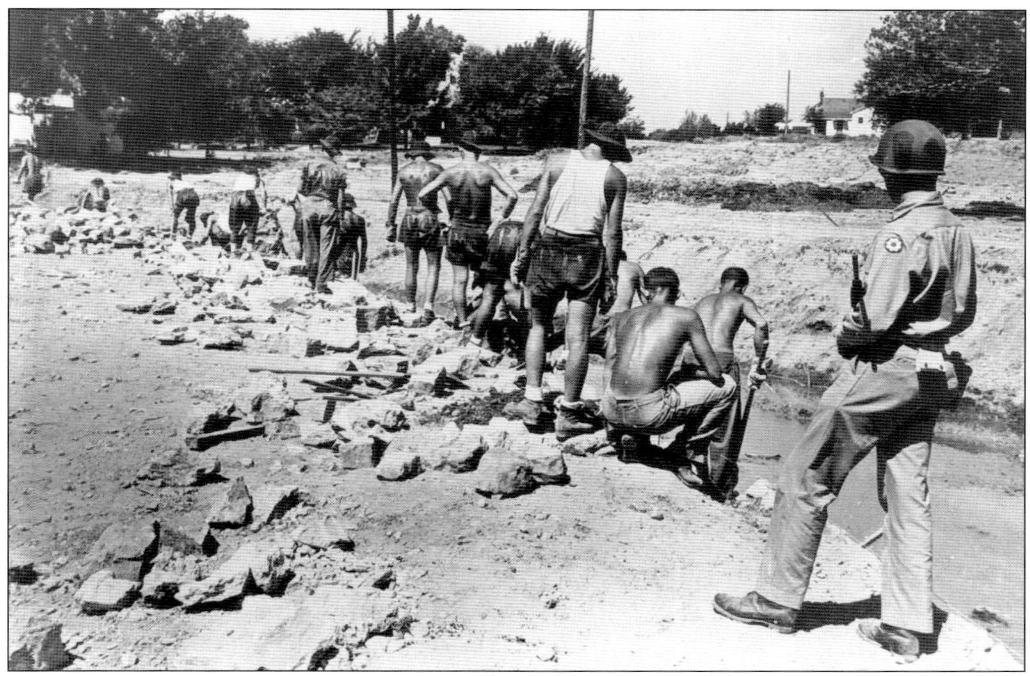

Two CCC camps were converted for use as smaller POW camps in Las Cruces. With an acute labor shortage in the Mesilla Valley, German and Italian POWs often worked on nearby farms. Local residents remember the Germans as sullen, while Italian POW sang and brought candy to at least one farmer's family. Some POWs liked the region so much that they later returned to visit or live there. (Southeastern New Mexico Historical Society.)

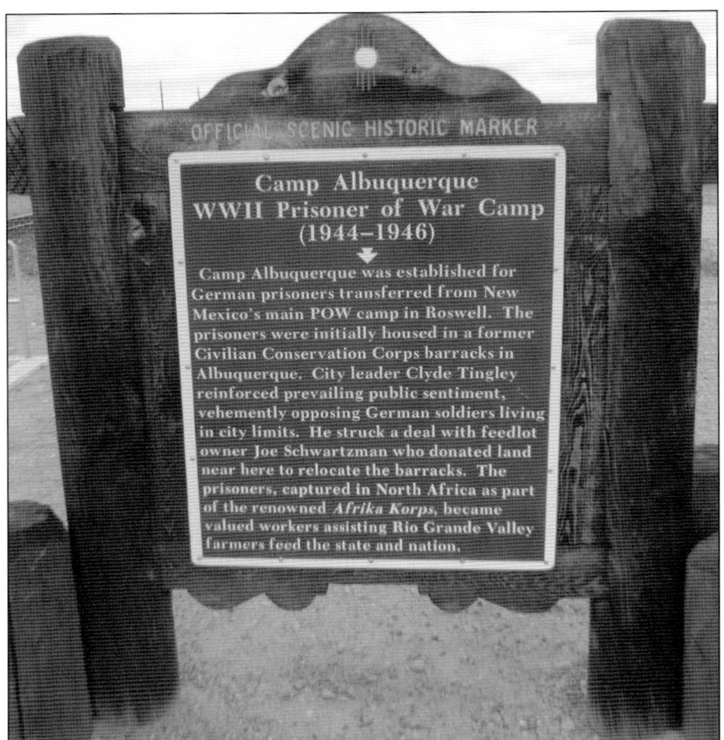

A former CCC camp near Albuquerque's Rio Grande Zoo became a small POW camp by 1943. POWs detained there were welcomed on local farms, where their labor was needed. However, nearby residents resented their presence so close to Albuquerque's Country Club neighborhood. The camp was moved to an eight-acre lot in the city's South Valley, where POW labor was used on farms as far south as Valencia County. (Richard Melzer.)

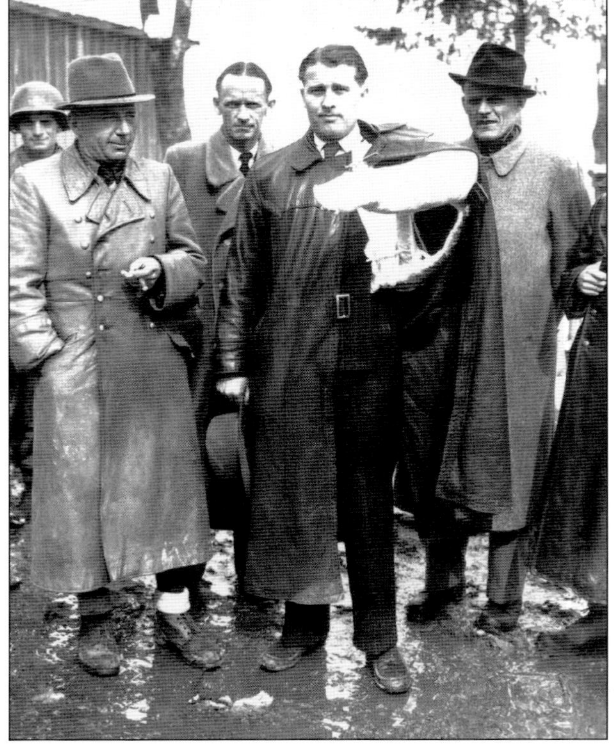

As the war in Europe ended, top German scientists, led by Wernher von Braun, surrendered to American forces rather than face capture by the Soviet Union. Von Braun, shown here in a cast, used his knowledge of German V-2 rockets to help develop similar American weapons in a program codenamed Operation Paperclip in southern New Mexico. The V-2 rocket became an essential part of the American defense system and space program. (Richard Melzer.)

Nine

Internment of Japanese Americans

Like most Americans on December 7, 1941, citizens of Japanese descent were shocked by the news that Japanese planes had bombed Pearl Harbor in a surprise attack that took 2,403 American military and civilian lives. The vast majority of Japanese Americans responded to the attack with outrage and an eagerness to help the United States as the war began.

Many Americans panicked after Pearl Harbor, believing that if the Japanese military could cause such destruction in Hawaii, it might well be prepared to attack other parts of the United States, especially the states along the Pacific coast. As a result of this wartime hysteria and longstanding prejudice against Asians, many suspected that Japanese Americans might assist in attacks to help their former mother country. Many US military and political leaders shared these concerns, including President Roosevelt and his chief advisors. On February 19, 1942, Roosevelt issued Executive Order No. 9066, ordering that as many as 120,000 men, women, and children of Japanese descent be rounded up and confined in isolated relocation camps, despite the lack of evidence that many, if any, had ever conspired with the enemy. Most families came from the West Coast, but others came from places like Hawaii and, eventually, Peru.

While the vast majority of Japanese families were forced to live in relocation camps in Western states, men who were considered particularly suspicious were separated from their families and sent to internment camps run, ironically, by the Department of Justice. Two of the main internment camps were located in Santa Fe and Lordsburg, largely due to their distance from the West Coast, where a Japanese attack might occur. Over 5,000 of these so-called dangerous men were detained in New Mexico's two camps from 1942 to 1946.

In 1988, the US Congress acknowledged the injustice of relocation and internment camps by apologizing for the government's acts and passing legislation that granted compensation to over 100,000 survivors of the camps. This gesture was important, but it could never compensate for the freedom, family unity, and dignity lost because of Executive Order No. 9066.

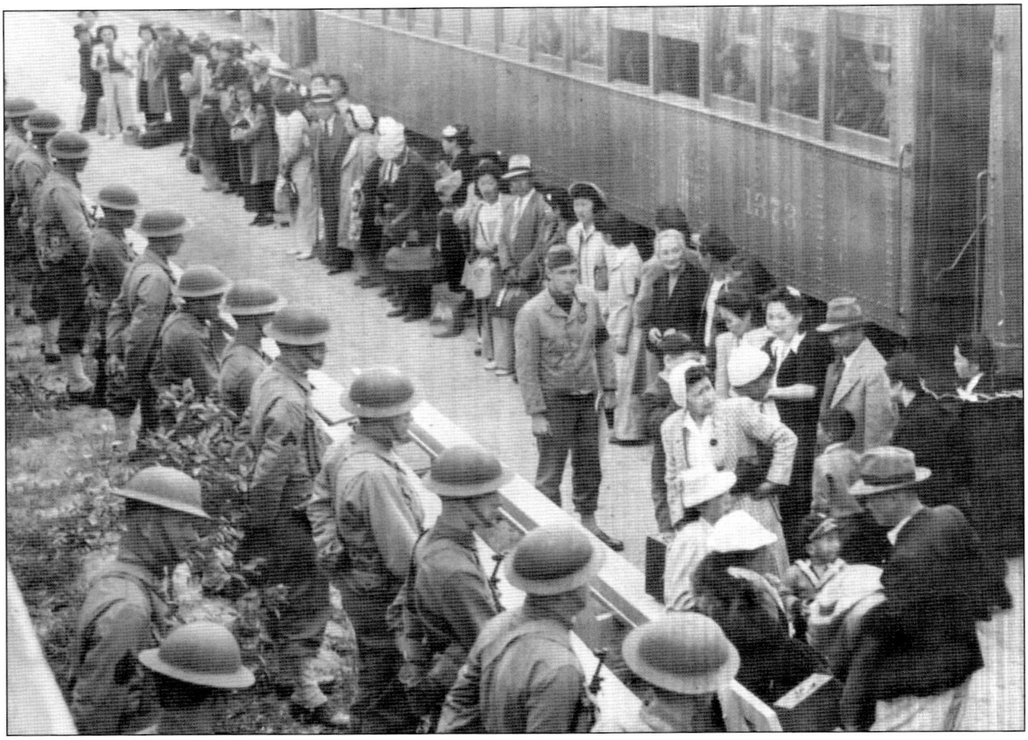

Families of Japanese descent had little time to settle their affairs before they reported to distant relocation camps. Armed guards and barbed wire fencing were constant reminders that these facilities were little more than prison camps. Clearly, their civil liberties were compromised, ironically in a war that was supposedly fought to defend freedom around the world. (Richard Melzer.)

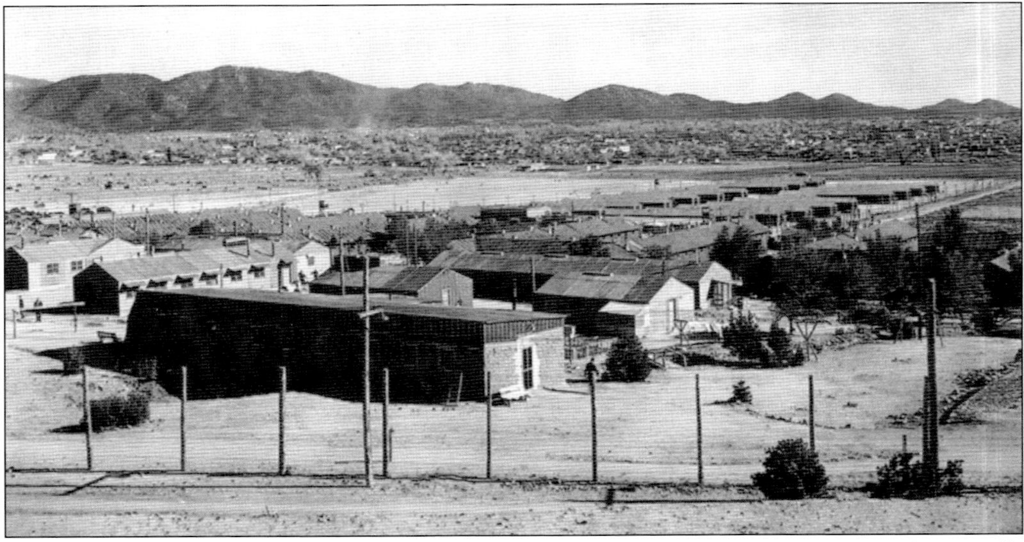

The first internees arrived in Santa Fe on March 14, 1942. The facility they entered had originally been a CCC camp. Converted into a prison camp, it was on the western outskirts of the state capital. In one of the strangest decisions of the entire war, the camp was within 35 miles of Los Alamos, supposedly the most secret military operation of the war. (US Department of Justice.)

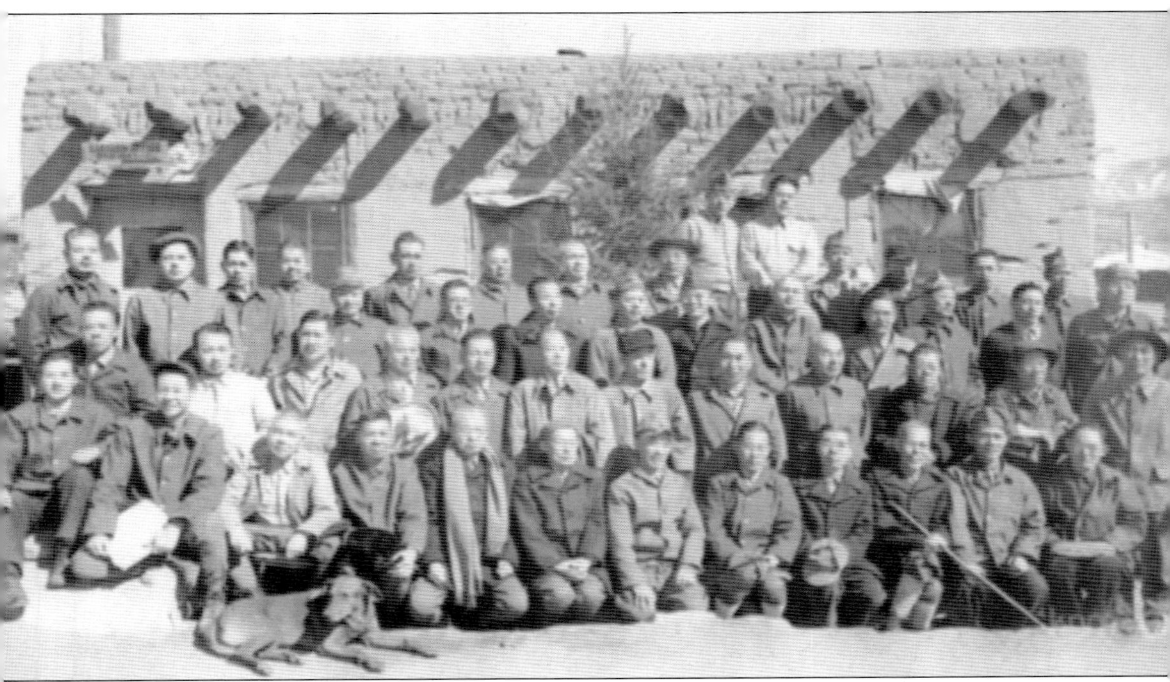

The FBI detained Japanese internees based on their so-called suspicious behavior, backgrounds, or skills. Some had been cultural, religious, or civic leaders in their West Coast communities. Some had had business connections with Japan. Others had been fishermen on boats with shortwave radios. Many knew martial arts. Clearly, some of these experiences and skills might be considered potentially dangerous, but most were not. This photograph of internees reflects many characteristics they shared. A majority were middle-aged, well-groomed members of the middle class. Most were so well educated that they taught classes, from English to engineering. Literate and artistic, they spent much of their time writing poems, painting, and polishing rocks found on the grounds in camp. Eager to be reunited with their families, they also spent much of their time appealing their cases, usually to no avail. (New Mexico Japanese-American Citizens League.)

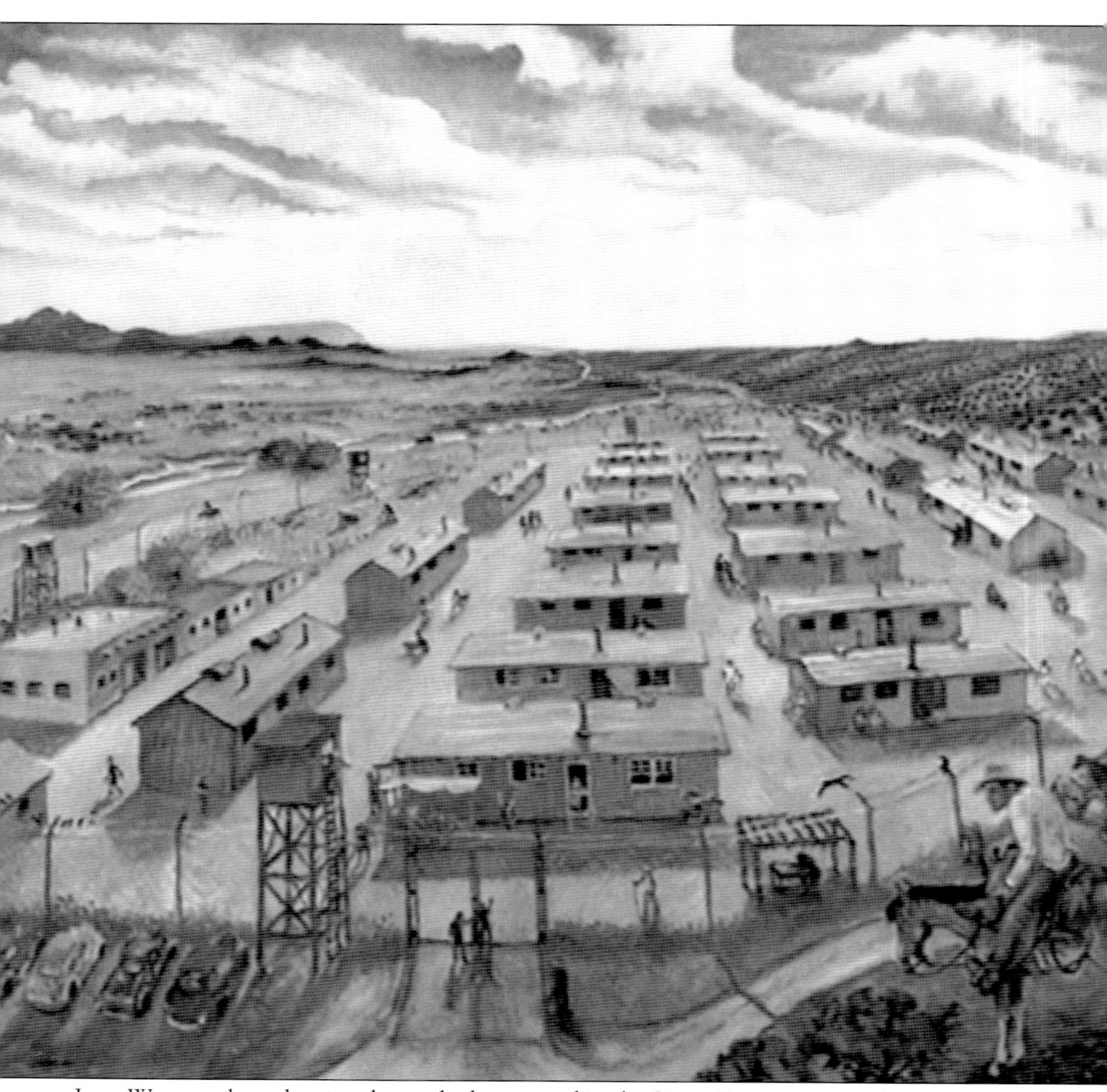

Jerry West, a talented artist who worked as a guard in the Santa Fe camp, painted many scenes of the facility. In this scene, West depicted the military-like barracks, main offices, exterior fencing, and watchtowers. Despite their desolate surroundings, internees were treated relatively well, with adequate food and shelter. With the exception of a brief riot on March 12, 1945, conditions remained calm inside the camp. On the other hand, many local residents in Santa Fe grew hostile to the internees, especially when they learned of the horrors of the Bataan Death March and wrongly assumed that the detained men must be Japanese POWs. In fact, many internees felt that they were in protective custody; guards claimed that there was no need to lock the camp's gate because few internees would risk their lives escaping into Santa Fe. (New Mexico Museum of Art.)

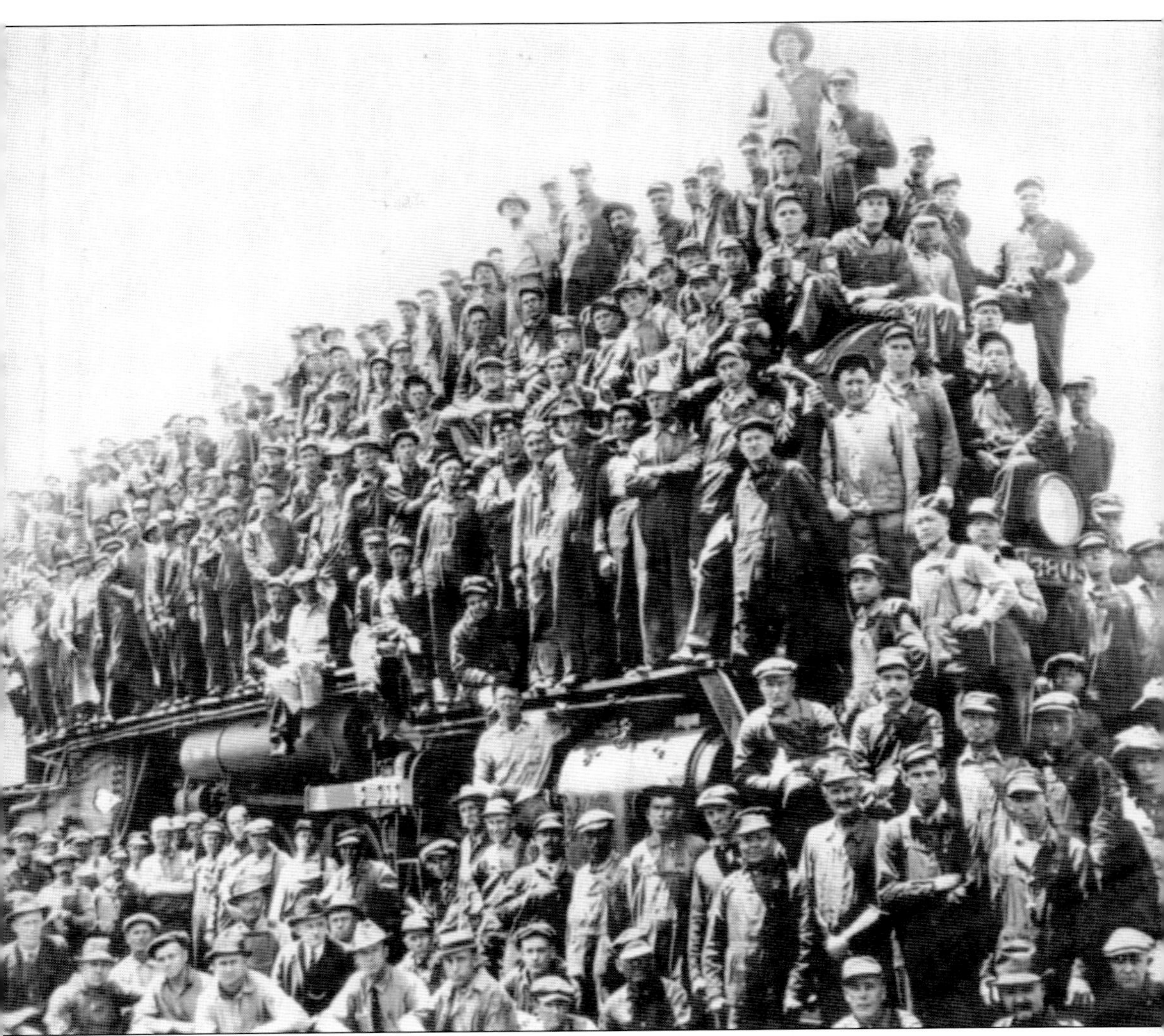

Many New Mexico towns and cities had resisted the creation of relocation camps near their communities. Some of these towns were just as adamant about protecting the rights of the Japanese American families who had worked side-by-side with them, as pictured here. Of the Japanese Americans who lived in Gallup, Grants, and Belen, none were forced into relocation camps. Thirty-five Japanese Americans, including seventeen children from Clovis who had not been well integrated into the community, were sent to camps. Tom Matsu of Belen and others who had worked for the Santa Fe Railway lost their jobs because they were wrongly believed to be security risks. In a letter to Gov. John E. Miles, Matsu's son James protested, "This isn't the American way. This is the Axis way." Thirty-one leading citizens of Belen also signed a petition to Miles, but Tom Matsu never regained his job. (Randy Dunston.)

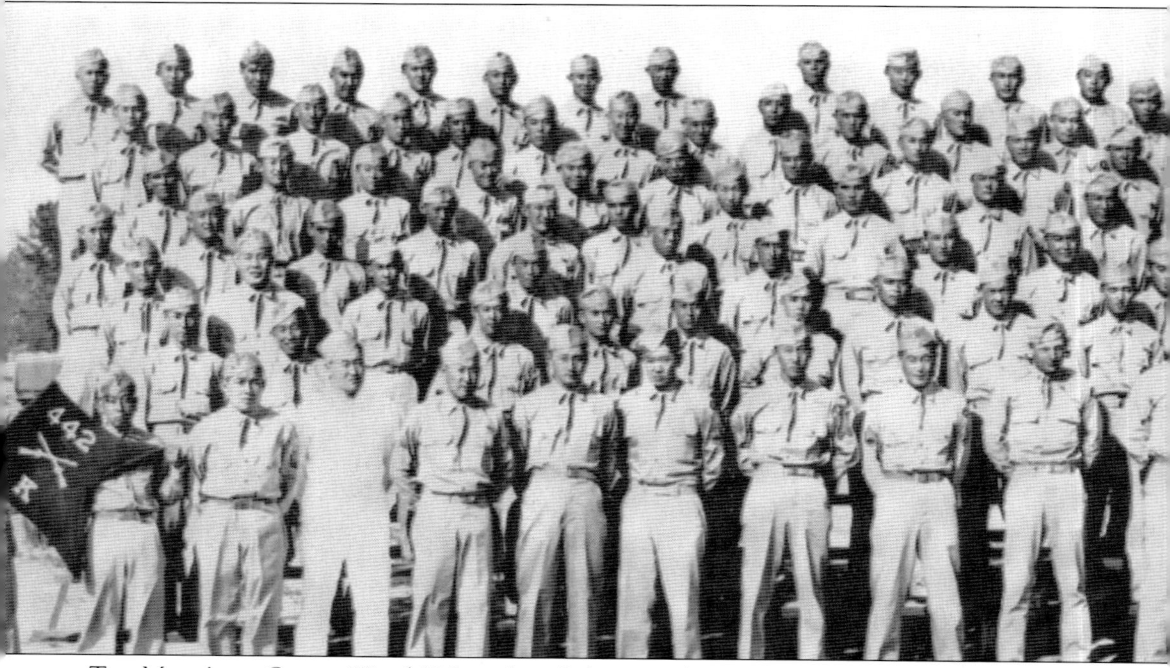

Tom Matsu's son George "Kotch" Matsu from Belen served in Company K of the 442nd Regimental Combat Team consisting of fellow Japanese Americans, most of whom had family members in relocation or internment camps. These loyal soldiers hoped to prove that their families did not

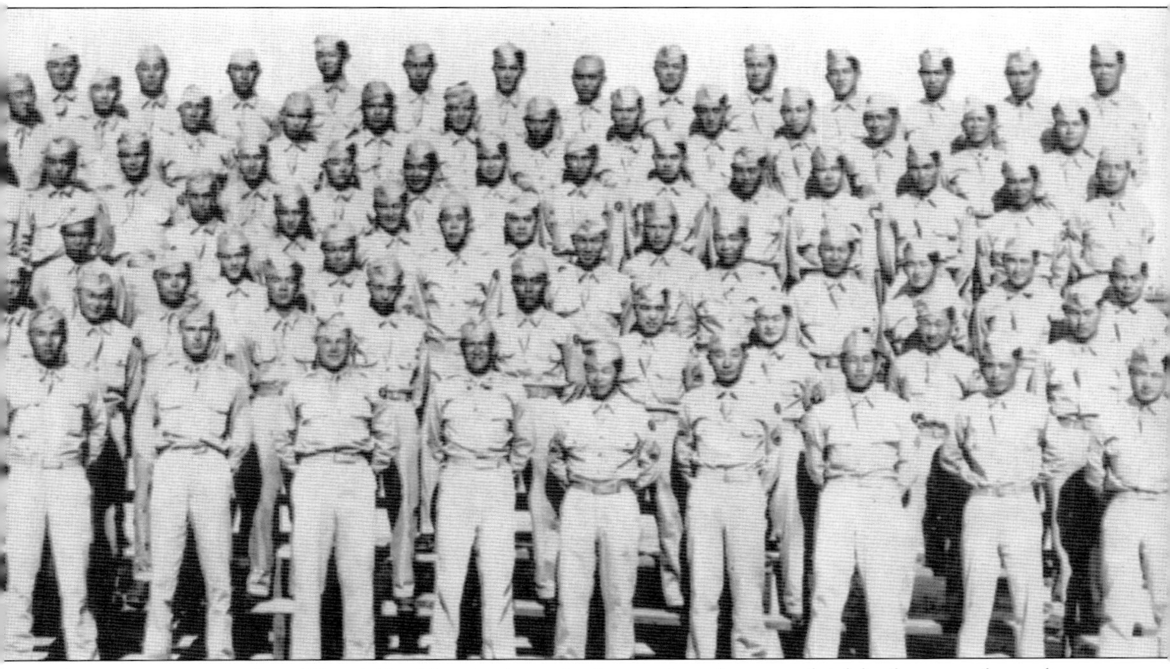

deserve incarceration. The 442nd fought bravely, becoming the most highly decorated combat unit in the US Army. (goforbroke.org.)

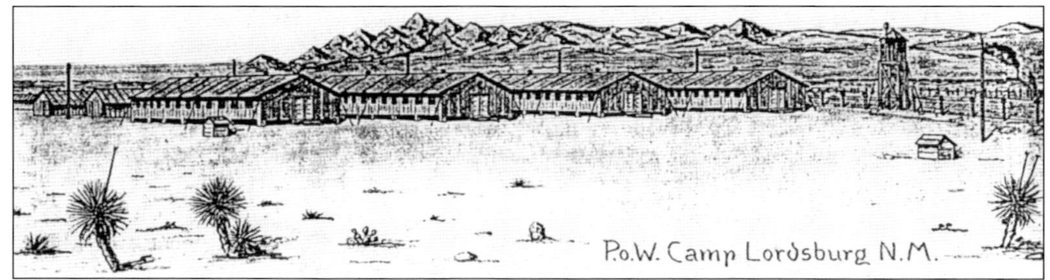

In June 1942, the US Department of Justice opened a second internment camp six miles southeast of Lordsburg in southern New Mexico. The camp included over 250 structures with enough room to house as many as 3,000 internees. The camp's exterior was much like the facility in Santa Fe, with barbed wire fences and watchtowers. Unlike the mild climate of Santa Fe, internees in Lordsburg faced months of strong winds and oppressive heat. (Mollie Pressler.)

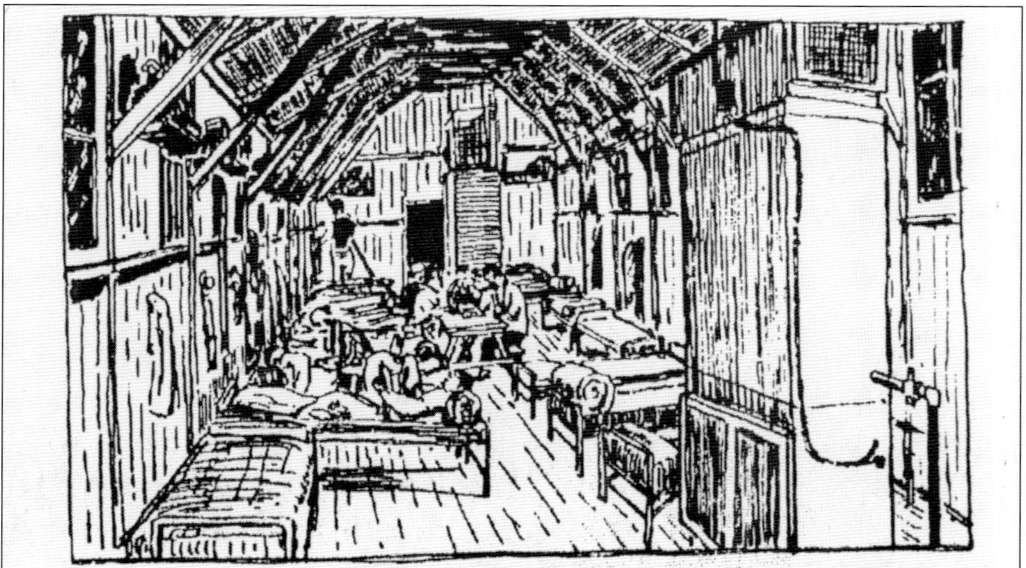

OUR BARRACK.. LORDSBURG INTERNMENT CAMP 7-4-42
COMPANY 10 - BARRACK #4

Japanese internees faced similar living conditions in Lordsburg as those experienced in Santa Fe. Barracks were spartan but clean. The men worked to improve their surroundings while spending much of their time in creative pursuits. Japanese internees were relocated in 1943 to be replaced by German and Italian POWs from 1943 to 1945. The camp was probably the only one in the United States to house all three groups. (Mollie Pressler.)

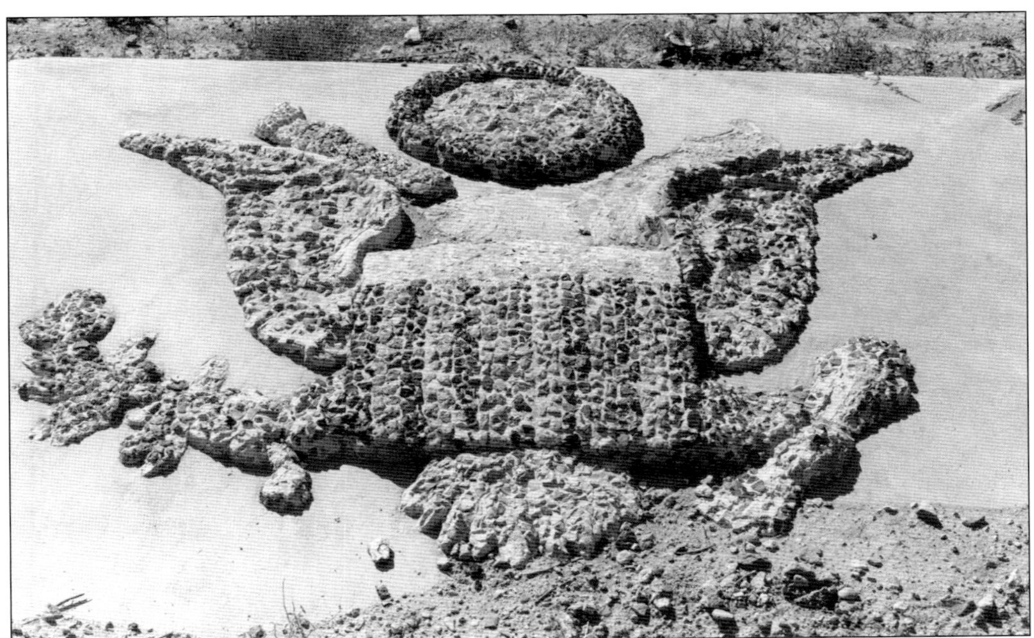

Lordsburg internees kept busy with work details, carpentry, cooking, and tending to a five-acre vegetable garden. While the men in Santa Fe favored rock art, those in Lordsburg used concrete for many of their creative works. Their finished art included birdbaths, drinking fountains, statues, and items found in a typical Japanese garden. The photographs shown here reflect their creative skills in the making of an American eagle (above) and a cactus garden (below). Depending on the commander in charge, Japanese culture was respected, and ceremonies were allowed in both Lordsburg and Santa Fe. For the Japanese New Year in 1943, some internees in each camp dressed as Geisha girls to perform a lion dance. (Both, Mollie Pressler.)

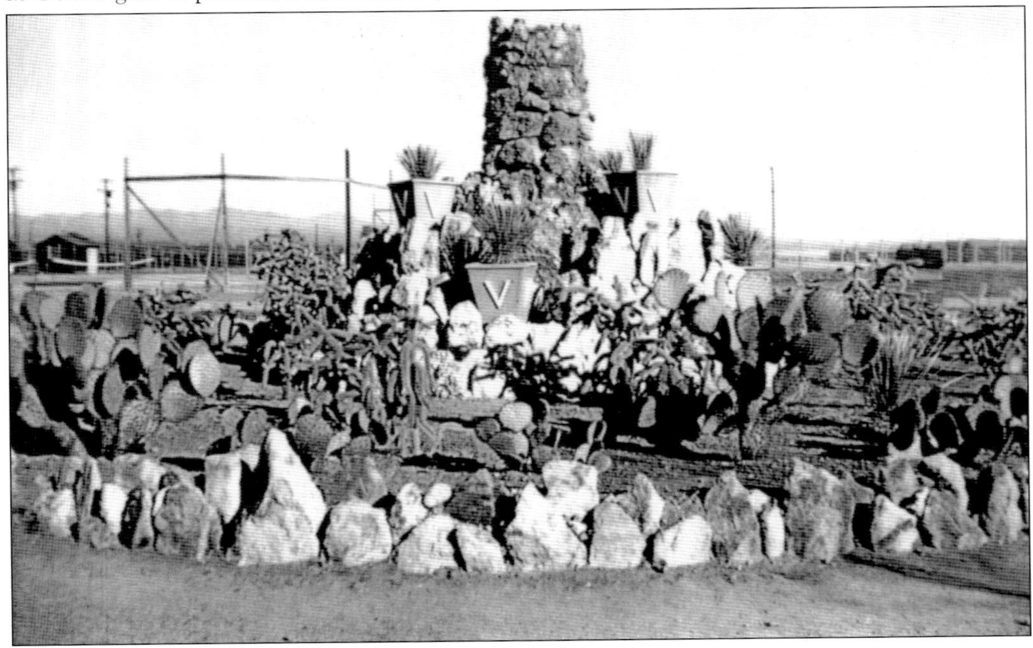

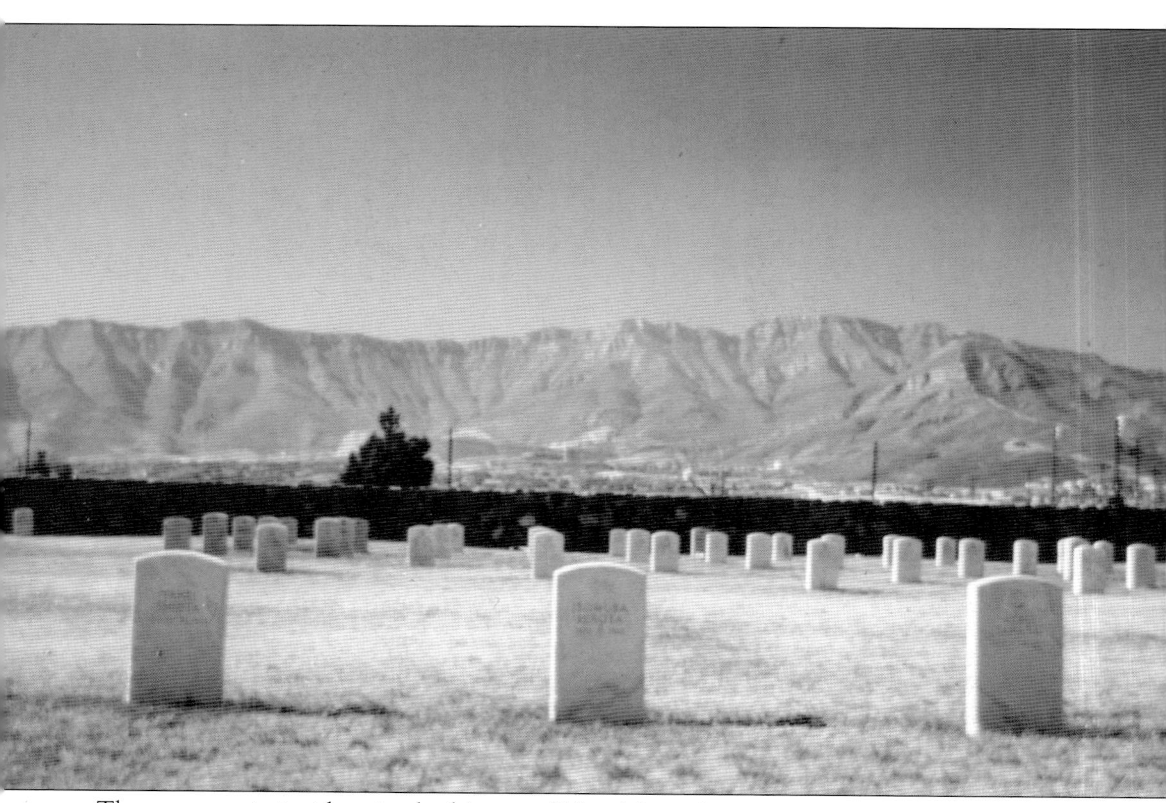

The most tragic incident in the history of New Mexico's two internment camps involved two internees who were shot and killed by a guard in Lordsburg. On the night of July 27, 1942, Toshiro Kobata and Isomura Hirota, just arrived by train with other new internees, were being brought to the camp's main gate. The two men lagged behind and stepped out of line at a turn in the path. We will never know if they could not see the path in the dark or planned to escape. Their guard assumed the worst and shot them at close range. Neither man survived. A court-martial was held; the guard was found not guilty of murder. A third internee, Tahara Ayao, was shot in an equally doubtful escape attempt. All three internees were buried at the national cemetery at Fort Bliss, Texas. (Mollie Pressler.)

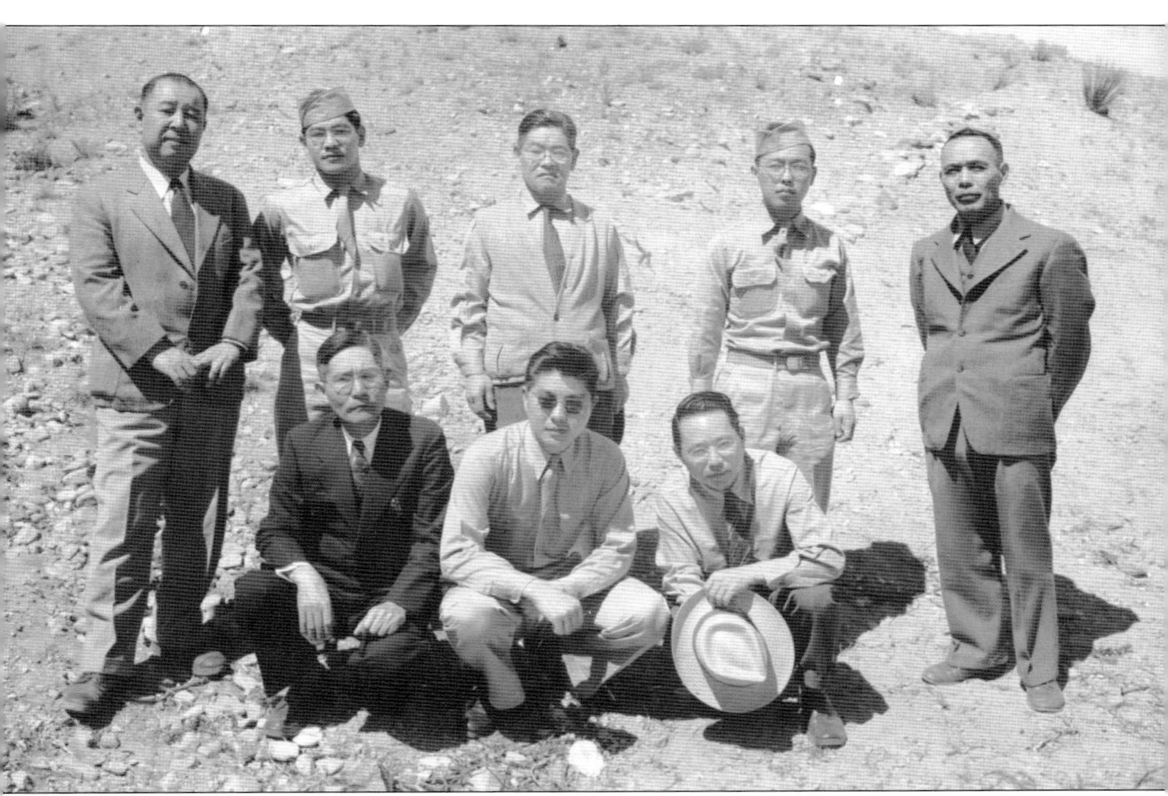

Many sons of the men detained in Santa Fe enlisted in the US Army to help prove not only their own loyalty but also the loyalty of their fathers who did not deserve incarceration. Historian Gail Y. Okawa has discovered an 11-page document listing the names of Hawaiian internees with from one to four sons in the military. With some as young as 18, most of these young men joined the 442nd Regimental Combat Team. Members of the 442nd fought bravely, with 68 percent receiving Purple Hearts. As shown in this photograph, some soldiers were able to visit their fathers, despite obstacles, including distance from their far-off military camps. Visits were limited to from one to two hours with armed soldiers standing guard. Seeing soldiers visit their interned fathers is ironic enough, but seeing wounded soldiers visit their interned fathers was perhaps the ultimate irony of the war. (The Shinoda family.)

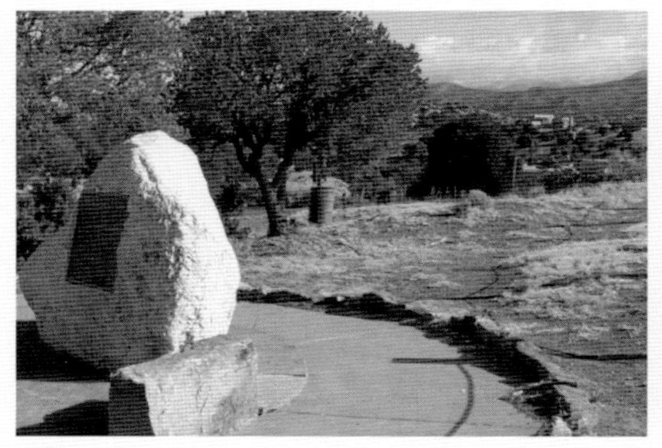

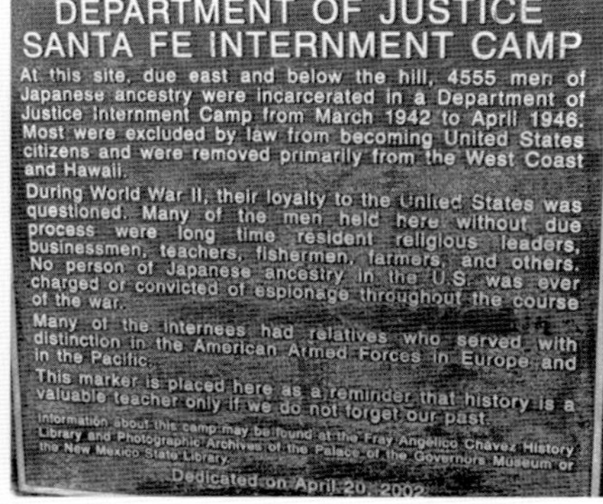

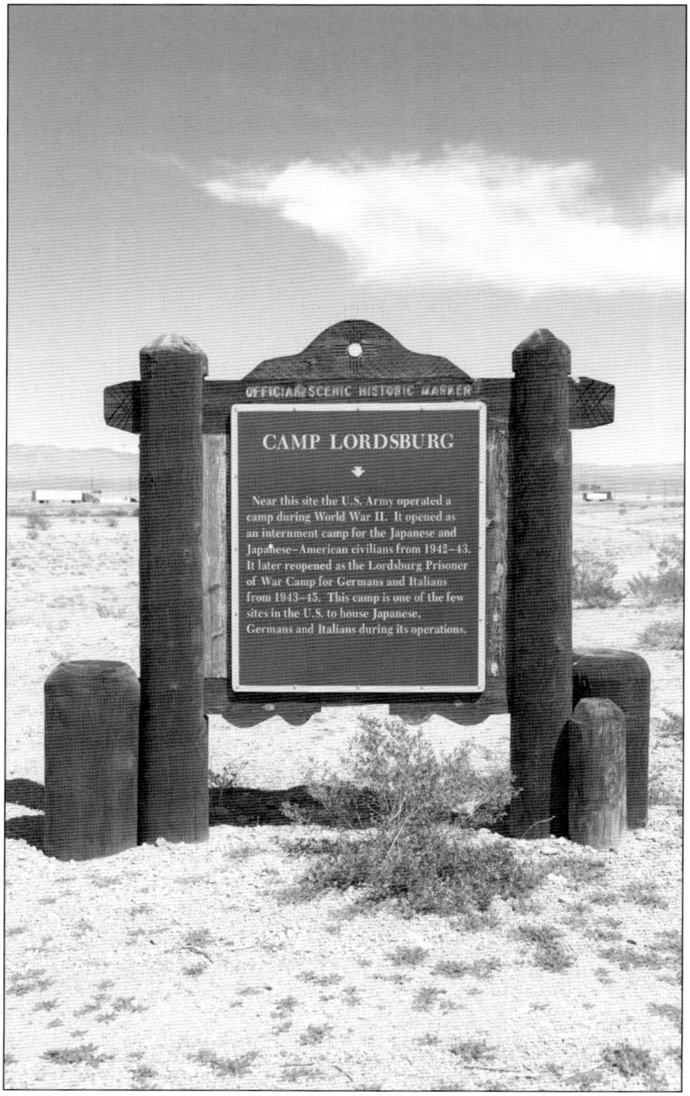

The Japanese internment camp in Santa Fe is long gone, but in 1999, local community leaders and descendants of the men imprisoned there believed that it should not be forgotten. They proposed that a monument be placed at Frank S. Ortiz Park overlooking the camp's 28-acre location, now a suburban neighborhood. Still confused that the camp had held Japanese POWs rather than internees, some Santa Feans, including several Bataan Death March survivors, vehemently opposed the monument. The Santa Fe City Council passed the proposal when Mayor Larry Delgado cast the tie-breaking vote in 1999. Designed by Faith Okuma, the 6.5-ton stone monument (above) was dedicated on April 20, 2002. Meanwhile, the internment camp near Lordsburg is remembered with a historical marker and a separate room at the Hidalgo County Historical Museum. (Above, Kermit Hill; left, New Mexico Department of Transportation.)

Ten

The Surrender

Just after 9:00 a.m. Tokyo time on September 2, 1945, a Japanese delegation led by Foreign Minister Maromu Shigimitsu boarded the USS *Missouri*, anchored in Tokyo Bay. In a ceremony presided over by Gen. Douglas MacArthur, the Japanese signed the instrument of surrender, ending the costliest war in the history of the world.

Nearly 50,000 New Mexico men and women directly participated in World War II. In fact, New Mexico had the highest per capita volunteer rate of any of the 48 states then in the Union. Of these brave souls, over 2,000 did not survive, making New Mexico the state with the highest casualty rate per capita in the nation. New Mexicans died at sea, in the air, and on the battlefields, including the only battle on US soil, the Aleutian Islands campaign in Alaska in May 1943. More than 800 died in Japanese prison camps and on hell ships.

New Mexico played a significant role in finally bringing the war to an end. The use of nuclear weapons designed, constructed, and tested in New Mexico, while not the only reason for the Japanese capitulation, helped convince Emperor Hirohito to override his military advisors and surrender. The Japanese did not know how many atomic bombs the United States could still use (in fact, there were none), but did know they faced a massive Allied invasion if they did not surrender unconditionally by the fall of 1945.

Although the nuclear weapon program is now viewed as the most important technical contribution of New Mexico to the successful prosecution of the war, it was not viewed as such at the time. The development of the proximity fuse at Johns Hopkins Applied Physics Laboratory and its testing by E.J. Workman and his team at Kirtland Army Air Field was viewed by the men at the front as more important. Testing and training with the Norden bombsight was also a crucial development supported in the Land of Enchantment.

While of great significance, the technical developments were not the only consequential contributions that New Mexico made to the war effort. From railroad workers to Navajo code talkers, from coal mining in Madrid to cotton farming in the Mesilla Valley, from war bond sales to rationing, from pilot training to weapons testing, from POW camps to Army air bases, New Mexico's participation in the war was broad, varied, and important. Only federal acts, especially the unjust internment of Japanese Americans, indirectly marred New Mexico's record in World War II.

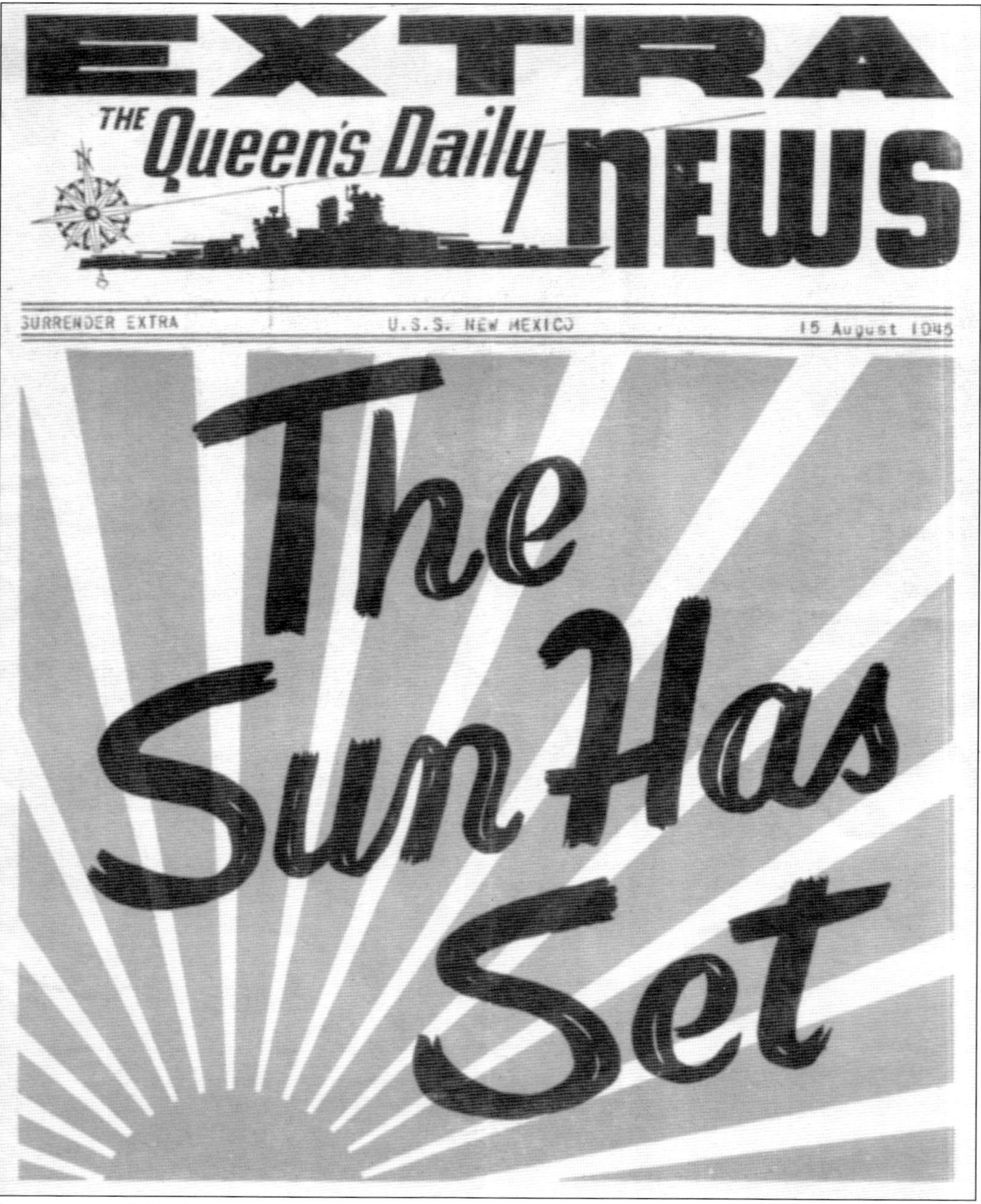

It is estimated that between 70 and 85 million people, or approximately three percent of the world's population, perished in the terrible years of World War II. Given New Mexico's important role in the Allies' victory, it was appropriate that the USS *New Mexico* was alongside the *Missouri* in Tokyo harbor when the surrender documents were signed. Sailors on the *New Mexico* later wrote of their memories of this event. By joining the *Missouri*, the *New Mexico* became the only naval vessel to have participated in the end of both World War I and World War II. Regrettably, the USS *Bullhead*, memorialized by a park in Albuquerque, was the last combatant vessel to be lost in the war. The August 15, 1945, issue of the *New Mexico's* onboard newsletter, *The Queen's Daily News*, proudly proclaimed the Allies' victory in an extra edition. (Greg Trapp.)

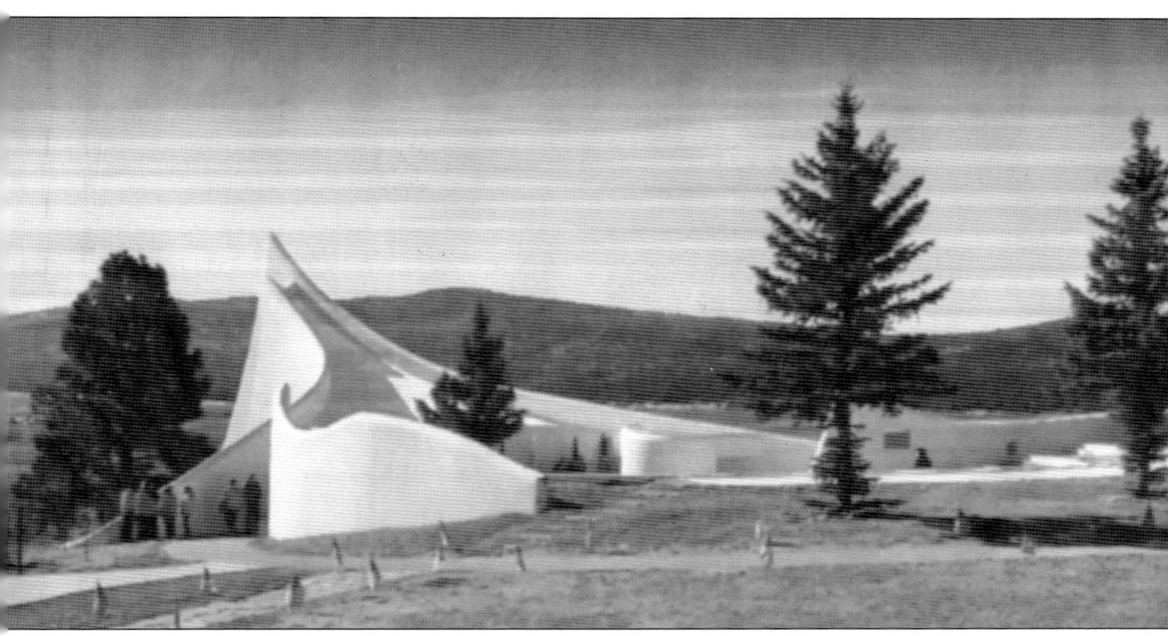

Any history of New Mexico's role in World War II would be incomplete without stressing the impact of the state's wartime contributions on the worldwide conflict that followed. No sooner had World War II ended than the United States and its allies confronted the Soviet Union in the Cold War. Rather than be abandoned, many facilities in New Mexico were retooled to meet the United States' new defense challenges. Former US Army air bases in Albuquerque, Alamogordo, Roswell, and Clovis became important US Air Force bases. Trinity Site became part of the White Sands Missile Range. Los Alamos remained open to develop new nuclear weapons. It was joined by Sandia National Labs with a similar mission. Mines near Grants helped produce uranium for the production of nuclear weapons. As in all previous wars, New Mexicans volunteered and suffered casualties at rates surpassing most other states, especially in Korea and Vietnam. Those killed in Vietnam are memorialized at a state park in Angel Fire, New Mexico, seen here. (Richard Melzer.)

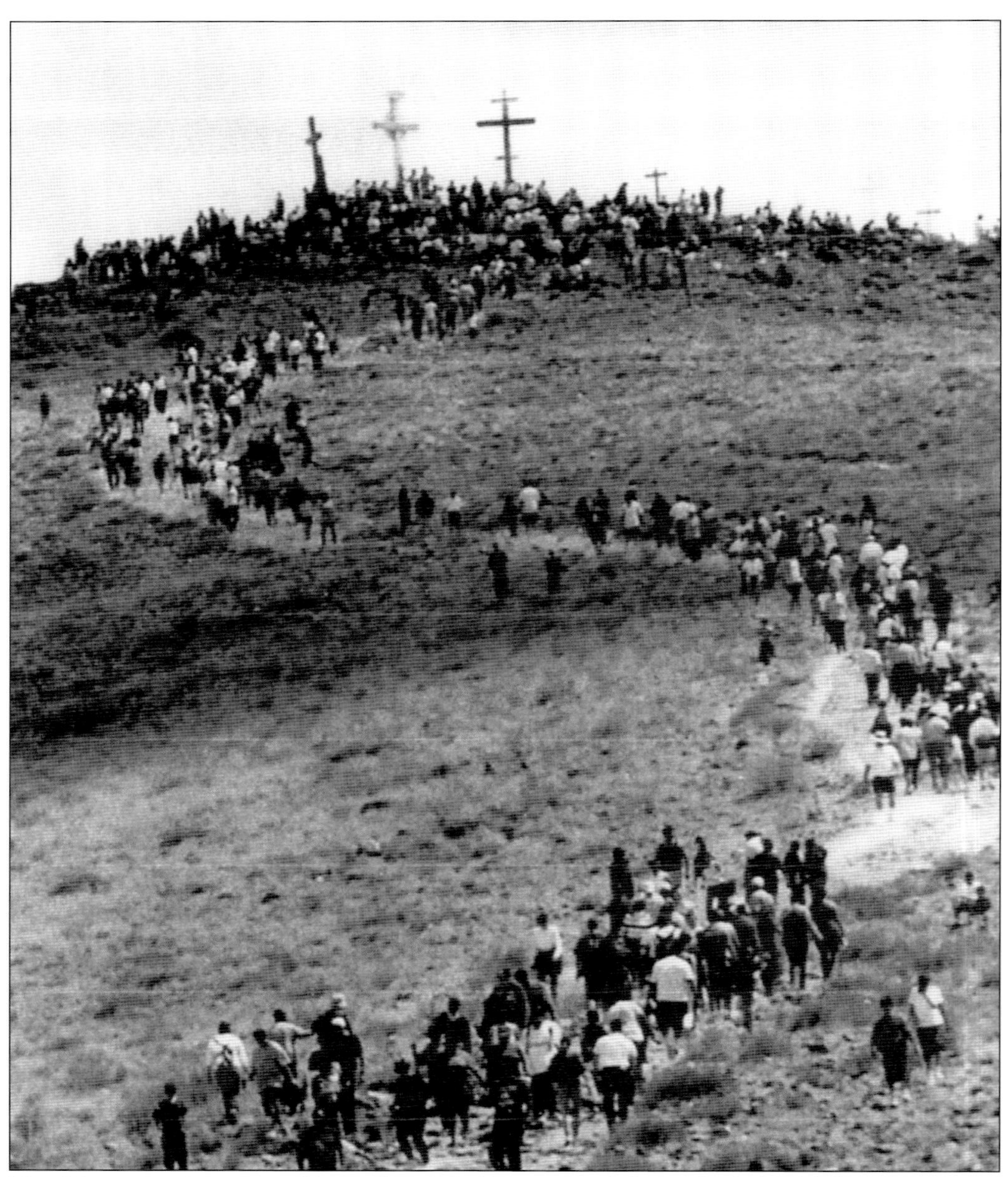

New Mexicans who returned home from World War II and those who helped fight at home were eager to memorialize their fallen colleagues and loved ones with monuments. One of the most impressive and meaningful is located in Tome in central New Mexico. Edwin Berry of Tome served in North Africa and Italy, where he experienced the horror of war in deeply personal ways, losing both a brother, Ramon, and a friend, Foch Romero. When Berry returned to Tome, he promised God that he would honor the memory of all those who died by placing a memorial atop the hill that overlooks his village. He kept his promise by almost singlehandedly finishing the monument in 1948. Today, the three crosses Edwin Berry erected have become a pilgrimage site for thousands of worshipers on Good Friday. The vast majority of those who climb the hill never realize the underlying secular significance of Berry's labor: to honor the sacrifices of all New Mexicans in World War II. (B.G. Burr.)

Bibliography

Andrews, Martha Shipman, ed. *The Whole Damned World: New Mexico Aggies at War, 1941–1945.* Albuquerque, NM: Rio Grande Books, 2009.

Baldwin, Ralph B. *The Deadly Fuze.* San Rafael, CA: Presidio Press, 1980.

Cave, Dorothy. *Beyond Courage: One Regiment Against Japan, 1941–1945.* Las Cruces, NM: Yucca Tree Press, 1992.

DeMark, Judith Boyce, ed. *Essays in Twentieth Century New Mexico History.* Albuquerque, NM: University of New Mexico Press, 1994.

Flint, Richard and Shirley Cushing Flint. *Overhaul: A History of the Albuquerque Locomotive Repair Shops.* Albuquerque, NM: University of New Mexico Press, 2021.

Melzer, Richard. *Breakdown: How the Secret of the Atomic Bomb Was Stolen During World War II.* Santa Fe, NM: Sunstone, 2000.

__________. *Ernie Pyle in the American Southwest.* Santa Fe, NM: Sunstone Press, 1996.

Nez, Chester with Judith Schiess Avila. *Code Talker.* New York, NY: Berkley Books, 2011.

Paul, Doris A. *The Navajo Code Talkers.* Bryn Mawr, PA: Dorrance and Company, 1973.

Payne, Sarah, ed. "Confinement in the Land of Enchantment." CLOE Project, 2018.

Rhodes, Richard. *The Making of the Atomic Bomb.* New York, NY: Simon and Schuster, 1986.

Rogers, Everett M. and Nancy R. Bartlit. *Silent Voices of World War II.* Santa Fe, NM: Sunstone Press, 2005.

Taylor, John M. *New Mexico's Navy.* Tome, NM: Techknowledge Press, 2018.

Taylor, John M., Richard Melzer, Dick Brown, and Greg Trapp. *USS* New Mexico*: BB-40.* Charleston, SC: Arcadia Publishing, 2018.

Thomas, Gerald W. *Victory in World War II: The New Mexico Story.* Las Cruces, NM: Rio Grande Historical Collections, New Mexico State University, 1994.